Endorsements

1. Mitchell Koza – Distinguished Professor of Management, Rutgers School of Business, Camden, New Jersey, USA

"This timely and well reasoned assessment of Global Boards provides a much welcome correction to the current distrust of Boards and the organizations they govern. Bravo!"

2. Professor David Hayward – Dean of the School of Global Studies, Social Science and Planning, RMIT University, Melbourne, Australia.

"A must read for those interested in the role that Boards might play in the vastly different global economy."

3. Dr Cliff Bowman – Professor of Strategic Management, Cranfield School of Management, UK

"A timely and insightful exploration of the impact of national cultures on boardroom behaviour."

4. David G. Altman, Ph.D, Executive Vice President, Research, Innovation & Product Development, Center for Creative Leadership, USA

"An insightful and powerful analysis of the global context of board oversight. Readable and highly relevant to the current day events."

5. Yasmin Allen – Director, Insurance Australia Group & Director, Macquarie Specialised Asset Management, Australia.

"Too many studies focus on the statutory role of the board and not enough on the reality of boardroom conduct. In this broad reaching study, the authors assess board dynamics globally. While it would be convenient for a standard set of behaviours and ideals to manifest, in fact, the opposite is true. Best in breed companies rely on diversity and contextual knowledge creates longer lasting wealth creation."

6. Professor Yvon Pesqueux – CNAM, Chair, Development Systems Organisation, France.

"The world is not so global, a board is not so perfect..."

7. Professor Frank Bournois – Directeur du CIFFOP, University Pantheon-Assas, Paris, France

"A most comprehensive and insightful treatment of boards, directors and governance on a global basis. A must read for all managers, directors and business school students."

8. Professor Peter Shergold – Macquarie Group Foundation Chair, Sydney, Australia

"A rich and fascinating global perspective on how the behaviour of Boards is shaped by the particularities of regional context."

9. Professor Marie McHugh – Professor of Organisational Behaviour, Ulster Business School

"Excellent book. Greatly advances our knowledge and understanding of the functioning of boards"

Also edited by Andrew Kakabadse and Nada Kakabadse

GOVERNANCE, STRATEGY AND POLICY: Seven Critical Essays

CORPORATE SOCIAL RESPONSIBILITY: Reconciling Aspiration with Application
(with Mette Morsing)

CSR IN PRACTICE: Delving Deep

Also by Andrew Kakabadse and Nada Kakabadse

LEADING THE BOARD

LEADING FOR SUCCESS: The Seven Sides to Great Leaders *(with Linda Lee-Davies)*

THE ELEPHANT HUNTERS: Chronicles of the Moneymen *(with Amielle Lake)*

Also by Andrew Kakabadse

SPIRITUAL MOTIVATION: New Thinking for Business Management
(with Jeremy Ramsden and Shuhei Aida)

Global Boards

One Desire, Many Realities

Edited by

Andrew Kakabadse
Professor of International Management Development, Cranfield University, School of Management, UK

and

Nada Kakabadse
Professor in Management and Business Research, Northampton University Business School, UK

First published 2009 by
PALGRAVE MACMILLAN

Palgrave Macmillan in the UK is an imprint of Macmillan Publishers Limited,
registered in England, company number 785998, of Houndmills, Basingstoke,
Hampshire RG21 6XS.

Palgrave Macmillan in the US is a division of St Martin's Press LLC,
175 Fifth Avenue, New York, NY 10010.

Palgrave Macmillan is the global academic imprint of the above companies
and has companies and representatives throughout the world.

Palgrave® and Macmillan® are registered trademarks in the United States,
the United Kingdom, Europe and other countries.

ISBN: 978–0–230–21212–1 hardback

This book is printed on paper suitable for recycling and made from fully
managed and sustained forest sources. Logging, pulping and manufacturing
processes are expected to conform to the environmental regulations of the
country of origin.

A catalogue record for this book is available from the British Library.

A catalog record for this book is available from the Library of Congress.

10 9 8 7 6 5 4 3 2 1
18 17 16 15 14 13 12 11 10 09

Printed and bound in Great Britain by
CPI Antony Rowe, Chippenham and Eastbourne

Contents

Tables

Figures

Acknowledgements

We are deeply grateful to Madeleine Fleure for her perseverance in typing draft after draft and her warm and pleasant demeanour in promptly responding to all queries and questions from contributors, research participants and all other parties.

We would also like to thank Sheena Darby for having arranged intricate travel itineraries and meeting schedules in the UK, Turkey and China.

Our grateful thanks also go to Alexi Mordashov, Vadim Makhov, Dmirty Afanasyev and Dmitry Kouptsov and the Severstal Corporation for their generous support in sponsoring the studies in this book through the Cranfield/Severstal research programme.

Last we are indebted to all of the managers and directors of the public and private organisations we surveyed and to the community representatives and politicians that we spoke to all of whom shaped the thinking and research that make up this book. Your experiences have provided an invaluable source of insight for so many people, for so many years to come.

Contributors

Dr Yang Chen Lecturer in Contemporary Chinese Studies Centre for East Asian Studies University of Bristol, UK.

John Cottrell PhD Candidate, Faculty of Business and Enterprise, Australian Graduate School of Entrepreneurship, Swinburne University of Technology, Hawthorn, Australia.

Andrew Kakabadse Professor of International Management Development, Cranfield University, School of Management, UK.

Nada Kakabadse Professor in Management and Business Research, University of Northampton, UK.

Abigail Levrau Doctor Assistant, member of the Management Committee, GUBERNA, Belgium.

Malcolm McIntosh Professor of Human Security and Sustainable Enterprise, Director, Applied Research Centre in Human Security (ARCHS), Coventry University, UK.

Dr Eleanor O'Higgins University College Dublin, School of Business and Visiting Fellow, London School of Economics and Political Science, UK.

Elina Oseichuk Lecturer, The Robert Gordon University, Aberdeen, Scotland.

Dr Jelena Petrovic Senior Lecturer, University of Wolverhampton Business School, UK.

Chris Pierce CEO of Global Governance Services Ltd, Australia.

Richard Sanders Professor of Contemporary Chinese Studies and Director of the China and Transitional Economies Research Centre, University of Northampton, UK.

Oleg Yu Tsvetkov Corporate Secretary JSC "Severstal," JSC Severstal, Russia.

Vladislav Udaltsov Assistant Strategy Director, OAO Severstal, Russia.

Lutgart Van den Berghe Executive Director, GUBERNA, Partner, Vlerick Leuven Gent Management School, Extra-Ordinary Professor, Ghent University, Belgium.

Hong Yang PhD candidate, Northampton Business School, University of Northampton, UK.

Orhan Yavuz CEO, Strategic Change Management Consultancy, Turkey.

Introduction

Andrew Kakabadse and Nada Kakabadse

Triggered by the mounting defaults of US housing loans, the autumn of 2008 witnessed a breathtaking global financial meltdown. Financial institutions turned to their Central Banks for short-term assistance as well as to Asian and Middle Eastern sovereign-wealth funds for equity injections. With these initial inputs of capital not having had the desired effect, the US and other Western governments provided additional substantial capital through stock acquisition, in effect nationalising the financial system. House prices, currency values, commodity values and commodity prices all speeded downwards. Economic downturn and recession became the reality of western and many developing economies. With the Federal Reserve (i.e., the Fed) and the Bank of England adopting an aggressive policy of "quantitative monetary easing measures" (QMEM), in effect printing dollars and pounds sterling, the economic outlook for the next years looks dark especially with the deluge of paper that is to enter the money market (*Khaleej Times*, 2008a, p. 33).

In the midst of such turmoil, the blame game started. Under fire came the "greedy and reckless investment bankers, particularly epitomised by Bernard Madoff, who was described on the front page of the *Financial Times* December 18th (2008), as being 'responsible for a $50 billion 'Ponzi' fraud scheme fraud'." The "hue and cry" was on for the fraudsters and the instigators of the corporate governance failures that "led" to this crisis. The clarion calls of, "where was the board in all this?" echoed through Wall Street, the City, Capital Hill and both houses of the UK's Parliament. Inadequate risk identification and assessment procedures, over generous compensation packages and board directors unable to act, became hot news for press and media alike.

Yet, the one theme that in December of 2008 was not given sufficient scrutiny was the integral nature of corporate and societal governance. In effect, sound corporate governance cannot be pursued until a foundation of equitable and transparent governance of the nation has been established. What is becoming increasingly clear through the collapse of the world's financial system is that such a foundation has been sadly lacking.

Since the 1913 introduction of US federal income tax, mortgage interest-payments become tax-deductible and in doing so, a fundamental element of the "American dream." To further facilitate that dream, Ronald Regan on his election to the White House in 1982, steadfastly cut the income tax paid by the wealthy. Tax paid by the wealthy in 1951 stood at 70 per cent of their total income, representing over 33 per cent of federal tax contribution. In 1983, it stood at 27 per cent of the total income of the rich, decreasing the contribution to federal tax receipts to less than 9 per cent. To cover this shortfall, the Regan administration embarked on a borrowing spree, first from savaging the huge surplus accumulated in the Social Security Trust Fund and then from other sources. In the 8 years of his presidency, Regan borrowed more money than the total of all Presidents from George Washington to Jimmy Carter combined (*The News*, 1977). Regan's tax cuts encouraged America to stop investing in infrastructure and to live on borrowed money.

Regan's trend was followed by consecutive administrations and by other western economies with the exception of Germany. In 1981, the US national debt stood at one trillion. By March 1996, it climbed to 4.8 trillion, reaching the 10 trillion mark in October 2008 (*US News*, 2008). Further, the challenges we currently face have been further compounded through mortgage reinvestment packages, known as mortgage backed securities or "collaterized mortgage obligations." These new securities have been traded as alternatives to government and corporate bonds. Through such initiatives, western governments encouraged householders to skew their investment portfolios in favour of real estate, encouraging them to turn their houses into ATMs. Over-valued loans, positioned by the rating agencies as triple A-rated investments, were pumped through the financial system across the globe.

In 2006, the economic output of entire world worth was around $48.6 trillion whilst the total market capitalisation of the world's stock market was $50.6 trillion. The total value of US and other international bonds stood at $67.9 trillion. However, the growth of derivatives between 2005 and 2007 was extraordinary, increasing from $298 trillion to $596 trillion. The collapse of our financial system was inevitable. For how long could this behaviour of investing in hot air and paper, encouraged by the US and UK governments, have continued?

As the last days of 2008 unfolded, one particularly strongly expressed point of view was that considerable blame for the current economic crisis lays with banker's remuneration packages that encouraged short-term thinking. Yet, all evidence suggests that unless bankers were incentivised to "get the next deal," the structure of the markets, as "created" and permitted by governments, would have someone else "win the deal." In this sense, the bankers were "appropriately remunerated" for their efforts. The truth is that chief executives, money managers and financial analysts have been driven by short-term targets to the point where corporate leaders felt such pressure to "deliver the numbers" that financial fudging was turned from a covert activity to a highly rewarded financial skill. This is nothing new. US President Woodrow Wilson (1913, p. 185) observed that,

> a great industrial nation is controlled by its system of credit. Our system of credit is privately concentrated. The growth of the nation, therefore, and all our activities are in the hands of a few men who, even if their action be honest and intended for the public interest, are necessarily concentrated upon the great undertakings in which their own money is involved and who necessarily, by very reason of their limitations, chill and check and destroy genuine freedom.

The utter irony is that "the system," on the one hand, disabled effective corporate responsibility and governance and yet "the system" piled substantial legal and administrative demands on corporate boards in order to uphold the highest standards of governance obligations. This is not today's phenomena. Contending with such contradiction and paradox is a 90-year-plus-old story. So, if boards are the stewards of governance and yet are restricted to act by government, what then is the role, purpose and contribution of boards?

Early studies of US boards highlight that although boards bear ultimate responsibility and accountability to shareholders, they acted as little more than "legal fiction" (Smith, 1958). As counter to that, Smith (1958) advocated that boards be transformed into free constituencies composed of capable and independent members. By the 1970s, Mace's (1971, 1972, 1973) studies found the board's role had strengthened acting as both provider of advice and counsel to the company president and offering disciplined action particularly in crisis situations, such as replacing the CEO. However, Mace (1971) also found that US boards had little influence on determining the objectives, strategies and policies of the corporation. Moreover, Mace (1971) established that US board members rarely asked discerning questions, were rarely involved in selection of the president of the corporation and the CEO was only replaced under extraordinary circumstances.

Studies in the 1990s surfaced that the passivity of boards continued. Although it was found that boards had become more involved in strategy determination (Judge and Zeithaml, 1992; Siciliano, 2005; Nadler et al., 2006), all too frequently, board member challenge was minimal and critical issues remained undiscussed (Lorsch and MacIver, 1989). Too many relied on the attitude and orientation of the President, Chairman and CEO, which for the vast majority of US corporations was the one and the same person. The responsibility to nurture an atmosphere of openness and dialogue relied too much on this one man or woman (Lorsch and MacIver, 1989).

More up to date European studies equally emphasise the strategy contribution of boards but also highlight that board dynamics really determine board functioning (Roberts et al., 2005; Jonnergard et al., 2004). Role separation of CEO and Chairman and a more balanced external, independent director ratio have been identified as considerably improving boardroom dialogue (Kakabadse and Kakabadse, 2008). Boardroom leadership exercised by the chairmen emerges as the determinant factor in terms of encouraging independent challenge and nurturing a board member mindset of independence.

The inquiry into board purpose, role and contribution continues. Partly driven by the present financial crisis but also by a genuine concern for governance improvement, major questions are being raised about the role of boards, particularly in the financial services sector, where excessive executive remuneration is seen by some as one critical factor in the "collapse" of the global banking system. The true effect of US determined Sarbannes Oxley legislation concerning the governance responsibility of boards has also come under scrutiny. Additionally, questions are being raised as to whether shareholder value should be substituted by a philosophy of stakeholder concern.

Yet, despite these concerns, whilst the global financial system displays an imbalance between the high savings/high surplus economies of Asia and the Gulf states and the recession riddled Western "free markets," the focus on board role and contribution as a way of "getting out of the mess" is likely to continue. For sure, boards are unlikely to fall "below the radar."

With such scrutiny and interest on boards, we the editors have invited contribution from an international gathering of scholars and practitioners and captured their contribution under the heading *Global Boards: One Desire, Many Realities*.

The tone for this text is set in Chapter 1, by Abigail Levrau and Lutgart Van de Burghe of the Vlerick Leuven Gent Management School, Belgium, who report a qualitative and quantitative study of board director performance. The authors draw attention to a gap in the literature between board role, purpose and functioning and the reality of boardroom practice. The concluding plea is that greater account be taken of board member behaviour and its effect on board conduct.

Chris Pierce, in Chapter 2, builds on the Levrau and Van de Berghe contribution by offering an insightful view of the varying approaches to board evaluation. Pierce identifies why board evaluation, considered a critical aspect of board performance, does not sufficiently take place. Despite this shortfall, Pierce does highlight the characteristics of successful evaluation. Chapter 2 concludes that the "hit and miss" nature of board performance evaluation cannot continue. If boards are increasingly going to provide that extra competitive and governance edge, tightening up on their performance assessment is a must.

John Cottrell in Chapter 3 agrees and provides insightful case analysis of board functioning in Australia. Despite the geographic isolation of Australia that John Cottrell terms as "the solitude of an island continent," the need to recognise and enhance the uniqueness of each board and enterprise in order to be locally and globally successful is the critical message to come through.

Thus, the first three chapters of this book implicitly refer to the power of context. The learning to draw from these chapters is to be aware of the context in which the board operates in order to appreciate the "true" nature of the board and board member performance.

Building on the theme of context, the next five chapters examine broader, cultural issues. In Chapter 4, we the editors, together with Dr Chen Yang, explore, through qualitative study, boardroom role, dynamics and relationships in China. The study concludes that social network ties, an aspect of 5000 years of Chinese civilisation, are powerful determinants of board performance and contribution. Such orientation is also identified as likely to lead to continued "localised practice," which some in the west view as unethical. The demand made in the concluding sections of the chapter is for greater transparency and the establishment of independent legal frameworks in order to break with the past and enable Chinese boards to have a meaningful role in the international community.

The theme of culture but at the local level continues. In Chapter 5, Elina Oseichuk, together with us, the editors, examine the workings of a board of an international joint venture (IJV) in Kazakhstan. Highlighted are the differences of expectation between external, non-Kazakh directors and the locals. Equally shown is the intricate interrelationship between government and corporation in a stakeholder society. Certain practices which are viewed as corrupt by Western standards are understood as "looking after our own people" and "maintaining local networks." In conclusion, this case study points to the need to understand the substantive influence of context surrounding each board in order to set the basis for trust and openness of dialogue between board members.

The cultural interpretation of context is continued in Chapter 6, where we, the editors, together with Orhan Yavuz, more specifically focus on the role, contribution and impact of the Turkish chairman. This in-depth qualitative study of Turkish boards and Chairmen emphatically points to the overwhelming influence of the Chair on the functioning of Turkish boards and Turkish companies. Turkish Chairmen emerge as relationally shrewd, strategically astute but unfortunately too embedded in their local culture to be able to support a governance policy framework that will encourage western interests to further invest in Turkey. The conclusion reached is similar to the Chinese study reported in Chapter 4 and that is, the necessity to stand above local practices that have remained deeply embedded for many hundreds of years. The sound governance of the Turkish business enterprise cannot be left to the idiosyncrasies of board members and chairmen. It is emphasised that government intervention is necessary but seemingly unlikely to be realised in the immediate future.

Pursuing the effect of local influence, in Chapter 7, Oleg Tsvetkov and Vlad Uldtatsov, together with us the editors, embark on an analysis of Russian corporate governance, in owner-managed corporations in the Russian steel industry. Cross-case analysis of four Russian steel companies reveals that board contribution is largely determined by the will and aspirations of the owner manager, irrespective of whether the individual is the Chairman or CEO of the company. The question that is raised is: how long can this last? The question of succession is loaming. Russian oligarchs are beginning to show their age. The leadership capability of direct family-related successors to fully take owner leadership responsibility is also questioned. The need to recruit independent NEDs on Russian steel boards is overwhelming, but the will to do so is seemingly not forthcoming.

Focusing now on the role of board members, Jelena Petrovic in Chapter 8, together with us, the editors, focuses on the contribution of international joint venture (IJV) directors to board effectiveness. A qualitative, exploratory case study of three Serbian foreign joint ventures points again to the power of context. Aside from having to negotiate through the different agendas of the parent companies and also individual IJV directors, the need to reach shared vision and to ascertain, trust and transparency is shown to be determined by appreciation of local ways of working. Certainly one theme consistently runs through this book, that of how board member interaction determines board effectiveness. What drives board member interaction? – the particularities of context. Understanding both local context and the mindset of the directors of each board is a necessary prelude to taking action to improve board performance.

In Chapter 9, Eleanor O'Higgins returns to the discussion of the role and contribution of the Chairman. In taking a broad and yet in-depth sweep of the literature, O'Higgins concludes the role of Chairman as pivotal to determining board and company performance. The message at the end of this chapter is that identifying, developing and recruiting the high-performing chairmen of the future have to be given absolute priority.

Searching for the high-quality directors of the future is further explored in Chapter 10, where Nada Kakabadse, Hong Yang and Richard Sanders examine the recruitment and evaluation of Chinese board directors. This qualitative study highlights the need for greater shareholder involvement in board director recruitment and evaluation. Further, poor monitoring mechanisms and lack of independence of board directors confirm the findings of previous chapters of the need for state intervention in the governance of Chinese boards.

The book finishes with a question from Malcolm McIntosh – are boards able to stand above the immediate and concern themselves with relevant, broader issues? The focus of Chapter 11 is on how boards need to adapt to address the challenges of climate change. Malcolm McIntosh's exploration of how ecological challenges can be effectively addressed highlights a theme previously raised, that of whether the current Anglo-American board is able to stand above the immediate and enter into other critical debates.

The reason for the title of this book, *Global Boards: One Desire, Many realities*, is that in conversation with many directors across the world, one desire has emerged, the aspiration for unified governance and shared board best practise. However, the investigation of this desire has surfaced as many realities about governance and boards as there are countries, cultures, boards and board directors. Our conclusion is that the essence of productive life is cosmopolitanism, diversity and respect for communities. Substantial variance of approaches exist to tackling strategic and policy challenges. Productively working together whilst talking account of context better allows for sustainable relations and longer-lasting wealth creation.

It is our hope that this unique collection of papers draws attention to the contextual richness of boards and in doing so highlights the ever more demanding role of the board director. Our point is that the high-performing board director of the future will integrate business skills with contextual insight and from that appreciation have the confidence to act in ways that he/she feels to be right, at times taking account of custom and convention and at other times, acting in spite of it.

References

Jonnergard, K., Karreman, M. and Svensson, C. (2004), The impact of changes in the corporate governance system on the boards of directors: experiences from Swedish listed companies, *International Studies of Management and Organization*, 34(2): 113–52.

Judge, W. Q. and Zeithaml, C. P. (1992), Institutional and strategic choice perspectives on board involvement in the strategic decision, *Academy of Management Journal*, 35(4): 766–94.

Kakabadse, A. and Kakabadse, N. (2008), *Leading the Board: The Six Disciplines of World-Class Chairman*, Palgrave, London.

Khaleej Times (2008a), Asset flow tug-of-war to buoy dollar next year, *Business*, 29 November, p. 33.

Lorsch, J. W. and MacIver, E. (1989), *Pawns or Potentates: The Reality of America's Corporate Boards*, Harvard University Graduate School of Business Administration, Boston, MA.

Mace, M. L. (1971), *Directors: Myth and Reality*, Harvard University Graduate School of Business Administration, Boston, MA.

Mace, M. L. (1972), The president and the board of directors, *Harvard Business Review*, pp. 37–49.

Mace, M. L. (1973), The president and the board of directors, *McKinsey Quarterly*, 4: 15–34.

Nadler, D. A., Behan, B. A. and Nadler, M. B. (eds) (2006), *Building Better Boards*, Jossey-Bass, San Francisco, CA.

Roberts, J., McNulty, T. and Stiles, P. (2005), Beyond agency conceptions of the work of the non-executive director: creating accountability in the boardroom, *British Journal of Management*, 16: S5–S26.

8   *Andrew Kakabadse and Nada Kakabadse*

8

888888
Siciliano, J. I. (2005), Board involvement in strategy and organizational performance, *Journal of General Management*, 30(4): 1–10.
Smith, E. (1958), Put the directors to work, *Harvard Business Review*, 41–8.
The News (1977), The national debts, 28 March, Saturday, Lynchburg, VA, p. A8.
US News (2008), National debt topped $10 trill this week, 3 October, http://www.topix.com/us/2008/10/national-debt-topped-10-trill-this-week (accessed 20 November 2008).
Wilson, W. (1913), quoted in Bayard Hale, *The New Freedom: A Call for the Emancipation of the Generous Energies of a People*, Doubleday, New York.

1
Identifying Key Determinants of Effective Boards of Directors

Abigail Levrau and Lutgart Van den Berghe

Introduction

Boards of directors are of interest to academics, the investment community, the business world and society at large. According to Cadbury (1999) this attention is understandable given the fact that boards of directors serve as a bridge between the shareholders, who provide capital, and management in charge of running the company. At the heart of the corporate governance debate is the view that the board of directors is the guardian of shareholders' interest (Dalton et al., 1998). Yet, boards are being criticized for failing to meet their governance responsibilities. Major institutional investors put pressure on (incompetent) directors and have long advocated changes in the board structure (Monks and Minow, 2001). Their call has been strengthened by many corporate governance reforms resulting from major corporate failures. The reforms put great emphasis on formal issues such as board independence, board leadership structure, board size and committees (Weil et al., 2002; Van den Berghe and De Ridder, 1999). These structural measures are assumed to be important means to enhance the power of the board, protect shareholders' interest, and hence, increase shareholder wealth (Becht et al., 2002; Westphal, 1998).

The interest of the investment and business community in the effectiveness of corporate boards undeniably stimulated academic research. Empirical studies on boards of directors are largely triggered by a common question, that is, whether boards of directors have an impact on corporate performance. Early research on US boards showed a sad picture as it concluded that boards of directors are rather passive, dominated by management and their impact is in fact minimal (Drucker, 1974; Lorsch and MacIver, 1989; Mace, 1971). From a different angle, an extensive body of research has examined the direct impact of board attributes on firm performance. By using a firm's financial performance as a proxy, scholars have been able to empirically test a board's effectiveness in protecting shareholders' interests. Most of these studies have, however, shown inconclusive results (see the reviews by Coles et al., 2001 and

Dalton et al., 1998). Another stream of research has investigated the influence of board attributes on the performance of board roles, suggesting an indirect causal relationship between boards of directors and company performance (see the reviews by Deutsch, 2005 and Johnson et al., 1996). A common feature of all these studies is the focus on a limited number of characteristics related to board composition, namely insider/outsider representation, board size and CEO duality. This comes as no surprise as (i) their importance is recognized by the various theoretical perspectives on board research (Zahra and Pearce, 1989), (ii) they are common targets of those who seek to reform the corporate governance processes (Dalton et al., 1998), and (iii) a vast majority of these studies rely on archival data gathering techniques and structural board measures provide the relative ease of data collection (Daily et al., 2003).

Notwithstanding the fact that market parties (investors, corporate governance activists and so on) and scholars attach great importance to the same board issues, there are few definitive and striking findings to link these structural board characteristics to performance outcomes (Daily et al., 2003). Due to the lack of clear and solid academic evidence, the appropriateness of these board measures as adequate proxies for understanding board effectiveness can be questioned. Almost two decades ago, Zahra and Pearce (1989) already argued that there is "a growing awareness of the need to understand better how boards can improve their effectiveness as instruments of corporate governance. The starting point for future research involves conducting extensive field work to understand better, document and operationalize board variables. More descriptive work is necessary before normative board models or theories can be advanced" (p. 327). Some scholars have tried to overcome the limitations in mainstream board research by examining the explanatory value of individual director characteristics (Van der Walt and Ingley, 2003; Kesner, 1988; Vance, 1978), board working style (Gabriellson and Winlund, 2000) and board processes (Cornforth, 2001) for the effectiveness of boards. In addition, recent qualitative research into boards of directors (Leblanc and Gillies, 2005; Roberts et al., 2005; Huse, 2005) as well as more practitioner literature (for example, Charan, 2005; Carter and Lorsch, 2004; Sonnenfeld, 2002) has brought the importance of studying boardroom dynamics to researchers' attention. Unfortunately the conduct of extensive field work (as called upon by Zahra and Pearce (1989)) remains limited, not in the least because of difficulties of gaining access to boardrooms and directors. Hence, a sufficient insight into the complex web of criteria which enables (or hampers) boards of directors to be effective in conducting their roles and ultimately creating shareholder wealth is, to a large extent, still lacking (Leblanc and Gillies, 2005).

The purpose of this study is to try to fill this void as much as possible, by identifying and exploring the broad variety of criteria that may influence board effectiveness. In particular, this paper addresses the following research question: *What are the key factors that contribute to the effectiveness of boards of directors?* We will investigate this question by means of a mixed methods research design, involving boards of directors of both listed and non-listed Belgian companies as well as other actors in the field. Particularly, we will explore a set of qualitative and quantitative data generated from a sample of directors, who expresses their views on the criteria of board effectiveness, based on their own (board) experience. This chapter is organized in four sections. First, we outline the theoretical background. The second section contains an explanation of the research methodology, focusing on the mixed methods research design. The third section presents the results of our study. We end this paper by discussing our findings and drawing conclusions.

Theoretical background

In studying boards of directors, academic research has been concerned with mainly three board characteristics: composition, leadership structure and size. They are commonly identified by the basic theoretical perspectives on boards of directors and by consequence assumed to be important proxies for understanding board effectiveness (Zahra and Pearce, 1989).

Board composition as key determinant

The bulk of academic research on boards of directors examines the role and the proportion of inside, outside and independent directors. In essence, two theories prevail to explain the reliance either on insider- or outsider-dominated boards. Agency theory, which dominates corporate governance research, is concerned with the conflicts of interest that may occur between the shareholders (principals) and the managers (agents). Separation of ownership and control provides the potential for managers to pursue actions which maximize their self-interest at the expense of the shareholders. The board of directors serves as an internal control mechanism in order to monitor management and to ensure shareholders' welfare (Fama and Jensen, 1983; Jensen and Meckling, 1976). In an agency perspective, effectiveness is presumed to be a function of board independence from management. Applied to the composition of the board of directors, agency theory prescribes a preponderance of independent outside directors. The opposite perspective is grounded in stewardship theory, which perceives managers as good stewards of the company assets. Managers have a range of non-financial motives, such as the intrinsic satisfaction of successful performance, the need for achievement and recognition and so on, which restrain them to misappropriate corporate resources at any price. Reallocation of control from shareholders to management leads to maximization of corporate profits and hence shareholder returns (Muth and Donaldson, 1998). Based on these assumptions, stewardship theory suggests a board of directors dominated by insiders. The empirical findings of academic research on board composition, however, do not reveal a consistent picture.

First, a rich body of literature has investigated the direct impact of board composition on a company's financial performance, but yielded mixed results. Several researchers have studied the effects of outsider-dominated boards on shareholder wealth and have found positive results. For example, Baysinger and Butler (1985) reported that firms with higher proportions of independent directors ended up with superior performance records (as measured by return on equity). Rosenstein and Wyatt (1997) found that a clearly identifiable announcement of the appointment of an outside director leads to positive effects on the firm's share price. In contrast, there are also a series of studies that do not support the postulated positive relationship. Agrawal and Knoeber (1996) and Coles et al. (2001) reported a negative impact of greater representation of outside directors on firm performance, as measured by Tobin' s Q respectively Market Value Added. In addition, Kesner's findings (1987) indicate a positive association between the proportion of inside directors and two indicators of firm financial performance, profit margin and return on assets. Still others are more reserved on the effects of board composition on corporate performance. Wagner et al. (1998) conclude that both greater insider and outsider representation can have a positive impact on performance while a meta-analyses by Dalton et al. (1998) demonstrates that there is virtually no substantive relationship between board composition and financial performance.

Another stream of empirical research suggests that board composition is related to the board's undertaking of its roles but again the results are mixed. A fair amount of evidence supports the assumption that outside directors have been effective in monitoring management and protecting shareholder interests. Outsider-dominated boards are significantly more likely to replace an underperforming CEO (Weisbach, 1988), to prevent management from paying greenmail (Kosnik, 1990), are more involved in restructuring decisions (Johnson et al., 1993) and are better able to distinguish between good and bad acquisitions (Byrd and Hickman, 1992). In contrast, some researchers do not support the notion that independent directors are effective guardians of shareholders' interest. For instance, no significant relationship was found between the proportion of independent directors and the adoption of a poison pill provision (Malette and Fowler, 1992) or the number of illegal acts committed by management (Kesner et al., 1986). Moreover, some results are rather in favour of insider-dominated boards. Research shows that the proportion of inside directors has a positive influence on R&D spending (Baysinger et al., 1991), innovation and diversification strategies (Hill and Snell, 1988) and is negatively associated with the incidence of golden parachute agreements (Cochran et al., 1985).

Board leadership structure as key determinant

A board leadership structure refers to whether or not there are separate persons who serve in the roles of CEO and chairman of the board. Agency theory as well as stewardship theory is also relevant to explain the leadership structure of boards. In an agency perspective, the separation of the roles of the CEO and chairman of the board is prescribed as a measure for more independent oversight. Splitting these roles dilutes the power of the CEO, avoids CEO entrenchment and reduces the potential for management to dominate the board. A separate board leadership structure provides the required check and balances and hence positively influences company performance (Zahra and Pearce, 1989). This view runs counter to other thinking about CEO duality. In fact, proponents of stewardship theory suggest that if the CEO also serves as the chairman, this duality provides unified firm leadership, builds trust and stimulates the motivation to perform. In this perspective, a joint leadership structure facilitates better firm performance (see for example Finkelstein and D'Aveni, 1994; Muth and Donaldson, 1998). Empirical research on the board leadership structure is rather limited and provides inconclusive results supporting both perspectives.

Only a limited number of studies have empirically examined the effects of CEO duality on firm performance. Donaldson and Davis (1991) and Coles et al. (2001) reported a positive relationship between a combined leadership structure and shareholder returns (as measured by return on equity), respectively, Economic Value Added. In contrast, Rechner and Dalton (1991) found that firms with a separate board leadership structure outperformed – over a 6-year time period – those relying upon a joint structure. However, a small amount of studies show no relationship between the board leadership structure and firm performance (for example, Dalton et al., 1998; Baliga et al., 1996; Chaganti et al., 1985). Another way of approaching this issue is by studying the joint effect of the board leadership structure and board composition. In this respect, a robust interaction effect is suggested between firm bankruptcy and board structure. Firms that combine the CEO and chairman roles and that have lower representation of independent directors are associated with bankruptcy (Daily and Dalton, 1994a, 1994b).

Board size as key determinant

Board size is a well-studied board characteristic for two different reasons. First, the size of the board is believed to have an impact on firm performance. In particular, in accordance with agency theory, the number of directors frequently serves as an indicator of CEO domination of the board. Increasing the number of directors makes it more difficult for the CEO to dominate the board and hence enables the board to better monitor management and corporate performance (Zahra and Pearce, 1989). Besides, the importance of board size is also recognized by resource dependency theory. The central postulate of this theory is that external parties hold resources that a business organization perceives as crucial to the realization of its internal objectives (Pfeffer and Salancik, 1978). In order to acquire and maintain these resources, a company seeks to establish links with its environment and the board of directors is a vehicle to do so. According to this perspective, a larger board of directors is assumed to be more capable of co-opting external influences, thus obtaining valuable resources that are inevitable for corporate success (Johnson et al., 1996). Based on these assumptions, a positive association between board size and corporate performance became conventional wisdom but the evidence of empirical research on this issue is rather inconsistent. Some early studies provide positive evidence for varying industries. According to Provan (1980), board size is one of the strongest predictors of organizational effectiveness in the human service sector. Chaganti et al. (1985) compared the board size of failed and non-failed firms in the retailing industry and found that larger boards were associated with a higher rate of corporate survival. Pearce and Zahra (1992) found a significant positive relationship between board size and different measures of financial performance, using data from Fortune 500 industrial companies. In contrast, more recent studies reported opposite results. Yermack (1996) found a negative relationship between board size and firm market value, using a sample of large US public companies. Similar results were reported using European data. Eisenberg et al. (1998) studied small non-listed Finnish firms and found a negative correlation between a firm's profitability and the size of its board, while the study of Conyon and Peck (1998) shows an inverse relationship between return on shareholders' equity and board size for five European countries.

Second, from a completely different angle, boards of directors are approached as decision-making groups. In this respect, board size serves as a proxy measure of directors' expertise. Larger boards are likely to have more knowledge and skill at their disposal and the ability of boards to draw on a variety of perspectives likely contributes to the quality of the decision making (Forbes and Milliken, 1999). However, expanding the number of directors might significantly inhibit the working of a board, due to the potential group dynamic problems associated with larger groups (Jensen, 1993). Consequently, larger boards may be hampered in reaching a consensus on important decisions (Forbes and Milliken, 1999). A limited number of studies empirically examined the influence of board size with respect to strategic decision making. Judge and Zeithaml (1992) found that board size was negatively associated with board involvement in strategic decisions, concluding that when boards get too large, effective debate and discussion are limited and the interaction between individual members is lower. Goodstein et al. (1994) have explored the effects of board size on strategic changes initiated by organizations. Their results indicate that large boards have limited effectiveness in directing strategic change during periods of environmental turbulence. Also Golden and Zajac (2001) found that strategic change is significantly affected by board size. In particular, their findings indicate that an increase in board size is negatively related to strategic change for larger boards.

To summarize, the above-mentioned studies show that there is no robust evidence on the relationship between structural characteristics of boards of directors and board or company performance. Although these studies revealed interesting and useful insights, the absence of clear empirical support of substantive relationships casts doubt on both the efficacy of agency theory as the dominant governance theory and the appropriateness of structural board measures as adequate proxies for understanding board effectiveness. In particular, the vast majority of empirical studies are being criticized for using a too narrow focus in assessing the effectiveness of boards in performing their governance role and its contribution to firm financial performance (Daily et al., 2003). It seems that our knowledge on the effectiveness of boards is hampered not only by the applied data gathering techniques but also by inadequate attention to the potentially large number of intervening variables between board characteristics and performance outcomes (Roberts et al., 2005; Pettigrew, 1992).

Methods

As indicated above, the vast majority of studies on boards of directors have relied upon quantitative data gathering techniques (Daily et al., 2003). These techniques include mainly large-scale archival data, while a subset of board studies has also used questionnaires. Although these techniques offer the advantage to analyse the data in a consistent way, their access to process-oriented data is restricted (Daily et al., 2003). Some scholars have overcome this limitation by using in-dept interviews (Roberts et al., 2005; Pettigrew and McNulty, 1995; Demb and Neubauer, 1992; Lorsch and MacIver, 1989) and direct observation techniques (Huse and Schoning, 2004; Leblanc and Gillies, 2003). Their research provides an important qualitative counter-balance to the traditional surveys on boards of directors.

In our study, we build upon the strengths of both approaches by opting for a mixed methods research design (Teddlie and Tashakkori, 2003). More specifically, we opted for a sequential exploratory design (Creswell et al., 2003). A specific feature of this design is its two-phase approach whereby the collection and analysis of the qualitative data in an initial phase is followed by a phase of quantitative data collection and analysis. More specifically, in the first (qualitative) research phase we try to identify – by means of interviews – the full set of criteria that potentially contribute to the effectiveness of boards. The results are then used to construct a rating survey for the second (quantitative) research phase which helps us in elaborating and interpreting the qualitative findings. Furthermore, the research design implies completely different samples and data collection techniques for the two phases.

Sample and date collection for the qualitative phase

Sample. For the first qualitative research phase, we selected purposively utilizing a critical cases sampling scheme (Collins et al., 2006). This means we intentionally limited the sample to members of the boards of directors of Belgian listed companies because we believed that they are well placed to provide us with compelling insights into the determinants of board effectiveness. A sample of 147 directors of Belgian companies listed on Euronext Brussels were contacted and asked to participate in a large-scale in-depth study on corporate governance in Belgium. Our sample included different directors' roles such as chairman, independent directors, non-executive directors and CEOs. Information on the companies listed on Euronext Brussels was found on the Euronext website (www.euronext.com). Information on the boards of directors was retrieved from multiple sources such as the company's annual report, its website and the Belfirst database. Of the initial 147 directors that were contacted, 104 (response rate = 71 per cent) agreed to participate. Table 1.1 presents our sample in terms of directors' roles.

Data collection. Data were collected during interviews with directors of Belgian listed companies. For the purpose of this study, a standardized open-ended question was used (Johnson and Turner, 2003). In particular, the directors were asked to sum up what they perceived as the most important ingredients of a good board of directors. In this respect, multiple answers could be given. We deliberately opted not to use the term 'effective' to avoid misunderstanding because the concept of effectiveness may yield different interpretations. Therefore, we used the word 'good'. By phrasing the question in a more neutral way, we believed that each respondent had the same

Table 1.1   (Qualitative) sample per directors' role

Directors' role	Number	
Chairmen	41	
Chairman = CEO		18
Chairman = independent director		11
Chairman = non-executive director		12
Executive directors	35	
CEOs		30
Other executives		5
Non-executive directors	25	
Independent directors		21
Non-executive shareholders' representatives		4
Secretary-generals	3	
Total	104	

Source: Compiled by the authors.

understanding of the question, which diminishes bias in the answers. In addition, by using an open-ended question we were able to fully capture a broad spectrum of criteria.

Sample and data collection for the quantitative phase

Sample. For the second quantitative research phase, we selected purposively utilizing a convenience sampling scheme (Collins et al., 2006). This means we have chosen individuals that are conveniently available and willing to participate in the study. A sample of 715 members of the Belgian Governance Institute were contacted and asked to participate in our study. Members include (i) directors with different roles (such as chairmen, and independent, non-executive or executive directors) representing boards of directors of listed as well as non-listed companies, and (ii) actors in the field of corporate governance (advisors, lawyers, academics and so on). Of the initial 715 directors that were contacted, 166 (response rate = 23 per cent) respondents were engaged in the quantitative research phase. Next, in order to avoid overlap between the samples, we excluded the respondents who previously participated in the interviews. Incomplete responses were also rejected from the sample resulting in 150 (response rate = 21 per cent). The sample can be divided into two groups of respondents. We labelled a group "directors," representing those persons who sit on boards of directors of Belgian companies, and another group received the label "experts," representing actors in the field of corporate governance (see Table 1.2).

Data collection. Two small written questionnaires were used to collect the quantitative data. The aim of the questionnaires was to reveal further gradation between various criteria which are assumed to contribute to the effectiveness of boards. For that purpose, we opted for structured closed-ended questionnaires whereby the response category took the form of rankings. The ten questionnaire items were based on the themes (representing groupings of similar criteria) derived from the open-ended question in the qualitative phase. To avoid misunderstanding, we clearly defined what was meant by board effectiveness. In particular, board effectiveness was defined as "the

Table 1.2   (Quantitative) sample per group of respondents

Respondent	Number	
Directors	119	
Representing listed companies		12
Representing non-listed companies		107
Experts	31	
Total	150	

Source: Compiled by the authors.

degree the board is able to carry out its strategic and monitoring tasks." Furthermore, we also indicated how the rankings should be interpreted. To minimize response bias, the respondents received the questionnaires in two steps. As previously explained, the first questionnaire was submitted to the respondents who were asked to rank the items according to their importance (1 most important to 10 least important). After a period of time, the respondents received the second form and were asked to indicate to what extent there is room for improvement in practice (1 needs most improvement to 10 needs least improvement).

Results

Qualitative analysis

The interviews yielded a broad set of responses regarding criteria that constitute a good corporate board, as perceived by the directors. The qualitative data were analysed by coding using the ATLAS.ti software. As recommended in the literature (Miles and Huberman, 1984), we developed a coding list, based upon the literature on boards of directors, insights into the corporate governance codes and complemented the list with themes that emerged during data analysis. This resulted in 31 qualitative codes. The codes resemble as close as possible the directors' responses. In a next step, we grouped codes that were related to similar concepts and entered these groupings as 'families' in ATLAS.ti (see Appendix A). The creation of families is a way to form clusters and allow easier handling of coded material (ATLAS.ti, 2004). In addition, we used a basic form of counting during the analysis process because it allowed us to more fully describe the variety of criteria that were cited during the interviews and it helped to maintain analytical integrity (Onwuegbuzie and Teddlie, 2003). Table 1.3 provides a summary of the results. A detailed overview of the frequencies of each code within a family can be found in Appendix B.

The findings presented in Table 1.3 show that aspects related to the composition of the board are by far most frequently reported by a great number of directors. Board culture that expresses more intangible aspects of the board of directors resides in second place, closely followed by the operations of the board. The less frequently mentioned cluster refers to the relationship of the board with management. In what follows, each of the themes will be described in more detail.

Board composition.[1] In directors' perceptions, in order to be effective, the board of directors needs to have the appropriate structure. This involves several related dimensions. The most frequently cited dimension refers to diversity. The board should comprise a mix of people having different personalities, educational, occupational and functional backgrounds. As some directors pointed out: 'A board of directors composed of "clones" does not

Table 1.3 Ingredients of a good corporate board-director' perspectives

Families	Number of respondents who referred to this theme	% of respondents (N = 104)	Frequency this theme was reported
Theme 1: board composition	99	95%	N = 101
Theme 2: board culture	53	51%	N = 55
Theme 3: operation of the board	49	47%	N = 54
Theme 4: board tasks	34	33%	N = 37
Theme 5: debate/decision making	28	27%	N = 29
Theme 6: individual norms	25	24%	N = 28
Theme 7: relationships between board members	23	22%	N = 23
Theme 8: board management relationship	6	6%	N = 7

Source: Compiled by the authors.

work.' However, although diversity seems to be top of mind, it is closely followed by the dimension of complementarity. Having different skills at the disposal of boards is a minimum requirement but they must be complementary. One director summarized this using the following metaphor: "It is the mayonnaise that counts within a board, thanks to the different oils present." The third dimension relates to the competence of individual directors. Beyond diversity and complementarity this dimension was cited separately as one of the key criteria. Individual directors should have a minimum degree of knowledge and experience. It boils down to the capacity and quality of the people sitting on the board. Within the cluster relating to board composition, the proportion of independent directors and the size of the board were among the least frequently mentioned criteria. In the cases where these criteria came across, it was noted that the board of directors should pursue a balance between executive directors, shareholders' representatives and independent directors. Moreover, the board of directors should not be too large.

Board culture.[2] Directors directed also much attention to the more intangible side of board conduct. We labelled this theme 'board culture' referring to a set of informal unwritten rules that regulate board and directors' behaviour. The frequencies of the reported issues within this theme are very close. Most important, there should be openness and transparency. Directors should have the ability to express their views and a culture of open debate should reign. This implies that matters should be treated inside the boardroom and not 'behind the scene'. One director formulated it as follows: "There should be no taboo. All subjects ought to be touched upon. Directors should utter their opposition against a principle. Freedom of thought is very important." Second, involvement is also perceived as an important criterion. In contrast to a ceremonial, passive board, a good board of directors is active, interested and of benefit to a company. Third, the general atmosphere or climate determines to some extent the way board members are expected to behave. This refers to a sense of humour, positive and constructive attitude, degree of professionalism and so on. Other dimensions with respect to board culture, but less often reported, are the fact that the board members need to pursue a common vision or interest and to be vigilant and critical.

Operation of the board.[3] It seems that directors attach much importance to the operation of the board of directors. In particular, the preparation of a board meeting was often cited as a key issue. This relates to the make-up of a board agenda and even more vital to the documents the directors receive in advance. A director commented: "A good board must be conscientiously prepared; sufficient information must be provided for each point on the agenda in such a manner that it allows directors to decide with full knowledge during board meetings." Next, the role of the chairman was acknowledged. One director put it as follows: "The chairman is the driving force... he is responsible for an efficient course of board meeting, he is the one who takes the plunge in case of conflict, who dare to stick its neck out...in addition, he is the hinge between shareholders, management and the board." Finally, some aspects, which were less frequently reported, were related to the conduct of board meetings such as the length of board meetings (not too long), the quality of (management) presentations, time management and so on.

Board tasks.[4] From a different perspective, a good board of directors was viewed in relation to the tasks it performs. Particularly, directors place emphasis on the strategic role of the board. As pointed out by the directors, the board should be involved in determining the long-term strategic direction of the company. In doing so, two additional comments are of interest. First, the board must have some insight into the evolution of the business environment. One director explained: "A good board of directors is able to see the present, whilst keeping an eye on the future." Second, the board must be able to translate the shareholder's strategic ambitions to management. One director expressed this as follows: "See the company through the eyes of the shareholder." In second order, the support role was mentioned. This role refers to the support the board of directors provides to management by means of challenging, advising and stimulating management. Some directors summarized this as follows: "A good board brings out the best in its management." Less attention is paid to the monitoring role of the board and more to the context that enables a board to fulfil it tasks. The latter refers to the degree of delegation of power within the corporate governance tripod.

Debate/decision making.[5] This theme views the board of directors as a decision-making group. In particular, the occurrence and quality of the debate(s) are perceived as key criteria within this cluster. The board is not a rubber-stamping body. Real, in-depth discussion should take place but the deliberations should be characterized by neutrality and objectivity. Or as one director stated: "One should play the ball, not the man." To a less extent, reference was also made to the fact that directors should make a contribution in the discussions by sharing information or knowledge and the fact that the board should make decisions.

Individual norms.[6] We have already touched upon the capacity and quality of the individual directors when discussing the composition of the board. In addition, more behavioural characteristics were highlighted during the interviews which we labelled as 'individual norms'. First, the personality of individual directors seems to matter. In particular, aspects such as integrity, ethics, attitude, ego and so on were mentioned. Second, it includes the commitment of individual directors referring to the personal enthusiasm, interest and availability of people sitting on a board. The least important characteristics are the independence of and preparation by individual directors.

Relationship between the board members.[7] Directors also paid some attention to the interpersonal relationships between the board members. Although the frequencies are quite low, some related dimensions could be singled out. First, boards need the right chemistry and to foster cohesiveness. Second, informal contacts and interaction among the directors must be stimulated. Third, the board of directors must function as a team. Finally, trust and respect between the members needs to be valued.

Board–management relationship.[8] The last theme refers to dimensions regarding the relationship between the board and management, which could not be grouped within the support role of the board. More specifically, this cluster relates to the contact, symbioses with and trust in management, as well as to the quality of management. In fact, only a few directors mentioned the reliance of the board on a strong and honest management as a key criterion for its effectiveness.

Quantitative analysis

The previous section has provided a descriptive analysis of the variety of criteria that potentially contribute to the effectiveness of boards. By means of two written questionnaires, the qualitative findings are further elaborated. More specifically, the questionnaires offered respondents a set of ten determinants of board effectiveness. These determinants are not mutually exclusive, as some are closely related. The first questionnaire was aimed at getting a more profound insight into the importance rate of a select number of suggested determinants on a quantitative base. Descriptive statistics for the full sample are given in Table 1.4 in while Appendix C provides the detailed frequency table.

The results in Table 1.4 show that a relationship of trust between the board and CEO/management is perceived to be the most important determinant of board effectiveness. The next-best determinants are the composition of the board in terms of complementary expertises, and a constructive critical attitude of board members. In contrast, a chairman who seeks consensus and board members who get along very well appear to be of little importance for the effectiveness of boards.

In order to reveal a more fine-grained view on the importance rate, we have divided our sample into two groups. The first group represents the "directors" while the second group represents the "experts." In fact, we are interested to see if directors' perceptions on the determinants of board effectiveness differ from those of experts in the field of corporate governance. Table 1.5 presents the descriptive statistics for both groups.

The descriptive results in Table 1.5 indicate some differences between the perceptions of directors and experts with respect to the importance rate, as only three of the ten suggest that the determinants rank the same (trust between the board and CEO/management, sufficient and timely information, consensus-seeking by the chairman). The views of directors and experts diverge, in particular, regarding the importance of board members'

Table 1.4   Descriptive statistics of importance rate for the full sample ($N = 150$)

Determinants of board effectiveness	In top 3*		Rank
	No.	%	
Trust between the board of directors and CEO/management	76	50.6	1
Complementarity with respect to background, expertise and experience	68	45.3	2
Board members show a constructive critical attitude	68	45.3	2
The board of directors includes a mix of executives, independent directors and non-executives representing the shareholders	61	40.06	4
The board members are well prepared	60	40.0	5
The information is sufficient and on time	49	32.6	6
All directors actively participate in the discussions	29	19.3	7
Divergent opinions are tolerated	22	14.6	8
The chairman seeks consensus	11	7.3	9
Board members get along very well	6	4.0	10

Note: *Denotes the frequency the item received a ranking score ≤3.

Source: Compiled by the authors.

Table 1.5 Descriptive statistics of importance rate for sub-samples

Determinants of board effectiveness	Directors (N = 119)			Experts (N = 31)		
	In top 3*			In top 3*		
	No.	%	Rank	No.	%	Rank
Trust between the board of directors and CEO/management	59	49.6	1	17	54.8	1
Board members show a constructive critical attitude	58	48.7	2	13	32.3	5
Complementarity with respect to background expertise and experience	51	42.9	3	17	54.8	1
The board of directors includes a mix of executives, independent directors and non–executives representing the shareholders	47	39.5	4	14	45.2	3
The board members are well prepared	46	38.7	5	14	45.2	3
The information is sufficient and on time	37	31.1	6	12	38.7	6
All directors actively participate in the discussions	27	22.7	7	2	6.5	8
Divergent opinions are tolerated	17	14.3	8	5	16.1	7
The chairman seeks consensus	10	8.4	9	1	3.2	9
Board members get along very well	5	4.2	10	1	3.2	9

Note: *Denotes the frequency the item received a ranking score ≤3.
Source: Compiled by the authors.

constructive critical attitude. The deviation in the ranking score is the greatest for this determinant (ranked 2nd for directors while 5th for experts). Although our data set can be claimed for statistical ordinal testing, it does not fulfil the requirements for the computation of a Pearson chi-square correlation coefficient mainly because of low frequencies per cell (with respect to the responses of the expert group).

The second questionnaire was used to explore how the suggested determinants occur in practice. In particular, it yielded quantitative data reflecting respondents' perceptions on the (same) listed items in terms of their need for improvement. Descriptives of the corrigible rate for the full sample are given in Table 1.6 while Appendix C provides the detailed frequency table.

The results in Table 1.6 indicate that the preparation of board members, a sufficient and timely information flow and the active participation in discussions by all directors are most capable of improvement. In contrast, consensus-driven deliberations, guided by the chairman, and a good relationship among the board members are perceived to be least capable of improvement.

Table 1.6   Descriptive statistics of corrigible rate for the full sample ($N = 75$)

Determinants of board effectiveness	In top 3*		Rank
	No.	%	
The board members are well prepared	48	64.0	1
The information is sufficient and on time	43	57.3	2
All directors actively participate in the discussions	32	42.7	3
Complementarity with respect to background, expertise and experience	31	41.3	4
Board members show a constructive critical attitude	21	28.0	5
The board of directors includes a mix of executives, independent directors and non-executives representing the shareholders	21	28.0	6
Divergent opinions are tolerated	11	14.7	7
Trust between the board of directors and CEO management	8	10.7	8
The chairman seeks consensus	6	8.0	9
Board members get along very well	4	5.3	10

Note: *Denotes the frequency the item received a ranking score ≤ 3.

Source: Compiled by the authors.

Similar to the analysis of the importance scores, it is possible to reveal a more fine-grained view on the corrigible rate, by dividing our sample into two groups. The first group represents the directors while the second group represents the experts. In fact, we are interested to see if directors and experts view the need for improvement of the suggested determinants differently. Table 1.7 presents the descriptive statistics for both groups.

The descriptive results in Table 1.7 indicate great similarities between the perceptions of directors and experts with respect to the corrigible rate, as seven of the ten suggested determinants rank the same. The views of directors and experts seem only to diverge regarding the need for improvement of tolerating divergent opinions, trust between the board of directors and CEO/management and consensus seeking by the chairman. Although our data set can be claimed for statistical ordinal testing, it does not fulfil the requirements for the computation of a Pearson chi-square correlation coefficient mainly because of low frequencies per cell.

Finally, matching the importance rate of the determinants of board effectiveness to their corrigible rate reveals the gaps that exist, and at the same time points out the criteria that limit the board's potential to fulfil its strategic and monitoring role. Figure 1.1 illustrates the link between

Table 1.7 Descriptive statistics of corrigible rate for sub-samples

Determinants of board effectiveness	Directors (N = 56)			Experts (N = 19)		
	In top 3*			In top 3*		
	No.	%	Rank	No.	%	Rank
The board members are well prepared	37	66.1	1	11	57.9	1
The information is sufficient and on time	33	58.9	2	10	52.6	2
All directors actively participate in the discussions	25	44.6	3	7	36.8	3
Complementarity with respect to background expertise and experience	25	44.6	4	6	31.6	4
Board members show a constructive critical attitude	16	28.6	5	5	26.3	5
The board of directors includes a mix of executives, independent directors and non-executives representing the shareholders	16	28.6	5	5	26.3	5
Divergent opinions tolerated	6	10.7	7	5	26.3	5
Trust between the board of directors and CEO/management	6	10.7	8	2	10.5	9
The chairman seeks consensus	2	3.6	9	4	21.1	8
Board members get along very well	2	3.6	9	2	10.5	9

Note: *Denotes the frequency the item received a ranking score ≤3.
Source: Compiled by the authors.

the importance of determinants of board effectiveness and their need for improvement.

Quadrant 1 denotes determinants of board effectiveness representing "type 1," which we term *flashing lights*. In particular, this quadrant groups criteria which are perceived to be very important for the effectiveness of boards and at the same time require most improvement in practice. Put differently, the findings suggest that too little complementarity in terms of expertise absence of a critical attitude in discussions, insufficient diversity regarding directors' roles and unpreparedness of board members, may hamper the board in carrying out its duties.

Quadrant 2 denotes determinants of board effectiveness representing "type 2," which we term *challengers*. In particular, this quadrant groups criteria which are perceived to be very important for the effectiveness of boards while at the same time require only little or no improvement in practice. It appears that

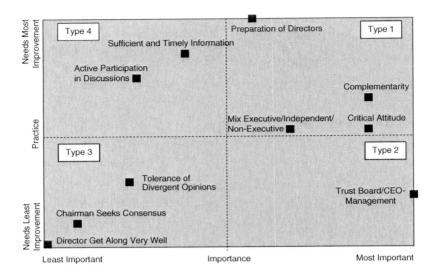

Figure 1.1 Linking importance and corrigible scores of determinants of board effectiveness[9]

Source: Compiled by the authors.

only one criterion fits into this quadrant, that is the relationship between the board and management. Although this relationship seems not to pose many problems in practice, the challenge to maintain a balance of trust between the board of directors and CEO/management inheres in the governance of every company. A relationship of trust can easily be broken at any point in time and therefore requires continuous effort of both governing bodies.

Quadrant 3 denotes determinants of board effectiveness representing "type 3," which we term *subordinates*. In particular, this quadrant groups criteria which are perceived to be of less importance for the effectiveness of boards and at the same time require only little or no improvement in practice. These criteria are perceived to be inferior compared to the other groups. Our findings suggest that when divergent opinions are tolerated in board meetings, the chairman seeks consensus or directors try to get along, does not significantly add value to the ability of a board in performing its roles (compared to types 1 and 2).

Quadrant 4 denotes determinants of board effectiveness representing "type 4," which we term *seducers*. In particular, this quadrant groups criteria which are perceived to be of less importance for the effectiveness of boards while at the same time being most corrigible in practice. The findings suggest that getting appropriate information beforehand and watching over an active participation of all directors in discussions are two criteria which should be addressed, but practice shows major shortcomings on these issues. Still, the danger exists that these criteria might mislead attention and effort from the more critical aspects of board effectiveness (types 1 and 2).

Discussion

Three major points emerge from this study. First, there appears to be a gap between a limited number of structural board measures consistently found in the literature and the broad set of criteria that are emphasized in directors' perceptions, in particular the systematic occurrence of a set of behavioural criteria of board effectiveness. Mainstream board research has been heavily influenced by a research tradition from financial economics and theories treating the board of directors as a "black box." Although boards of directors are frequently studied in academic research, scholars have traditionally focused on a limited number of characteristics such as board size, board composition and board leadership. These structural measures are commonly viewed as appropriate and adequate proxies for understanding board effectiveness, while the working processes of boards or individual directors' behaviour are rarely investigated. As such, the various research streams suggest that if the structure of a board is appropriate, the board should be able to fulfil its duties, and ultimately enhance corporate performance. However, little convincing evidence exists that these structural measures, which are presumed to contribute to the effectiveness of boards as guardians of shareholders' welfare, have had considerable impact on the financial performance of companies. Moreover, the data collected in this study reveal a huge discrepancy between the criteria found in academic literature and the perceptions of the directors themselves. Our qualitative findings have revealed an enlarged set of board attributes and suggest a more prominent role for intangible or "soft" factors as determinants for board effectiveness. More than half of the directors interviewed put great emphasis on the informal rules that regulate board and directors' behaviour ('board culture'), while more than a fourth stressed the importance of debate as a criterion for a good corporate board. The quantitative results retrieved from the questionnaires elaborate this qualitative evidence. They highlight the importance of trust between the board and CEO/management as well as the behaviour of board members with respect to their preparation, participation and critical attitude in boardroom deliberations. Our findings suggest that board of directors and board effectiveness, in particular, should also be understood through attributes reflecting the board's inner workings and not solely through attributes of board structure and composition. Besides, our findings are largely consistent and supported with evidence from other qualitative board studies. The latter have also drawn attention to the importance of the human element in board effectiveness. A climate of trust and candour, a culture of open dissent, collective wisdom, collective strength and behavioural expectations are some of the elements put forward to increase board performance (Leblanc and Gillies, 2005; Charan, 2005; Carter and Lorsch, 2004; Sonnenfeld, 2002).

A second major point is that the value of independence may be over-emphasized at the cost of the broader issue of diversity. Stimulated by the dominance of the agency perspective in corporate governance, board effectiveness has commonly been approached as the ability of boards to act independently from management. Board independence has been the cornerstone of the corporate governance debate, although considerable divergent views exist on both the right proportion of independent directors and their definition (Van den Berghe and Baelden, 2005; Daily et al., 1999). It is assumed that independent directors add real value to a company and arguments in favour of their appointment are well documented (Felton et al., 1995). Corporate governance reforms tend to support the plea for board independence by advocating that a critical mass of independent directors is essential for a board to be able to provide critical oversight. Although our findings also highlight the importance of having a sufficient mix of directors' roles in terms of executives, non-executives and independent directors, they suggest that competencies, diversity and complementarity are more pivotal attributes for board effectiveness. These criteria were among the most cited in the interviews and the dimension of complementarity systematically received high rankings in the questionnaires. Still, the issue of diversity is largely neglected in board research in spite of the fact that a small number of studies already presented interesting findings. For example, Golden and Zajac (2001) found that specific types of directors' expertise or experience are influential in shaping the orientation of a board towards strategic change. In addition, corporate governance and shareholder activists are increasingly becoming convinced of the benefit of diversity in terms of improved decision making. Boards have commonly been viewed as homogenous groups of executives and non-executives directors who are cut from the same cloth and it is argued that this uniformity undermines the quality and variety of boardroom debate (Grady, 1999). Consequently, institutional investors have begun to pressure companies to diversify their board composition with respect to gender, race and type of expertise. TIAA-CREF, for example, puts major focus on qualified directors who reflect a diversity of background and experience (TIAA-CREF, 2006).

A third major issue is that mainstream board research ignores to a large extent two additional conditions under which a board of directors can make an effective contribution to the strategic direction and control of a company. First, our findings suggest that board members should become sufficiently knowledgeable about the particular company context. During the interviews, the aspect of preparation of board meetings in terms of agenda and information provided to directors was frequently cited. The quantitative evidence endorsed this finding as both timely and sufficient information and the preparation of board members received high rankings scores as determinants of board effectiveness. The need to adequately inform board members is also recognized by other scholars involved in qualitative board research. It is generally accepted that non-executive and independent directors face a disadvantageous position with regard to information gathering. Non-executive and independent directors, who spend only a limited amount of time with the company, can never know as much as the executive directors. They depend largely on the goodwill of the management to obtain relevant and timely information. Consequently, it is assumed that in order to be able to perform their duties, directors need to be well informed at all times (Charan, 1998). The corporate scandals are only some examples of boards that knew too little too late. In addition, it is noted that a dysfunctional information flow may hinder the performance of boards. Some boards receive bundles of documents, but only a small part may be useful in gaining an understanding of the real issues the board should be addressing (Monk and Minow, 2001). Also Lorsch and MacIver (1989), in studying American boards, reported that information is often provided in such a complex way that directors have a problem in interpreting and using it. A study by Lawler et al. (2002) points out that those boards whose directors have a greater amount of relevant information appear to perform their roles more effectively than boards that are less well informed. Second, our findings suggest a pivotal role of the chairman in the effectiveness of boards. In particular, the qualitative data suggest that the leadership style of the chairman plays a major role in the way the board is able to carry out its duties. However, the academic governance literature traditionally looks at the issue of board leadership in quite narrow terms by focusing the discussion on the relationship of the chairman and the CEO. Especially, the question whether the two functions should be separated or not has received considerable attention and continues to be subject to much debate. Still, the effects of a separation of roles have not been consistently substantiated by empirical evidence. In addition, only a handful of studies exist, which have examined the role of the chairman and its impact on the effectiveness of boards. For example, Roberts (2002) documents how the unskilful management of board relationships and processes can easily disable a board in its decision making and performance. Based on the nature of chairman/chief executive relationships, he distinguishes three dysfunctional board dynamics – a competitive, personal and captured board – with negative consequences for board effectiveness. In addition, the earlier study of Pettigrew and McNulty (1995) already pointed to the key role a chairman plays in shaping board dynamics and transforming a 'minimalist' board to a 'maximalist' board, having a strong impact on the direction of a company. However, an unexpected finding in our study relates to the role of the chairman in board decision making. The results from the written questionnaire suggest that in order for the board to be effective, it is not important that a chairman seeks consensus. As such, this finding does not support the study of Hill (1995), who found that maintaining boardroom consensus was a fundamental value among all directors he surveyed and which was definitely the norm within the executive grouping. A possible explanation relates to the interpretation of the notion of consensus. Additional comments by directors revealed that consensus might be interpreted as 'unanimity' and consequently bias responses. They noted that a good board of directors reaches a decision that is supported by all board members even though there exists personal disagreement.

Conclusion

The purpose of this study was to get a better understanding of the various criteria that contribute to the effectiveness of boards. In order to do so, we conducted an in-depth review of the literature and complemented the insights with the findings of an extensive field study. The analysis is primarily intended to be exploratory and descriptive while using both qualitative and quantitative data. The first research phase is based on a large number of interviews and yielded a broad spectrum of criteria that constitute a good board of directors, as perceived by the directors. By coding the criteria and clustering them into separate groups we were able to grasp the variety of criteria. Moreover, the technique of counting (the frequency a criterion was mentioned) provided a first indication of which criteria matter more. The importance rate of a limited number of potential determinants of board effectiveness was further examined in the quantitative research phase by means of a written questionnaire. In addition, a second questionnaire was used to further elaborate the findings by exploring how the suggested determinants occur in practice. The overall results raised three major issues that were then discussed more in-depth. What becomes clear by our research is that many aspects of board effectiveness are invisible to 'outsiders' and as a result poorly understood. Most researchers have remained at a considerable distance from actual board practice, partly because of difficulties of gaining access. Therefore, they focus their attention on a small number of structural board characteristics leading to inconclusive findings. Our findings suggest that this ambiguity in current research evidence can to some extent be attributed to the ignorance of a wide range of interconnected structural (such as diversity and competence) and more behavioural factors (such as trust, attitude, norms and conduct) which actually shape the effectiveness of boards in performing their roles.

Various avenues of further research can be identified. First, our study is limited to a description of a broad set of criteria that are presumed to have an impact on board effectiveness. At this stage, we are unable to pronounce upon the way the different criteria interact. More research is required to examine the interrelationship between the criteria in order to develop a new theoretical model for board effectiveness or to adjust and refine existing board models. It is also advocated to test the identified relationships on a large scale to validate the new proxies that can be used to measure board effectiveness. Second, no reference was made to contingencies which may influence the effectiveness of boards and hence directors' perceptions. In particular, it can be stated that specific board attributes that are beneficial for one company may turn out to be detrimental to another. Therefore, it is suggested to get a better insight into the context and to identify the conditions under which a board can or will be effective in performing its roles. Third, the findings of the study also point to the need of a multi-disciplinary approach in board research. The latter should not only be restricted to the use of different research techniques but also incorporate relevant literature, such as literature on group effectiveness, TMT decision making, organizational demography and so on.

This study makes at least three contributions to the corporate governance literature. The first contribution stems from the study of boards of directors in a non-US context using an alternative research methodology. In spite of the intense research interest in corporate governance systems and mechanisms around the world (Shleifer and Vishny, 1997), most (empirical) studies on boards of directors have been carried out by using samples of large US corporations and are inspired by quantitative US research traditions (Huse, 2005). In contrast, qualitative studies on boards of directors as well as research of boards in European contexts are still very scarce. Our research contributes to reduce the observed gap in the existing board literature by studying boards of directors in a Belgian context with a qualitative-oriented research approach (mixed methods design). Second, our study also emphasizes the potential importance of board diversity as additional (structural) measure of board composition. Rather than approaching the board of directors exclusively in terms of insiders versus outsiders, researchers should consider to integrate measures of diversity that reflect the differences in backgrounds, experiences and skills (Kosnik, 1990). Third, this study also stresses the need to examine the inner workings of boards. A common feature of mainstream board research is the treatment of the board of directors as a "black box" (Daily et al., 2003). The inconclusive findings of studying direct relationships between board characteristics and performance outcomes, however, raise doubt on the explanatory power of these input–output models. One way to make progress in board research is to develop and adopt indirect research models that take into account more behavioural aspects of board conduct.

Acknowledgements

This paper was presented at the 'Research on Friday Seminar' at the Vlerick Leuven Ghent Management School on 29 September 2006; the TEW

Working Paper Forum on 5 October 2006; the Roundtable 'board effectiveness' organized by the Belgian Governance Institute on 8 October 2006; the 3rd PhD Workshop on Corporate Governance, the European Institute for Advanced Studies in Management (EIASM), Brussels, 9–10 November 2006. We wish to thank Annick Willem and Dave Bouckenooghe for their helpful comments on earlier drafts of this chapter. We also would like to thank the colleagues of the Belgian Governance Institute who assisted us in carrying out the many interviews. We express our gratitude to the participants of the various workshops this paper was presented at. Their feedback was of added value for improving our own insights. Finally, this research was made possible by the support of the Belgian Governance Institute and, in particular, by its member network.

Appendix A

Table A.1   Debate/decision making

Code	Interpretation/definition
Occurrence	Refers to the fact that discussions take place; no rubber stamping
Quality	Refers to the characteristics of the discussions such as neutral, objective, in-depth, open, critical, emotionless, based on facts, to the point and so on
Contribution	Related to the participation on the discussions and the assumption that members contribute during the discussions (for example, sharing of knowledge, information, ideas and so on)
Decision	Refers to the fact that decisions are taken

Table A.2   Board culture

Active involvement	Refers to the fact that a board is interested and involved in the company; it takes initiatives, learns and contributes in contrast to a formal, passive board
Openness	Refers to an open culture, the possibility or ability to express an opinion, transparency and so on
Critical	Refers to a critical attitude/behaviour
Common values or goals	Refers to the fact that group members have a common denominator
Atmosphere climate	Relates to other unwritten rules or standards such as humour, a positive and constructive mind, professionalism, passion for excellence.

Table A.3   Individual norms

Commitment	Refers to the fact that individuals are interested, involved and available (sufficient time)
Preparation	Refers to the fact that individual members are prepared (for example, read the documents)
Personality	Relates to characteristics of the personality of individual members such as humility, ego, attitude, sense of responsibility, integrity, ethical
Independence	Refers to the courage of individual members to speak up and show an independent mind

Table A.4   Relationships among the board members

Cohesiveness	Refers to the chemistry and the fact that board members cohere
Respect	Refers to the fact that the board members respect each other
Team	Refers to the fact that board members operate as a team/group
Trust	Refers to the trust among the board members
Contact	Refers to the interaction, dynamic and informal contacts between the board members

Table A.5   Board tasks

Context	Refers to the conditions which are necessary to fulfil the tasks (for example, delegation, position within the CG tripod)
Control	Relates to the monitoring tasks a board is expected to fulfil (financial, legal, internal governance and so on).
Strategy	Relates to the involvement of the board in the strategic process
Support	Relates to the interaction of the board with its management (challenging, stimulating, sounding board, advising and so on)

Table A.6   Board management relationship

Relationship with management	Relates to the contact, symbioses with and trust in management, as well as to the quality of management

Table A.7   Board composition

Competence	Refers to the fact that experienced, high quality and competent members are sitting on the board
Complementarity	Refers to the fact that members complement each other
Diversity	Refers to the fact that members differ in background, views, experience, nationality and so on
Mix	Refers to the fact that various categories of directors are represented (executives, non-executives and independent directors)
Size	Relates to the limitation on the number of directors

Table A.8   Operations of the board

Meeting	Relates to the characteristics of the board meeting such as frequency, timing, presentations and minutes
Preparation	Refers to the fact that the board meeting should be well prepared in terms of agenda and information provided to the members
Chairmanship	Relates to the quality and role of the chairmen of the board

Appendix B

Table B.1   Detailed overview of elements of cluster 1

Board composition	Number of respondents who mentioned this element	% of respondents (N = 104)	Frequency this element is reported
Diversity	30	28.85%	N = 31
Complementarity	27	25.96%	N = 27
Competence	25	24.04%	N = 25
Mix (executive/ non-executive)	10	9.62%	N = 11
Size	7	6.73%	N = 7
Total	99	95.19%	N = 101

Table B.2 Detailed overview of elements of cluster 2

Board culture	Number of respondents who mentioned this element	% of respondents ($N = 104$)	Frequency this element is reported
Openness	17	16.35%	$N = 17$
Active involvement	15	14.42%	$N = 15$
Atmosphere climate	11	10.58%	$N = 12$
Common values or goals	6	5.77%	$N = 7$
Critical	4	3.85%	$N = 4$
Total	53	50.96%	$N = 55$

Table B.3 Detailed overview of elements of cluster 3

Operations of the board	Number of respondents who mentioned this element	% of respondents ($N = 104$)	Frequency this element is reported
Preparation	23	22.12%	$N = 27$
Chairmanship	18	17.31%	$N = 18$
Meeting	8	7.69%	$N = 9$
Total	49	47.12%	$N = 54$

Table B.4 Detailed overview of elements of cluster 4

Board tasks	Number of respondents who mentioned this element	% of respondents ($N = 104$)	Frequency this element is reported
Strategy	15	14.42%	$N = 17$
Support	9	8.65%	$N = 9$
Context	5	4.81%	$N = 6$
Control	5	4.81%	$N = 5$
Total	34	32.69%	$N = 37$

Table B.5   Detailed overview of elements of cluster 5

Debate/decision making	Number of respondents who mentioned this element	% of respondents ($N = 104$)	Frequency this element is reported
Quality	10	9.62%	$N = 11$
Occurrence	10	9.62%	$N = 10$
Contribution	5	4.81%	$N = 5$
Decision	3	2.88%	$N = 3$
Total	28	26.92%	$N = 29$

Table B.6   Detailed overview of elements of cluster 6

Individual norms	Number of respondents who mentioned this element	% of respondents ($N = 104$)	Frequency this element is reported
Personality	9	8.65%	$N = 10$
Commitment	8	7.69%	$N = 10$
Independence	6	5.77%	$N = 6$
Preparation	2	1.92%	$N = 2$
Total	25	24.04%	$N = 28$

Table B.7   Detailed overview of elements of cluster 7

Relationship among the board members	Number of respondents who mentioned this element	% of respondents ($N = 104$)	Frequency this element is reported
Cohesiveness	8	7.69%	$N = 8$
Contact	5	4.81%	$N = 5$
Team	5	4.81%	$N = 5$
Respect	3	2.88%	$N = 3$
Trust	2	1.92%	$N = 2$
Total	23	22.12%	$N = 23$

Table B.8   Detailed overview of elements of cluster 8

Board management relationship	Number of respondents who mentioned this element	% of respondents ($N = 104$)	Frequency this element is reported
Relationship with management	6	5.77%	$N = 7$
Total	6	5.77%	$N = 7$

Appendix C

Table C.1 Frequency table of importance ranking scores for the full sample ($N = 150$)

Determinants of board effectiveness	1*	2	3	4	5	6	7	8	9	10**
The board of directors includes a mix of executive, independent directors and non-executives representing the shareholders	24.0%	11.3%	5.3%	6.0%	8.7%	7.3%	8.7%	8.7%	8.7%	11.3%
The board members are well prepared	8.7%	12.7%	18.7%	18.7%	16.7%	10.7%	7.3%	5.3%	1.3%	0.0%
All directors actively participate in the discussions	4.0%	4.7%	10.7%	11.3%	12.0%	12.0%	12.7%	13.3%	12.7%	6.7%
Board members show a constructive critical attitude	10.7%	18.7%	16.0%	18.0%	8.0%	16.0%	6.7%	3.3%	1.3%	1.3%
Trust between the board of directors and CEO/management	25.3%	12.0%	13.3%	8.0%	8.0%	9.3%	10.7%	7.3%	4.7%	1.3%

Continued

Table C.1 Continued

Determinants of board effectiveness	1*	2	3	4	5	6	7	8	9	10**
The chairman seeks consensus	2.0%	2.0%	3.3%	2.0%	7.3%	7.3%	16.0%	16.7%	31.3%	12.0%
The information is sufficient and on time	5.3%	14.0%	13.3%	12.0%	16.0%	13.3%	9.3%	8.7%	4.7%	3.3%
Divergent opinions are tolerated	3.3%	2.7%	8.7%	12.0%	12.0%	15.3%	14.0%	19.3%	11.3%	1.3%
Complementarity with respect to background expertise and experience	15.3%	20.0%	10.0%	10.7%	10.7%	7.3%	10.7%	8.0%	5.3%	2.0%
Board members get along very well	1.3%	2.0%	0.7%	1.3%	0.7%	1.3%	4.0%	9.3%	18.7%	60.7%

Note: *Score 1 denotes 'item is most important'.
**Score 10 denotes 'item is least important'.

Table C.2 Frequency table of corrigible ranking scores for the full sample ($N = 75$)

Determinants of board effectiveness	1*	2	3	4	5	6	7	8	9	10**
The board of directors includes a mix of executive, independent directors and non-executives representing the shareholders	13.3%	6.7%	8.0%	6.7%	4.0%	6.7%	9.3%	10.7%	18.7%	16.0%
The board members are well prepared	20.0%	25.3%	18.7%	12.0%	12.0%	6.7%	1.3%	0.0%	2.7%	1.3%
All directors actively participate in the discussions	8.0%	14.7%	20.0%	20.0%	4.0%	10.7%	9.3%	6.7%	4.0%	2.7%
Board members show a constructive critical attitude	4.0%	9.3%	14.7%	21.3%	13.3%	13.3%	8.0%	8.0%	2.7%	5.3%
Trust between the board of directors and CEO/management	0.0%	5.3%	5.3%	4.0%	10.7%	8.0%	21.3%	16.0%	20.0%	9.3%
The chairman seeks consensus	0.0%	2.7%	5.3%	1.3%	16.0%	13.3%	12.0%	14.7%	16.0%	18.7%
The information is sufficient and on time	29.3%	17.3%	10.7%	5.3%	13.3%	4.0%	5.3%	5.3%	5.3%	4.0%
Divergent opinions are tolerated	6.7%	4.0%	4.0%	8.0%	12.0%	18.7%	20.0%	14.7%	10.7%	1.3%
Complementarity with respect to background expertise and experience	17.3%	13.3%	10.7%	16.0%	12.0%	12.0%	2.7%	8.0%	4.0%	4.0%
Board members get along very well	1.3%	1.3%	2.7%	5.3%	2.7%	6.7%	10.7%	16.0%	16.0%	37.3%

Note: *Score 1 denotes 'item needs most improvement'.
**Score 10 denotes 'item needs least improvement'.

Notes

1. See AppendixB, Table B.1.
2. See Appendix B, Table B.2.
3. See Appendix B, Table B.3.
4. See Appendix B, Table B.4.
5. See Appendix B, Table B.5.
6. See Appendix B, Table B.6.
7. See Appendix B, Table B.7.
8. See Appendix B, Table B.8.
9. For the sake of presenting the results more clearly in the picture, we have reserved the values of the importance and corrigible scores.

References

Agrawal, A. and Knoeber, C.R. (1996). Firm performance and mechanisms to control agency problems between managers and shareholders. *Journal of Financial and Quantitative Analysis*, 31(3) 377–97.

Baliga, B.R., Moyer, R.C. and Rao, R.S. (1996). CEO duality and firm performance: what's the fuss? *Strategic Management Journal*, 17 41–3.

Baysinger, B.D. and Butler, H.N. (1985). Corporate governance and the board of directors: performance effects of changes in board composition. *Journal of Law, Economics and Organization*, 1(Fall) 101–24.

Baysinger, B.D., Kosnik, R.D. and Turk, T.A. (1991). Effects of board and ownership structure on corporate R&D strategy. *Academy of Management Journal*, 34 205–14.

Becht, M., Bolton, P. and Röel, A. (2002). Corporate governance and control. Working paper 9371, National Bureau of Economic Research.

Byrd, J.W. and Hickman, K.A. (1992). Do outside directors monitor managers? Evidence from tender offer bids. *Journal of Financial Economics*, 32 195–221.

Cadbury, A. (1999). What are the trends in corporate governance? How will they impact your company. *Long Range Planning*, 32(1) 12–19.

Carter, C.B. and Lorsch, J.W. (2004). *Back to the Drawing Board. Designing Corporate Boards for a Complex World*. Harvard Business School Press. Boston, MA.

Chaganti R., Mahajan, V. and Sharma, S. (1985). Corporate board size. composition and corporate failures in retailing industry. *Journal of Management Studies*, 22 400–16.

Charan, R. (1998). *Boards at Work. How Corporate Boards Create Competitive Advantage*. JosseyBass, a Wiley Company, CA.

Charan, R. (2005). *Boards That Deliver. Advancing Corporate Governance – From Compliance to Competitive Advantage*. Jossey-Bass, a Wiley Company, CA.

Cochran, R.L., Wood, R.A. and Jones, R.B. (1985). The composition of boards of directors and the incidence of golden parachutes. *Academy of Management Journal*, 28(3) 664–71.

Coles, J.W., McWilliams, V.B. and Sen, N. (2001). An examination of the relationship of governance mechanisms to performance. *Journal of Management*, 27(1) 23–50.

Collins, K.M.T., Onwuegbuzie, A.J. and Jiao, Q.G. (2006). Prevalence of mixed methods sampling designs in social science research. Paper presented at the Annual Meeting of the American Educational Research Association, San Francisco, CA, 1–7 April 2006.

Conyon, M.J. and Peck, S.I. (1998). Board size and corporate performance: evidence from European countries. *European Journal of Finance*, 4(3) 291–304.

Cornforth, C. (2001). What makes boards effective? An examination of the relationships between board inputs, structures, processes and effectiveness of non-profit organisations. *Corporate Governance: An International Review*, 9(3) 217–27.

Creswell, J.W., Plano Clark, V.L., Gutmann., M.L. and Hanson, W.E. (2003). Advanced mixed methods research designs. In C. Teddlie and A. Tashakkori (Eds), *Handbook of Mixed Methods in Social and Behavioural Research*. Sage Publications, Thousand Oaks, CA.

Daily, C.M. and Dalton, D.R. (1994a). Bankruptcy and corporate governance: the impact of board composition and structure. *Academy of Management Journal*, 37(6) 1603–17.

Daily, C.M. and Dalton, D.R. (1994b). Corporate governance and the bankrupt firm: an empirical assessment. *Strategic Management Journal*, 15 643–54.

Daily, C.M., Dalton, D.R. and Cannella Jr, A.A. (2003). Corporate governance: decades of dialogue and data. *Academy of Management Review*, 28(3) 371–82.

Daily, C.M., Johnson, J.L. and Dalton, D.R. (1999). On the measurement of board composition: poor consistency and a serious mismatch of theory and operationalization. *Decision Sciences*, 30(1) 83–106.

Dalton, D.R., Daily, C.M., Ellstrand, A.E. and Johnson, J.L. (1998). Meta-analytic reviews of board composition, leadership structure and financial performance. *Strategic Management Journal*, 19(3) 269–90.

Demb, A. and Neubauer, F.-F. (1992). *The Corporate Board. Confronting the Paradoxes*. Oxford University Press, Oxford.

Deutsch, Y. (2005). The impact of board composition on firms' critical decisions: a meta-analytic review. *Journal of Management*, 31(3) 424–44.

Donaldson, L. and Davis, J.H. (1991). Stewardship theory or agency theory: CEO governance and shareholder returns. *Australian Journal of Management*, 16 49–64.

Drucker, P.F. (1974). *Management: Tasks, Responsibilities, Practices*. Harper and Row, New York.

Eisenberg, T., Sundgren, S. and Wells, M.T. (1998). Larger board size and decreasing firm value in small firms. *Journal of Financial Economics*, 48 35–54.

Fama, E.F. and Jensen, M.C. (1983). Separation of ownership and control. *Journal of Law and Economics*, 26(2) 327–49.

Felton, R.F., Hudnut, A. and Witt, V. (1995). Building a stronger board. *The McKinsey Quarterly*, 2 163–75.

Finkelstein, S. and D'Aveni, R.A. (1994). CEO duality as a double-edged sword: how boards of directors balance entrenchment avoidance and unity of command. *Academy of Management Journal*, 37 1079–108.

Forbes, D.P. and Milliken, F. (1999). Cognition and corporate governance: understanding board of directors as strategic decision-making groups. *Academy of Management Review*, 24(3) 489–505.

Gabriellson, J. and Winlund, H. (2000). Boards of directors in small and medium-sized industrial firms: examining the effects of the board's working style on board task performance. *Entrepreneurship and Regional Development*, 12 311–30.

Golden, B.R. and Zajac, E.J. (2001). When will boards influence strategy? Inclination × power strategic change. *Strategic Management Journal*, 22(12) 1087–111.

Goodstein, J., Gautam, K. and Boeker, W. (1994). The effects of board size and diversity on strategic change. *Strategic Management Journal*, 15(3) 241–50.

Grady, D. (1999). No more board games! *The McKinsey Quarterly*, 3 17–25.

Hill, S. (1995). The social organization of boards of directors. *British Journal of Sociology*, 46(2) 245–78.

Hill, C.W.L. and Snell, S.A. (1988). External control. Corporate strategy and firm performance in research-intensive industries. *Strategic Management Journal*, 9 577–90.

Huse, M. and Schoning, M. (2004). Group dynamics and decision processes in boards of directors: observations from flies on the wall. Paper prepared for the 20th EGOS Colloquium, Ljubljana, Slovenia, 1–3 July.

Huse, M. (2005). Accountability and creating accountability: a framework for exploring behavioural perspectives of corporate governance. *British Journal of Management,* 16(1), 65–79.

Jensen, M.C. (1993). The modern industrial revolution. Exit and failure of internal control systems. *Journal of Finance,* 48(3) 831–80.

Jensen, M.C. and Meckling, W.H. (1976). Theory of the firm: managerial behaviour, agency costs and ownership structure. *Journal of Financial Economics,* 3(4) 305–60.

Johnson, J.L., Daily, C.M. and Ellstrand, A.E. (1996). Boards of directors: a review and research agenda. *Journal of Management,* 22(3) 409–38.

Johnson, R.A., Hoskisson, R.E. and Hitt, M.A. (1993). Board of director involvement in restructuring: the effects of board versus managerial controls and characteristics. *Strategic Management Journal,* 14(4) 33–50.

Johnson, R.B. and Turner, L.A. (2003). Data collection strategies in mixed methods research. In A. Tashakkori and C. Teddlie (Eds), *Handbook of Mixed Methods in Social and Behavioral Research* (pp. 297–319). Sage Publications, Thousand Oaks, CA.

Judge, W.Q. and Zeithaml, C.P. (1992). Institutional and strategic choice perspectives on board involvement in the strategic decision process. *Academy of Management Journal,* 35(4) 766–94.

Kesner, I.F. (1987). Directors' stock ownership and organizational performance: an investigation of Fortune 500 companies. *Journal of Management,* 13(3) 499–508.

Kesner, I.F. (1988). Directors' characteristics and committee membership: an investigation of type, occupation, tenure and gender. *Academy of Management Journal,* 31 66–84.

Kesner, I.F., Victor, B. and Lamont, B. (1986). Board composition and the commission of illegal acts an investigation of Fortune 500 companies. *Academy of Management Journal,* 29(4) 789–99.

Kosnik, R.D. (1990). Effects of board demography and directors' incentives on corporate greenmail decisions. *Academy of Management Journal,* 33 129–51.

Lawler, E.E., III., Finegold, D., Benson, G.S. and Conger, J.A (2002). Corporate boards: keys to effectiveness. *Organizational Dynamics,* 30(4) 310–24.

Leblanc, R. and Gillies, J. (2003). Improving board decision-making: an inside view. Paper presented at the 6th International Conference on Corporate Governance and Direction, Henley Management College, 6–8 Oct.

Leblanc, R. and Gillies, J. (2005). *Inside the Board Room. How Boards Really Work and the Coming Revolution in Corporate Governance.* Jossey-Bass, a Wiley Company, CA.

Lorsch, J.W. and MacIver, E. (1989). *Pawns or Potentates. The Reality of America's Corporate Boards.* Harvard Business School Press, Boston, MA.

Mace, M.L.G. (1971). *Directors: Myth and Reality.* Division of Research Graduate School of Business Administration Harvard University, Boston.

Malette, P. and Fowler, K.L. (1992). Effects of board composition and stock ownership on the adoption of poison pills. *Academy of Management Journal,* 35(5) 1010–35.

Miles, M. and Huberman, A. (1984). Drawing valid meaning from qualitative data: toward a shared craft. *Educational Researcher,* 13 20–30.

Monks, R.A.G. and Minow, N. (2001). *Corporate Governance.* 2nd edition, Blackwell, Oxford.

Muth, M.M. and Donaldson, L. (1998). Stewardship theory and board structure: a contingency approach. *Corporate Governance – An International Review,* 6(1) 5–27.

Onwuegbuzie, A.J. and Teddlie, C. (2003). A framework for analyzing data in mixed methods research. In C. Teddlie and A. Tashakkori (Eds), *Handbook of Mixed Methods in Social and Behavioural Research*. Sage Publications, Thousand Oaks, CA.

Pearce II, J.A. and Zahra, S.A. (1992). Board composition from a strategic contingency perspective. *Journal of Management Studies*, 29(4) 411–38.

Pettigrew, A. (1992). On studying managerial elites. *Strategic Management Journal*, 13(8) 163–82.

Pettigrew, A. and McNulty, T. (1995). Power and influence in and around the boardroom. *Human Relations*, 48(8) 845–73.

Pfeffer, J. and Salancik, G.R. (1978). *The External Control of Organisations: A Resource Dependence Perspective*. Harper and Row, New York.

Provan, K.G. (1980). Board power and organizational effectiveness among human service agencies. *Academy of Management Journal*, 23 221–36.

Rechner, P.K. and Dalton, D.R. (1991). CEO duality and organizational performance: a longitudinal analysis. *Strategic Management Journal*, 12(2) 155–60.

Roberts, J.T. (2002). Building the complementary board. The work of the Plc Chairman. *Long Range Planning*, 35 493–520.

Roberts, J.T., McNulty, P. and Stiles, P. (2005). Beyond agency conceptions of the work of the non-executive directors: creating accountability in the boardroom. *British Journal of Management*, 16(Special Issue) S5–6.

Rosenstein, S. and Wyatt, J.G. (1997). Inside directors, board effectiveness and shareholder wealth. *Journal of Financial Economics*, 44(2) 229–250

Shleifer, A. and Vishny, R. (1997). A survey of corporate governance. *Journal of Finance*, 52(2) 737–83.

Sonnenfeld, J.A. (2002). What makes great boards great. *Harvard Business Review*, 8 106–13.

Teddlie, C. and Tashakkori, A. (2003). *Handbook of Mixed Methods in Social and Behavioural Research*. Sage Publications, Thousand Oaks, CA.

TIAA-CREF (Teachers Insurance and Annuity Association-College Retirement Equities Fund). (2006). Policy Statement of Corporate Governance. New York. http://www.tiaa-cref.org/pubs/html/governance policy/index.html

Vance, S.C. (1978). Corporate governance: assessing corporate performance by boardroom attributes. *Journal of Business Research*, 6 203–30.

Van den Berghe, L. and Baelden, T. (2005). The complex relation between director independence and board effectiveness. *Corporate Governance: International Journal of Business in Society*, 5(5) 58–84.

Van den Berghe, L. and De Ridder, L. (1999). *International Standardisation of Good Corporate Governance*. Kluwer, Dordrecht.

Van der Walt, N. and Ingley, C. (2003). Board dynamics and the influence of professional background, gender and ethnic diversity of directors. *Corporate Governance: An International Review*, 11 218–34.

Wagner, J.A.., Stimpert, J.L. and Fubara, E.I. (1998). Board composition and organizational performance: two studies of insider/outsider effects. *Journal of Management Studies*, 35(5) 655–77.

Weil, Gotshal and Manges, L.L.P. (2002). Comparative study of corporate governance codes relevant to the European Union and its member states. Final Report & Annexes I–III on behalf of the European Commission Internal Market Directorate General, in consultation with EASD (European Association of Securities Dealers) and ECGN (European Corporate Governance Network).

Weisbach, M.S. (1988). Outside directors and CEO turnover. *Journal of Financial Economics*, 20 431–60.

Westphal, J.D. (1998). Board games: how CEOs adapt to increases in structural board independence from management. *Administrative Science Quarterly,* 43(3) 511–37.

Yerack, D. (1996). Higher market valuation of companies with a small board of directors. *Journal of Financial Economics,* 40(2) 185–211.

Zahra, S.A. and Pearce II, J.A. (1989). Boards of directors and corporate financial performance: a review and integrative model. *Journal of Management,* 15(2) 291–334.

2
International Board Evaluation: Trends and Practices

Chris Pierce

Introduction

Most successful companies have formal procedures to regularly evaluate the performance of their employees and organizational performance. However, until comparatively recently very few companies have evaluated the effectiveness of their board. In 2002, Professor Jeffrey Sonnenfeld commented that effective board evaluation was simply not taking place:

> I can't think of a single work group whose performance gets assessed less rigorously than corporate boards. (Sonnenfeld, J., 2002)

The situation has moved on significantly in recent years. Board evaluation has rapidly become one of the key areas for developing boards.

This chapter explores the drivers for board evaluation and explains why board evaluation has grown in importance. It also describes a typical board evaluation process and lists the typical areas of board dysfunction that a board evaluation might identify as a development need for the chairman to focus upon. The chapter also reviews common reasons given by directors for not introducing board evaluation. The final section of the chapter discusses recent international experiences in this area.

The drivers for board evaluation

Corporate governance codes and regulations

National corporate governance standards and codes are increasingly recommending that boards evaluate their effectiveness.

Australia

> Companies should disclose the process for evaluating the performance of the board, its committees and individual directors. (ASX, 2007)

Canada

> The board, its committees and each individual director should be regularly assessed regarding his, her or its effectiveness and contribution. An assessment should consider
>
> (a) in the case of the board or a board committee, its mandate or charter, and
>
> (b) in the case of an individual director, the applicable position description(s), as well as the competencies and skills each individual director is expected to bring to the board. (TSX, 2006)

UK

> The board should undertake a formal and rigorous annual evaluation of its own performance and that of its committees and individual directors. (The Combined Code, 2008)

USA

> Listed companies must have a nominating/corporate governance committee composed entirely of independent directors. The nominating/corporate governance committee must have a written charter that addresses: the committee's purpose and responsibilities – which, at minimum, must: . . . . oversee the evaluation of the board and management. (NYSE, 2003)

However, board evaluation is not just occurring in English speaking countries.

Spain

The Principles of Good Corporate Governance for Unlisted Companies in Spain (ICA, 2005, p. 21) recommends that the boards of all unlisted companies should periodically assess its performance, its directors' performance and board committees' performance (if any). The board should also make an annual evaluation of its chief executive and this evaluation should be coordinated by the non-executive chairman (or by the senior independent director/lead director/principal director when the chairman is an executive) who will subsequently submit the results to the chief executive. In addition, the Spanish Unified Code (2006, pp. 14–15) recommends that the boards of all listed companies should evaluate the quality and efficiency of the board's stewardship, and how well the chairman and chief executive have carried out their duties and the performance of its committees. This evaluation should be conducted on an annual basis.

Financial institutional and shareowner pressure

Financial institutions are increasingly recommending that the boards of the companies that they invest in should undertake regular evaluations.

For example, the US Teacher Insurance and Annuity Association – College Retirement Equities Fund (TIAA-Cref) – is one of the largest financial services companies in the United States, with $420 billion in assets under management as of 30 June 2008. Their Policy Statement on Corporate Governance states:

> The board should conduct an annual evaluation of its performance and that of its key committees. Evaluation criteria linked to board and committee responsibilities and goals should be set forth in the charter and governance policies. In addition to providing director orientation and education, the board should consider other ways to strengthen director performance, including individual director evaluations. (College Retirement Equities Fund, 2007)

Director development and board development

Institutes of Directors and Corporate Governance Associations around the world are growing in number and membership. Many of them are providing directors and boards with an increased understanding of the value and benefits of undertaking a board evaluation.

Examples of courses stressing the importance of board evaluation include:

- In the United States, the National Association of Corporate Directors (NACD) Certificate in Director Education flagship programme has a course objective focused upon improving board effectiveness through leading governance practices in board evaluations (National Association of Corporate Directors).
- In the Middle East, the Mudara Board Development Programmes in Jordan, Morocco, UAE and Saudi Arabia cover the topic of board evaluation in some detail and there is case study role play on this topic in their current series (Mudara, 2008).

Internal drivers

Many boards are using the board evaluation process as a development tool to create a key source of superior organization performance leading to a competitive advantage. In addition, there is a general desire amongst the chairman and the other board members to be more professional. The reasons for initiating an evaluation process typically include:

- Allowing the board to assess the value it creates for the company
- Allowing the board to assess the efficiency of its internal functioning
- Acting as an early warning system to the board which will allow changes to be implemented before more deep rooted problems set in

- Identifying board development areas (the processes do not tend to use the word weaknesses!) and providing an opportunity for the board to take action to improve itself.

The board evaluation process

Typical questions that directors should ask prior to an evaluation include:

- Is the board clear on its function and responsibilities?
- Is each director clear on their role?
- Do the committees understand their roles?

If the answer to any of these questions is no, then it is advisable (and cost effective) for the board or committees to remedy the situation themselves before the evaluation takes place.

Once it has been decided by the board that a board evaluation is appropriate, key questions need to be asked that include:

- What performance metrics will be used?
  It is essential that the board members understand on what basis they will be evaluated. Typical areas of assessment include board role, structure and functioning, control environment and processes, relationships with shareholders and key stakeholders, and commitment to corporate governance.
- Who will collect the information?
  The board has a choice to allow the evaluation to be conducted in house by the chairman or the company secretary or to be conducted by an external independent evaluator. Good practice recommends the latter since the chairman and or the company secretary role and functions should be part of the evaluation and are therefore clearly conflicted in terms of objectivity and independence. For example, if the board is concerned about the quality of board's papers that it is receiving, it is clearly inappropriate for the company secretary to be in charge of the evaluation process.
- How will the information be collected and reported?
  Confidentiality is extremely important, so the method of collection and storage of information is extremely important. All contributions by directors should be anonymous and non-attributable. This can be quite problematic with small sized boards since it is often very difficult to disguise the source of sensitive and critical comments.

A typical evaluation process comprises:

- Formulating the evaluation instrument(s) normally involving questionnaires and one to one confidential interviews

- A presentation to the board involving a description of the process
- A questionnaire being completed privately by directors individually
- Confidential interviews on a one-to-one basis being undertaken with discussions focusing upon issues raised in the questionnaire
- The data being collated and analysed by the evaluator
- A presentation and board discussion involving the development of a plan to remedy any deficiencies that have been identified.

One technique for reducing directors' opposition to the evaluation process is to recast them as "performance improvement plans." Performance improvement plans (PIPs) emphasize the objective of the exercise as one of improving performance, rather than criticizing performance or behaviour. Treating reviews as a forward-looking planning process rather than a backward-looking critique may make the process appear more goal oriented and positive.

Board evaluations are inevitably challenging for board members. The evaluation process can be made easier, however, by using external expert facilitators and by treating it as a forward-looking process whose goal is the improvement of the board workings, rather than an implicit critique.

Reporting board evaluation

The threshold of reporting on board evaluation is rising. An example of good practice in this field is Barclays. The following information has been taken from the Barclays Bank Annual Report, 2008.

Characteristics of a dysfunctional board

The characteristics of a dysfunctional board that a board evaluation might identify as a major development need may include:

- **Wrong size**
  Many boards are either too large or too small rather than being just right (this is sometimes called the goldilocks' syndrome named after the fairy tale). If this is the case the evaluation should recommend that the chairman should consider altering the board size by either:
  - requesting the nominations committee initiate recruitment, selection and appointment processes or
  - taking appropriate steps to remove directors.
- **Insufficient range of expertise**
  If this is the case the evaluation should recommend that the chairman should consider requesting the nominations committee to initiate a study of the personal skills, knowledge and attributes required by the board

- **Inadequate information provision**
  If this is the case the evaluation should recommend that the chairman should ask the company secretary to remedy the situation.
- **Inadequate debates and few overt disagreements or differences of opinion**
  If this is the case the evaluation should recommend that the chairman should consider encouraging non executive directors to be more independent,
- **Decisions are made by small inner groups outside of the board**
  If this is the case the evaluation should recommend that the chairman should consider reviewing the statement of reserved powers.
- **Have few reviews to see if the decisions were correct**
  If this is the case the evaluation should recommend that the chairman should consider initiating a regular review of material decisions made by the board.
- **Fail to identify the risks facing the company**
  If this is the case the evaluation should recommend that the chairman should consider initiating a regular review of the company's risk profile.
- **Fail to keep the company's finances under review**
  If this is the case the evaluation should recommend that the chairman should consider initiating a regular review of the financial health of the company.

In nearly every case remedying board dysfunction is the chairman's responsibility since they have the ultimate responsibility for managing all aspects of board meetings.

Common reasons why evaluations do not take place

In practice, there is often considerable reluctance to initiate a board evaluation process. Common reasons why evaluations do not take place include:

- Some directors may feel uncomfortable about being evaluated. They are often very comfortable about evaluating others (e.g., the CEO and other senior management), but when it is their turn to be evaluated they raise many different objections.
- Pressures of day-to-day activities cause the board to delay the introduction of evaluation. Often the evaluator experiences great difficulty in communicating with the CEO since the CEO often gives priority to running the business and wishes the issue of running the board to the chairman.
- Evaluation might be perceived as a sign that the board lacks trust or confidence in the Chairman or CEO's performance.
- The board feels it lacks the skills and expertise to undertake effective evaluations.

- The board has not been emphasizing planning or evaluation. There are no performance targets for the board, committees or executive managers.
- The board is dysfunctional board.
- The CEO, chairman and/or founder may be dominating the board and be concerned at the issues that an evaluation may raise.
- Previous board evaluations have proven to be ineffective.

Characteristics of successful evaluations

Characteristics of successful evaluations include:

- The purpose, objectives, process and outcomes of the evaluation have been fully explained and discussed with all concerned parties prior to the evaluation commencing.
- Strict confidentiality is maintained at all times.
- The board, chairman and the CEO should play a key role in developing and approving the process.
- The assessment should be a regular annual process.
- Benchmarks of board, committee, executive and company effectiveness should be used as indicators of performance wherever possible. Often external evaluators will bring comparative board performance data that internal evaluators would not be able to provide.
- The evaluation should be in a written format and discussed by all concerned parties.
- After the meeting, the chairman should provide the full board with a report.
- The process should be evaluated in order to improve the process the next time when an evaluation is undertaken in the following year.

International experiences

Australian experience

Some of the leading edge work in board evaluation in Australia has been developed by Geoffrey Kiel, Gavin Nicholson and Mary Jane Barclay from Competitive Dynamics Pty Ltd. Their frameworks are outlined in the excellent book *Board, Director and CEO Evaluation* published by McGraw-Hill in 2005 (Kiel et al., 2005).

Canadian experience

Some of the leading edge work in board evaluation is taking place in Canada. For example, Richard Leblanc has developed a very interesting proprietal framework based upon his research published in *Inside the Boardroom* (Leblanc and Gillies, 2005). In addition, Davide Anderson has been writing many excellent articles in the Canadian professional press concerning board evaluation processes.

Middle East experience

Very few companies have introduced board evaluation processes in the Middle East. One of the few organizations to do so has been the Dubai International Foreign Exchange (DIFX).

Board Evaluation Case Study : DIFX

A performance evaluation of the collective board and its committees was undertaken in January 2007. The evaluation was conducted by an independent consultant and involved the completion of questionnaires followed by one-to-one meetings or telephone interviews with the consultant. The findings of the evaluation identified that the board and its committees were functioning well and conformed to best international corporate governance practices. No changes to either board or committees processes was recommended; however, a number of development areas were highlighted. These areas were reviewed and discussed in detail at board and committee meetings and appropriate action was taken in order to develop and enhance performance and processes.

Source: DIFX Annual Review 2006.

UK experience

The Combined Code recommends that

> the board should undertake a formal and rigorous annual evaluation of its own performance and that of its committees and individual directors. *The Combined Code* (2008)

As a result of board evaluations being recommended as good practice in the Combined Code in 2003, all of the top 100 companies on the London Stock Exchange now undertake an evaluation process.

However, a recent Institute of Chartered Secretaries and Administrators (ICSA) survey in August 2008 has revealed that only 16 per cent of the top 200 companies on the London Stock Exchange undertake an externally developed or managed evaluation process (ICSA, 2008).

BP is typical of UK companies when it states on its website that:

> The Board will evaluate its own processes and performance including the work of its committees, to ensure its on-going effectiveness as a high performing board.

This self-evaluation does not obtain many the benefits that might arise if an independent external evaluation process is put in place.

ICSA argues that if companies do not benchmark board processes by using an external facilitator, then evaluations will become less valuable over time and may become the equivalent of "children marking their own homework." ICSA has identified that many board directors do not understand their role of evaluating the effectiveness of each of the main board executive directors.

ICSA Corporate Services currently provide an excellent board evaluation service for all types of companies.

Conclusion

Companies around the world in recent years have increasingly seen their boards as a major source of competitive edge. Board evaluations are now becoming widely perceived as a method of identifying and developing the effectiveness of the board. In the very near future, it is anticipated that board evaluation processes amongst successful companies will be external, rigorous and common place.

References

ASX (2007), Revised corporate governance principles and recommendations, ASX Corporate Governance Council, Sydney. Available at www.ecgi.org.

Barclays Bank Annual Report (2008), Available at www.barclays.com (accessed 18/11/2008).

College Retirement Equities Fund (2007), *Policy Statement on Corporate Governance*, Teacher Insurance and Annuity Association, New York, p. 14. Available at www.tiaa-cref.org/pubs/pdf/goverrnance_policy.pdf.

DIFX, Dubai International Foreign Exchange Annual Review (2006), www.difx.ae (accessed 18/11/2008).

ICA, Instituto de Consejeros Administradores (2005), *Principles of Good Governance*, ICA, Madrid www.iconsejeros.com accessed 18/11/2008

ICSA, Institute of Chartered Secretaries and Administrators (2008), *Survey on Board Evaluation Practices in the UK*, ICSA, London.

Kiel, G., Nicholson, G. and Barclay, M. (2005), *Board, Director and CEO Evaluation*, McGraw-Hill, Sydney.

Leblanc, R. and Gillies, J. (2005), *Inside the Boardroom*, Wiley, Toronto.

Mudara (2008), Middle East and North Africa Institute of Directors, Dubai, www.NACDonline.org (accessed 18/11/2008).

National Association of Corporate Directors (NACD), Washington, DC, www.NACDonline.org.

NYSE (2003), Final NYSE corporate governance rules, Available at www.ecgi.org.

Sonnenfeld, J. (2002), What makes great boards great, *Harvard Business Review*, 80(9), 113.

Spanish Unified Code (2006), Comisión Nacional del Mercado de Valores (CNMV), Madrid, available in English at www.ecgi.org.

The Combined Code (2008), Financial Reporting Council, London, p. 9. Available at www.ecgi.org/codes/all_codes.php

Toronto Stock Exchange (TSX) (2006), *Corporate Governance Guidelines*, TSX, Toronto, www.TSX.com (accessed 18/11/2008).

3
Governance Down-under: An Overview of Corporate Governance in Australia

John Cottrell

Introduction

Australia's small but highly developed corporate and financial systems compare well internationally. Building from a low post-World War 2 base the Australian economy thrived, initially "on the sheep's back" and latterly from an ever expanding "mine and ship" commodities boom. The non-farm/mining sectors moved steadily from manufacturing to services. The highly developed financial services sector grew rapidly from the 1990s to offer leading superannuation and unit trust structures and reforms. Corporate governance systems that evolved from a United Kingdom "principles"-based parentage have endured and continued to flourish. Arguably influenced by a stream of US management theory and market-linked "rules"-based governance guidance, Australia has maintained its principles-based governance system and become a leading international participant in good corporate governance notwithstanding many high-profile homegrown corporate scandals and collapses. In a country of avid adopters, corporate Australia has set a leading pace in the separation of the roles of chairman and CEO across its major publicly listed corporations coupled with strong measures for determining non-executive director independence. The "down-under" effect of corporate isolation in the southern hemisphere and the entrepreneurial thirst for scarce capital required to develop a large sparsely populated island continent has undoubtedly driven Australia's corporate leaders to steer a fine path between the governance paradox that seemingly conflicts the northern hemisphere.

The island continent

Mainland Australia is the Earth's largest island but smallest and driest continent located down-under in the southern hemisphere. Its ocean territory is the third largest in the world spanning three oceans: the Indian; the Pacific and the Southern. With a land area 80 per cent of mainland United States it supports only 15 per cent of its population (21 million), most of whom live along the coastal fringes (DFAT). With an economy of around $AUD1.3 trillion, some 6 per cent of the United States, Australia has highly developed legal, corporate and financial systems: all internationally well recognised. The financial services sector includes world-class equity and debt securities markets that sit favourably on the world time zone immediately following the United States. These are underpinned by a strong national corporate governance system operating in a vibrant free-market economy. With traditionally strong United Kingdom, European and United States relationships, Australian trade is now more reliant on Japan, China and other Asian economies. As such, Australia's trading and corporate governance are now balanced between Anglo-American and Eurasian relationships.

Scarcity of labour and the vastness of the land and new wealth based on farming, mining and trade made Australia a land of opportunity. From 1900 to 1914 great progress was made in developing Australia's agricultural and manufacturing capacities, and in setting up institutions for government and needed social services. The period between the wars was one of reconstruction. After 1945 Australia entered a boom period. The economy developed strongly through the 1950s on the back of major nation-building projects. Home ownership rose dramatically from around 40 per cent in 1947 to more than 70 per cent by the 1960s, and remains at this level today. Australians are active investors: in 2006 approximately 7.3 million people or 46 per cent of the Australian population owned shares either directly or indirectly via a managed fund or self-managed superannuation fund. Thirty-eight per cent were direct investors in the Australian share market (ASX).

Business environment

The Commonwealth of Australia was formed in 1901 through the federation of six states under a single constitution. The system of government is based on the liberal democratic tradition, and institutions and practices reflect a British heritage and North American influence, though they remain uniquely Australian. The responsibility for governing Australian is shared between three levels of government: the federal, state and local government authorities. The legal system is founded on the concepts of the rule of law, justice and equality before the law, and in its common law system, principles such as procedural fairness, judicial precedent, prospective legislation and the separation of powers are fundamental. The judiciary is separate from the legislative and executive arms of government, and in interpreting and applying the law judges act independently of governments.

Financial services sector

Australia is a major regional financial centre with an important place in the global financial system. Its foreign exchange market is ranked seventh in the world by turnover and the Australian dollar is the sixth most actively traded currency in the world (after the US dollar, the Euro, the Japanese yen, the UK pound and the Swiss franc) due largely to its commodities backing. With globally recognised niche expertise in areas of each of insurance, banking, securities and asset/funds management, Australia is recognised for innovation in consumer credit and mortgage finance, including in the non-bank sector (Australian Services Roundtable, 2008). Australia has progressively developed the status as the Asia-Pacific centre for funds management and since the 1990s has attracted global financial institutions. A universal, compulsory employer-funded pension scheme was introduced in 1986 and with a current 9 per cent contribution rate Australia's investment funds asset pool stands at over $AUD1 trillion positioning it as the largest in the Asia-Pacific region and the fourth largest in the world.

Corporate Australia

"Driven by principles or rules governance is an impost on the majority as a result of the actions of the minority of owners, directors and managers who succumb to self-indulgence and recklessness." This prophetic advice of Sykes (1998) on the cycle of "greed and folly" that has administered "two centuries of pain" to the Australian corporate scene appears to have fallen on deaf ears as corporate carnage continued into the late 1990s and the early 2000s, and as a result of the demise of Wall Street and the global financial contagion, manifested again in 2008 with the collapse of corporate balance sheets.

Sykes went on to remind us that big crashes follow big booms and although the Great Depression of the 1930s was the worst in our history, it was not accompanied by many corporate collapses because there had been no sizeable boom in Australia in the 1920s. But in the 1840s, the 1890s and the 1970s, booms were followed by waves of collapses. Clearly, by the 1980s we had forgotten the lessons of the 1890s. Nor is there any guarantee that we will not forget them again. "Businesses do not collapse through any iron rules of the economic cycle but because of the greed and folly of the people who run them. Well-run companies survive the most vicious economic downturns but badly run companies don't" (Sykes, 1998, p. x1).

Sykes (1994) wrote of a scenario that could be easily adapted to fit the events of 2008.

They were bold riders, all right. The corporate cowboys...rode our financial landscape as none had done before. They used tiny equity holdings as the basis for huge empires built on mountains of clay. They took the

savings of Australians, entrusted to our banks, and channelled them....
on a scale never been seen before.

On a broader scale Australia's vibrant business environment is driven by the small to medium enterprise (SME) sector in combination with substantial and mature listed and non-listed public, government business enterprise (GBE) and Not-for Profit (NFP) sectors. The 100 largest enterprises are big employers and big income earners for Australia and a major force in the economy (DFAT).

Regulatory environment

A brilliant legal invention and so important for modern society is how The Hon Justice Michael Kirby referred to the company (McDermott, 2005). He continued: "little could those who gave birth to this legal fiction have imagined the dominance that companies would come to enjoy in the national economy, in global markets and world power." As Justice of the Supreme Court of Australia Justice Kirby (Kirby 1998) remarked that

> The seeds for the idea of a corporation, a body having a legal personality separate from that of its shareholders, can be traced in English law at least to the reign of Queen Elizabeth I when Crown monopolies were established to help exploit high risk investments in the overseas colonies, settlements and trading posts of the Crown. Charter companies that were established with a monopoly from the Crown provided the origin of the notion of a body independent of the investors, which was permitted, by law, to engage in sometimes risky and speculative commercial ventures but with only limited personal liability in the adventurers. The modern reincarnation of laws on bankruptcy, intellectual property and corporations had to wait to the reign of Queen Victoria when the basic legal foundations of the modern capitalist economy were enacted by the Parliament at Westminster. The British colonies took advantage of such laws which were often extended to apply to them and inherited the institutional and intellectual framework of law within which their fledgling economies could quickly flourish.

So began Australia's company law that Justice Kirby advised was to grow into a "national companies law that today must operate in a regional and global context that inevitably has an impact on corporate governance."

Australia's founding colonies (later states) initially modified the British legislation to meet their local requirements but in doing so established a fragmented system that continued well beyond the Federation in 1901. In a move to accommodate a national approach to companies legislation, the Uniform Companies Act was enacted by each of the states in 1961; however, complications continued as the increasingly national operating requirements of expanding corporations forced companies into duplicating actions, such as the issue of a prospectus to raise funds. What existed was a "jigsaw puzzle of regulation" (Dignam and Galanis, 2004). There was no single national regulator, a Corporations Law not embodied in a single statute and six disparate state-based stock exchanges.

In 1987 the six state-based stock exchanges were amalgamated to form the national Australian Stock Exchange (ASX), and in 1989 responsibility for the regulation of companies and securities law was transferred to the federal government under the auspices of the Corporations Act 1989 (Cwlth) and Australian Securities Commission Act 1989 (Cwlth). A number of the states challenged this transfer and by a six-to-one majority the High Court held that the Commonwealth had no power to make laws for the incorporation of companies. The 1989 Acts were subsequently amended by the Corporations Legislation Amendment Act 1990, which introduced uniform "national" companies legislation and administration. Following further court challenges to the federal government powers to enforce national corporations law the Commonwealth re-enacted the legislation based on the stronger constitutional footing of "powers conferred by the states" (Kiel and Nicholson, 2003, p. 26).

Corporations law

Since July 2001 corporate regulation in Australia has been governed under the following "national" Commonwealth of Australia Acts:

- Corporations Act 2001 (Cwlth)
- Australian Securities and Investment Commission Act 2001 (Cwlth).

Corporations Act 2001 (Cwlth)

The *Corporations Act 2001* (Cwlth) is an act of the Commonwealth of Australia setting out the laws dealing with business entities in Australia at federal and interstate level including companies, partnerships and managed investment schemes. As the principal legislation regulating companies in Australia, the Corporations Act regulates matters such as the formation and operation of companies, duties of officers, takeovers and fundraising. The Act gives statutory force to many common law principles and imposes a number of additional fiduciary duties on directors of incorporated bodies. Breach of statutory duties draws penalties under the Act that range up to $220,000. Officers may also be required to pay compensation or to account for profits, and in some cases directors may also be disqualified from office.

Companies established under the Corporations Act must be either proprietary companies or public companies. Proprietary companies cannot have more than 50 shareholders (excluding shareholders who are employees) and they are not permitted to engage in certain fundraising activities. Public companies have no limitation on the amount of people who can be shareholders and are permitted to engage in certain fundraising activities such as issuing shares to the public. Public companies can be limited by shares or by guarantee and unlimited with share capital. In recognition of the inherently risky nature of investment in Australia's mining industry the No-liability company was created. A No-liability company must have as its stated objects that it is solely a mining company and that it is not entitled to calls on the unpaid issue price of shares.

The duties imposed on directors and officers under the Corporations Act 2001 apply to many different organisational structures such as public companies, proprietary companies and incorporated associations. All directors must comply with basic legal requirements.

Part 2D.1 of the Act deals with "Duties and Powers" and specifies four main duties for directors:

- to act with all the care and diligence that a reasonable person might be expected to show in the role (s 180) [see *Business Judgment Rule* (BJT), below],
- to act in good faith in the best interests of the company and for a proper purpose (s 181),
- to not improperly use their position for personal gain or to the detriment to the company (s 182),
- to not improperly use the information they gain in the course of their director duties for personal gain or to the detriment to the company (s 183), in association with the general concept
- to not trade whilst insolvent or where they suspect the company might be insolvent (s 588G).

Other significant duties and responsibilities for directors include

- taking reasonable steps to ensure that a company complies with its obligations in the Corporations Act related to keeping of financial records and financial reporting (s 344);
- disclosing matters relating to the affairs of the company in which a director or an officer has a material personal interest (s 191), particularly in the context of the requirement that public companies obtain shareholder approval for related party transactions (s 208) and, if necessary, obtaining approval for related party transactions;
- lodging information with the Australian Securities and Investments Commission (ASIC) (s 188–190); and
- for listed companies, *continuous disclosure* of significant information (ASX, 2007).

In addition to the Corporations Act, other legislation imposes responsibilities on directors. These operate under occupational health and safety (OH&S),

Trade Practices, Tax and Environmental Protection laws. Certain industries may also have specific legislation with which directors must comply.

Penalties apply for breaches. For a breach of Sections 181–183 (above) the penalty can result in disqualification from being a director and a fine of up to $200,000. Where intentional dishonesty or recklessness is involved criminal penalties may also apply and may include prison sentences on top of the civil penalties. Breaches of other parts of the Corporations Act and other legislation can result in directors being banned from acting as a company director for extended periods.

A "Business Judgment Rule" (BJR) applies to the duty to act with care and diligence (s 180). Section 180(2) requires that

- a director or other officer of a corporation who makes a business judgment is taken to meet the requirements of subsection 180(1) above, and their equivalent duties at common law and in equity, in respect of the judgment if they
- make the judgment in good faith for a proper purpose;
- do not have a material personal interest in the subject matter of the judgment;
- inform themselves about the subject matter of the judgment to the extent that they reasonably believe to be appropriate; and
- rationally believe that the judgment is in the best interests of the corporation.

The section further provides that the director's or officer's belief that the judgment is in the best interests of the corporation is a rational one unless the belief is one that no reasonable person in their position would hold (Corporations Act, 2001).

Case (common) law

Case law has been important to the development of Australia's corporate governance particularly in providing added meaning to the roles and responsibilities of boards and directors. This influence can be seen through the following three cases.

AWA

In AWA Ltd v Daniels t/as Deloitte Haskins and Sells and Others (1992) a clear distinction was drawn between executive and non-executive directors. The case, and its appeal, raised two issues of particular importance to all directors concerning the level of care and diligence required between non-executive and executive directors and to what extent directors can delegate actions and still perform with sufficient care and diligence. Section 180(1) of the Corporations Act 2001 requires that the standard of care and diligence is that of a "reasonable person" (Kiel and Nicholson, 2003, p. 52).

HIH insurance group (HIH)

HIH was a major Australian insurance provider that failed in 2001 recording Australia's largest corporate loss. Justice Owen headed the Royal Commission established to inquire into and prepare a report on the reasons for and the circumstances surrounding the failure of HIH. He noted, "by and large the people who were involved were not inherently bad or in some way set upon being part of a corporate disaster. HIH is a reminder, if one is needed, that a drastic fall from corporate grace can occur if those in charge lose their way" (HIH, 2003a).

In his summation on the corporate governance of HIH, Justice Owen found that

> The key to good corporate governance lies in substance, not form. It is about the way the directors of a company create and develop a model to fit the circumstances of that company and then test it periodically for its practical effectiveness. It is about the directors taking control of a regime they have established and for which they are responsible. These concepts do not lend themselves easily to specification in something such as a code of best practice. (HIH, 2003b)

Greaves case

Of major concern to the boardrooms of Australia are the Greaves Case and its implications on the responsibilities and liabilities of a Chairman (AICD, 2006). The 2003 case of ASIC v Rich involved One.Tel, a listed company that was placed into liquidation in 2001. ASIC commenced actions against One. Tel's non-executive chairman John Greaves for breaches of statutory duty of care and diligence. Mr Greaves was a chartered accountant with substantial commercial experience and held additional responsibilities through his role as chairman of OneTel's Finance and Audit Committee. ASIC was interested in the extended duty of care not the duties of the company chairman per se and specifically Greaves duties of that of a chairman who was also chairman of the audit committee: having regard to the circumstances of the company and qualifications of the individual involved (Kalokerinos, 2007). The court found in favour of ASIC and banned Greaves from being a director and fined him $20 million.

Regulators

Regulation of the Australian corporate system rests with the following organisations.

Australian Securities and Investments Commission (ASIC)

ASIC regulates Australian companies, financial markets, financial services organisations and professionals who deal and advise in investments, superannuation, insurance, deposit taking and credit. It functions as the following regulators:

- The *corporate regulator*, ASIC is responsible for ensuring that company directors and officers carry out their duties honestly, diligently and in the best interests of their company.
- The *markets regulator*, ASIC assesses how effectively authorised financial markets are complying with their legal obligations to operate fair, orderly and transparent markets. It also advises the minister about authorising new markets.
- The *financial services regulator*, ASIC licenses and monitors financial services businesses to ensure that they operate efficiently, honestly and fairly. These businesses typically deal in superannuation, managed funds, shares and company securities, derivatives, and insurance.

ASIC contributes to Australia's economic reputation and well-being by ensuring that Australia's financial markets are fair and transparent, supported by confident and informed investors and consumers.

Australian Securities Exchange (ASX)

The ASX group was created in 2006 through the merger of the Australian Stock Exchange and the Sydney Futures Exchange and is among the top eight equity markets in the world. The ASX equities market has over 2000 listed equity companies with a market cap of over $1.5 trillion. Institutional business accounts for 50 per cent of equity transactions (ASX, 2008b). Through its subsidiary, ASX Markets Supervision, it is responsible for broker and listed company supervision. The ASX Corporate Governance Council sets the standard for corporate governance of listed companies in Australia under the ASX's Listing Rules.

Listing Rules. The rules govern the admission of entities to the official list, quotation of securities and suspension of securities from quotation and removal of entities from the official list. Compliance is a requirement for admission to the official list, and in addition to being contractually binding the rules are enforceable against listed entities and their associates under the Corporations Act. They create obligations that are additional and complementary to common law obligations and statutory obligations. ASX listed companies are required to adopt ASX Corporate Governance Principles and Recommendations (2007).

ASX Corporate governance principles and recommendations. Listed companies are obliged to adopt eight principles and report against their compliance with 26 recommendations ranging from board structure to remuneration and risk management. Introduced in 2003 the principles were updated in 2007 through reorganisation and amendment to remove areas of overlap with other regulation and to clarify the operation of certain principles (ASX, 2007), and

- to adopt the concept of "good practice" to replace the concept of best practice;
- to produce high quality and integrity in company approach;
- to not require a "one size fits all" approach to corporate governance, but instead provide suggestions for practices designed to optimise corporate performance and accountability in the interests of shareholders and the broader economy;
- to provide for the "if not, why not" approach – if a company considers that a recommendation is inappropriate to its particular circumstances, it has the flexibility not to adopt it – a flexibility tempered by the requirement to explain why.

The eight principles are as follows:

1. *Lay solid foundations for management and oversight* – Companies should establish and disclose the respective roles and responsibilities of the board and management.
2. *Structure the board to add value* – Companies should have a board of an effective composition, size and commitment to adequately discharge its responsibilities and duties.
3. *Promote ethical and responsible decision making* – Companies should actively promote ethical and responsible decision-making.
4. *Safeguard integrity in financial reporting* – Companies should have a structure to independently verify and safeguard the integrity of their financial reporting.
5. *Make timely and balanced disclosure* – Companies should promote timely and balanced disclosure of all material matters concerning the company.
6. *Respect the rights of shareholders* – Companies should respect the rights of shareholders and facilitate the effective exercise of those rights
7. *Recognise and manage risk* – Companies should establish a sound system of risk oversight and management and internal control.
8. *Remunerate fairly and responsibly* – Companies should ensure that the level and composition of remuneration is sufficient and reasonable and that its relationship to performance is clear.

Australian Prudential Regulation Authority (APRA)

Established on 1 July 1998, APRA is the prudential regulator of the Australian financial services industry overseeing banks, credit unions, building societies, general insurance and reinsurance companies, life insurance, friendly societies and most members of the superannuation industry.

Trade Practices Act (TPA)

The TPA is a Commonwealth statute. Its purpose is to enhance the welfare of Australians through the promotion of competition and fair-trading and provision for consumer protection. The Act deals with almost all aspects of the marketplace: the relationships between suppliers, wholesalers, retailers, competitors and customers (ACCC).

Australian Competition and Consumer Commission (ACCC)

The ACCC is an independent statutory authority formed in 1995 to administer the Trade Practices Act 1974 and other acts. It promotes competition and fair trade in the market place to benefit consumers, business and the community and also regulates national infrastructure industries. Its primary responsibility is to ensure that individuals and businesses comply with the Commonwealth's competition, fair-trading and consumer protection laws. It is the only national agency dealing generally with competition matters and the only agency with responsibility for enforcing the TPA and the state/territory application legislation (ACCC, 2008).

Environmental protection laws. The protection of the environment has become a major social, and therefore political, issue over the past few decades resulting in rapid changes in Australian government policy from both the state and federal level of government. In addition to monetary fines, penalties for breaches now involve the potential for criminal liability. Environment protection has placed increasing pressure on directors.

The Environment Protection and Biodiversity Conservation Act 1999 (EPBC) is the Australian Government's central piece of environmental legislation. It provides a legal framework to protect and manage nationally and internationally important flora, fauna, ecological communities and heritage places – defined in the Act as matters of national environmental significance.

Associations that influence the corporate governance debate

The following peak-body organisations have been leading the way in the development of Australia's corporate governance for over half a century. With respective focus on the roles of the company directors, the company secretary and the securities industry, they have provided broad, robust, professional and open debate together with policy submissions to government. In addition, they each provide ongoing high-level education to their members and associated industry participants.

Australian Institute of Company Directors (AICD)

Commencing as the Institute of Directors Australia in 1971, the AICD was formed in 1990 representing the interests of company directors in Australia. It has a membership of some 17,000 drawn from large and small organisations across all industries and from private, public and not-for-profit sectors. The AICD promotes professional directorship and good governance and delivers knowledge and continuing learning in the field of directorship.

Chartered Secretaries Australia (CSA)

Established by Royal Charter in 1902, CSA has as its objective "the promotion and advancement of effective governance and administration
of organisations in the private and public sectors through the continued
development and application of governance and administrative best practice." CSA is an integral part of the international Institute of Chartered
Secretaries & Administrators founded in London in 1891.

Financial Services Institute of Australasia (FINSIA)

Formed in 2005 through the merger of the Securities Institute of Australia
and the Australasian Institute of Banking and Finance, FINSIA's representation covers the entire spectrum of financial services across Australasia –
including the wealth management, banking and finance, and capital
markets sectors.

Corporate governance

With unique local issues to address the Australian governance debate is also
well connected globally through government, commerce and industry peak-
body associations moving over time with the cycles of corporate scandals
and the subsequent moves by regulators to address past corporate excess.
Recognising a "one size does not fit all" corporate environment Australia's governance system is underpinned by the Corporations Act 2001 (Cwlth) administered by ASIC and covering all incorporated entities, together with the ASX
Listing Rules and Corporate Governance Principles and Recommendations for
publicly listed corporations. Australia's governance system is influenced not
only by its national and globally operating corporations. As the home to for-
eign-owned multinational corporations, many UK and US based, Australia's
governance system is subject to external factors with the most recent and
best demonstrated by the immediate flow-on effect from the introduction in
2002 of the US Sarbanes-Oxley (SOX) legislation and its heavy audit focused
compliance requirements. Australia's corporate regulatory environment was
subsequently updated with the Corporate Law Economic Reform Program
(Audit Reform and Corporate Disclosure) Act 2004, or CLERP 9 legislation,
with emphasis on enhanced accountability and transparency. These important changes to corporate governance included to

- expand the functions of the Financial Reporting Council (FRC, 2008) to
  oversee auditor independence;
- require the top 500 listed Australian companies to have audit
  committees;
- require auditors of listed companies to attend annual general meetings
  and answer reasonable questions about the audit;

- require auditors to report to ASIC any attempt to influence, coerce, manipulate or mislead them;
- protect any employee who reports a suspected breach of the law to ASIC, in good faith on reasonable grounds, from any retaliation in employment; and
- facilitate improved shareholder participation at company meetings in various ways, including by electronic means.

The introduction of these major pieces of financial legislation heralded "improved" financial governance, but, somewhat ironically, was to be followed by a period of creative financial engineering significantly increasing access to capital and inflating a leverage bubble that was pricked in late 2007 and burst on Wall Street in 2008 spawning a global financial crisis. Such was the magnitude and reach of this crisis, combined with the arrogance displayed by its Wall Street protagonist, that the global standing of US corporate governance and business ethics may have been irreparably damaged. The following period of deleveraging has put into question the direction of global corporate governance and in particular the influence of guiding "principles" versus the direct hand of "rules" (NACD, 2008).

In late 2008 the PIMCO Managing Director Bill Gross suggested: "We are now morphing towards a world where the government fist is being substituted for the invisible hand, where regulation trumps Wild West capitalism, and where corporate profits are no longer a function of leverage, cheap financing and the rather mindless ability to make a deal with other peoples money" (Gross, 2008). However, a broader cohort in the G20 leaders at their November 2008 meeting cautioned that using guiding principles rather than a new round of US SOX like governance regulation was preferable action to support the current credit crisis (*The Age*, 2008).

Moody's Investors Services (Moody's, 2008) suggest, "weaknesses in corporate governance uncovered by the credit crisis have focused regulatory and investor attention on what constitutes 'good' governance. This will have both near-term and long-term implications for U.S. and even non-U.S. corporations." Moody's advised that investors should focus on the following areas: Board oversight of risk management; executive compensation; board independence and skill sets; board practices, and succession planning.

Such high-level global debate and promotion of greater focus on the activities, capabilities and practices of company boards in the aftermath of failure in the American system of capitalism increases debate on key components of Anglo-American governance. In particular are the separation of the roles of chairman and CEO, reframing independence of non-executive directors and their role, and the extended leadership required to address the levels of abstraction necessary for boards to become more active in setting direction for the organisation whilst effectively overseeing the operations of management.

The Australian governance system, tested over recent decades of rampant capitalism with convergence to the US model, has established a sound foundation for good practice from which it can further enhance areas of transparency and corporate responsibility.

As a legal construct, Australian boards comprise a group of external and internal directors who function as a "social system" to direct and control the organisation (Bosch, 1995), forming as a group culture "a pattern of shared basic assumptions that the group learns as it solves its problems of external adaptation and internal integration" (Schein, 1997). The pronouncement that boards of directors are responsible for the "governance" of their companies through a "system by which companies are directed and controlled" (Cadbury, 1992, para 2.5) forms the basis of both the OECD and the Australian ASX Listing Rules and Corporate Governance Principles and Recommendations.

Along with its UK-based legal parentage Australia's corporate governance is grounded in "principles" rather than being reliant on a "black letter" regulatory system. With Australia business influenced by its inherent culture for fair play, its business managers actively shirk confrontation, preferring to be humanistic or "mates," unlike their counterparts in the United States, Germany or France. They must also contend with the "Tall Poppy Syndrome," a local cultural quirk with roots in Australia's colonial history, and the working class tribal ethos of egalitarianism, independence and resisting authority (Pumphrey, 2004).

From the late 1970s and with rapid growth of its securities and debt origination and trading systems, Australia has closely aligned with US competitive management and governance theory: accordingly its governance model has become increasingly influenced by a US governance debate, itself heavily influenced by a system entrenched in management control led by the combined chairman/CEO. As a consequence, Australia entered a period where US management was deemed highly preferable to local managers as a source of leading CEOs.

Following major local corporate scandals and import of the US SOX-driven compliance measures, recent focus of boards of directors has been on the monitoring of management conformance, and, as such, directors have experienced a period of compromise in their desire to become more engaged with improving performance and the setting of long-term strategic direction for the organisation (Cottrell, 2007). However, drawing on worldview Australia has created a leading corporate governance environment. The separation of the roles of chairman and CEO and boards led by independent chairs has provided the fundamentals that underpin the Australian governance system enabling it to largely avoid the US Lead Independent Director (LID) and UK Senior Independent Director (SID) structures requiring the interface of an "independent outside" director to take onboard and respond to the issues of shareholder concern unable to be dealt with by the compromised chair/CEO duality.

With highly developed and active market-capital system and investment markets Australia has moved in tandem with the UK and USA in having high levels of institutional shareholdings in its major publicly listed corporations. These corporations have in turn confronted the significant challenges of increasingly competitive market-driven short-term performance demands, demands that place increased pressure of accountability of boards of directors and oftentimes manifest in high turnover of CEOs.

Early development

As early as the 1970s, Australia's foremost company directors showed leadership in board governance and espoused the separation of the roles of chairman and CEO (Dunlop, 1972). Not until some 20 years later with the series of reports that led to the introduction of the UK Combined Code in 2003 did separation of these roles begin to gain prominence internationally. Whilst the UK has slowly moved to the separation of these roles, corporate USA appears to have committed to the CEO/chairman duality notwithstanding major academic and shareholder activist argument for change. Over the past 10 years, S&P 500 boards have moved slowly but steadily towards separate chair and CEO roles. Sixty-one per cent still have a combined chair/CEO, down from 84 per cent in 1998. Although 39 per cent now separate these roles, only 16 per cent have a truly independent chair (Spencer Stuart, 2008).

Corporate governance in the larger economy of the USA has drawn more on the accounting/audit-based Treadwell Report (1987) and the Committee of Sponsoring Organisation (COSO) report (1992) whereas in the UK the Corporate Code (2003) established itself as the world leader of corporate governance guidance, largely due to the breadth and depth of a series of lead-up reports: led by the 1992 Cadbury report (Internal control) through to the 2003 Higgs report (Role of Non-executive directors). However, according to Lipton (2008, p. 2), following decades of scandals and exposures of corporate excess and the resulting effects of shareholder activism, the USA may have been on the verge of "the eclipse of the public corporation." Arguing that a "forced migration from director-centric governance to shareholder-centric governance, along with the concomitant transformation of the role of the board from guiding and advising management to ensuring compliance and performing due diligence," potential directors may be dissuaded or existing directors caused to become increasingly risk-averse such that they "lose the entrepreneurial spirit that has made American business great."

Insider or outsider system?

Australia's corporate governance system can be seen to be aligned with the UK and US "outsider" model of ownership and control. It has a highly regarded and well-developed securities and financial markets. In addition, it has a corporate model that advocates at all levels of regulation a preference for the separation of role of independent non-executive chairman and CEO, and the appointment of independent non-executive directors. Cheffins (2001) adds support with "those who have sought to categorise Australia's version of corporate capitalism say that it follows the 'Anglo-American' or 'Anglo-Saxon' economic model." An important reason why this characterisation seems apt is that Australia has a "shareholder economy" and that the stock market is a well-established feature of the corporate economy. However, Dignam and Galanis (2004) argue that the corporate governance system of Australia's listed market in fact has many of the characteristics associated with insider systems, namely

- significant blockholders engaged in private rent extraction;
- institutional investor powerlessness;
- a strong relationship between management and blockholders, which results in a weak market for corporate control; and
- a historic weakness in public and private securities regulation, which allows the creation and perpetuation of crucial blocks to information flow.

Dignam and Galanis conclude by suggesting a compromise indicating that the Australian system may be currently in a state of flux, moving, as opined by Cheffins, from an insider to an outsider system as its real and shareholder economy grows to allow for greater separation of ownership and control.

The relatively small size of the Australian economy is important in rationalising the development of its corporate governance systems. Australia has arguably blended best practice from the Anglo-American and Eurasian systems with the Australian legal structure, and cognisant of its corporate culture has developed a sophisticated system meeting the needs of its local and international constituents.

Roles and responsibilities

Boards and directors

The board of directors acts on behalf of shareholders in overseeing and governing a company. To many Australian directors this equates to "monitor and review" whilst others, and mainly non-executive directors, contend that value-adding, principally through strong focus on long-term settings, is their desired primary role (Cottrell, 2007). Kakabadse and Kakabadse, (2008, p. 80) advises that for reasons more due to the unique geography of Australia, the board more proactively determines strategy and vision (Kakabadse and Kakabadse, 2008, pp. 80 and 99) To perform their overarching role the AICD recommends that directors must have independence of mind and need to be able to act independently of the management of the company. By law they must always act in the interests of the company. In addition, they need to exercise their responsibility collectively and to work in a collegial manner (AICD, 2006). The perception of responsibilities of directors remains divided. Responses to questions on directors' roles and responsibilities received in a 2006 Australian government Parliamentary Joint Committee varied from "a director would be failing in his or her duties if consideration was given to any factors other than maximising profit" to "the 'enlightened self-interest' interpretation of directors' duties argues that directors may consider and act upon the legitimate interests of stakeholders other than shareholders, to the extent that these interests are relevant to the corporation" (Chapman, 2006, p. xiii). This dichotomy sets the scene of a system in transition from responsibility to "shareholder" towards broader "stakeholder" responsibilities.

Major Australian boards have been structured to lead on many fronts, but central to this leadership are the roles of the chairman and chief executive, see Figure 3.1.

A primary role of the board is to ensure that the organisation can adapt to competitive and other inputs through appropriate direction, resource and cultural settings and meet the variety of its environment. Itself a complex social system the board of directors is required to adapt its decision making to meet these multiple leadership demands. The Australian board, functioning as a union of independent directors (chairman and non-executive directors) and executive directors (CEO and Management), operates under the ownership and control model. The law regards directors to be equally liable in their decision-making, but each has specific individual and collective vital roles in this process. The Greaves Case however is a reminder that this generally

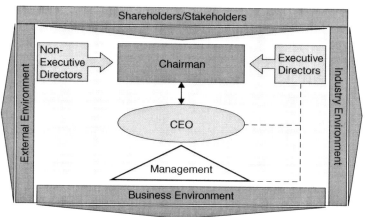

Figure 3.1   The Australian corporate board
Source: Compiled by the authors.

accepted view of director equality in decision-making has been challenged with the elevation of the role responsibilities of the chairman (AICD, 2006). Being a director is about being a leader – inclusive, open, inquiring, supportive, intelligent and decisive and embracing a culture of corporate governance as part of their commitment to enhancing the performance of the company that they serve (Hall, 2001). Evolving from the strong background of independent non-executive chairman, major Australian boards are proactive and "the more proactive Australian chairman requires a more proactive board" (Kakabadse and Kakabadse, 2008, p. 54), and champion high-quality participatory and anticipatory teamwork with open dialogue and strong decision-making. "It's in the culture. It's part of the psyche" (Pumphrey, D., as quoted in Kakabadse and Kakabadse, 2008, p. 83).

The responsibilities of the Australian board are specified in corporation board charter's and includes roles that the board specifically reserve for itself. The balance of responsibilities are delegated, mainly to the CEO, and accompanied with the levels of authority for each delegation.

Chairman

There is no more significant factor in determining effective board governance than the leadership qualities of the chair (Leblanc and Gillies, 2005, p. 201). In Australia's major listed corporations, the chairman's role is an increasingly recognised vital leadership role. In response to questions posed to unlock key roles of the chair, Kakabadse and Kakabadse (2008, p. 31) suggests that "to further understand these questions consider the role of chairmen in Australia. Here it has been traditionally a non-executive post" explaining that this is more due to its geographic isolation and the need to look internationally for executive talent. But, "in these circumstances, who attends to the balance, stability, and long-term future of the company? The chairman does."

The role of the chair is not defined in the Corporations Act 2001. The "first among equals" the chair is appointed by fellow board members not shareholders, and acts as the link between the board and the CEO. Rather than being formalised by law the many functions of the chair have evolved by custom. They include distinct responsibilities inside and outside the boardroom including the following:

- *Inside the boardroom*: establishing and maintaining effective working relationship with the CEO, setting the tone for the board, chairing board meetings and setting agendas and ensuring appropriate information, ensuring director contributions and reaching consensus when making decisions, board evaluation, CEO's employment/evaluation/succession.
- *Outside the boardroom*: communicating with shareholders/stakeholders, chairing shareholder meetings, ensuring compliance with ASX Listing Rules and continuous disclosure requirements, engaging with large institutional investors.

CEO

The Australian Chief Executive Officer (CEO) is employed by the board and is the most senior executive and the operational head in an organisation. In Australian corporations it has become customary for the CEO to be appointed to the board and given the role managing director, an executive director. The terms are now often used interchangeably notwithstanding that there are differences in their responsibilities. This crucial role is in practice split.

As the MD,

- function as a director working with the board to set strategic direction and other goal setting and roles reserved for the board, and
- communicate management's perspective and alert the board to growing issues.

As the CEO,

- working closely with the chairman and relying on clear direction, mentoring and support;
- manages the day to day operations of the organisation, its people and resources including the development of corporate strategy for board approval; and
- overseeing the effective implementation of the board's strategy and ensuring that the organisation's structure and processes meet the strategic and cultural needs of the organisation.

Executive directors

Legally, Australian executive directors have the same duties and responsibilities as other directors despite being both an employee and board director. Their deep understanding of the business can be invaluable to the board in raising and evaluating important issues. On the other hand, tensions have been known to exist when executive directors see little value in the input from non-executive directors.

There will be times when the board believes a conflict of interest may be evident and for the board to meet without any management present. Similarly, executive directors may also absent themselves from parts of board meetings to deal with real or perceived conflicts of interests, such as when the CEOs' performance or remuneration are being discussed, or for board meetings with the external auditor. Such conflicts are subject to decision by the board.

Non-executive directors

In Australia there is a preference for directors to be non-executive *and* independent, especially in ASX listed companies. Proxy advisers are increasingly rating companies on the independence of the board as a sign of their adherence to principles of good governance. The perceived advantage of non-executive directors is their independence and objectivity – their ability to act in the best interests of the company is not compromised. Other ways in which non-executive directors add value include bringing an independent and fresh perspective to decision making and demonstrating relevant competency, experience and ethical behaviour (AICD, 2007a).

An independent non-executive director is one without existing relationships with an organisation that might materially interfere with his or her ability to work in the best interests of the organisation. The ASX Corporate Governance Council takes the view that no director who is a former employee of a listed company is considered "independent" until 5 years after their employment ended. All directors, whether executive or non-executive, must comply with basic legal requirements under the Corporations Act 2001.

Board committees

Board committees are not essential for good governance; however, as the workload for boards has increased, committees have become the workhorses for many organisations. The following statistics from a study of Australian boards indicate the use of board committees (Korn/Ferry, 2007).

Audit Committee:

- 95 per cent of the total sample and 100 per cent of the top 50 have an audit committee, indicating that boards are complying with CLERP 9 legislation.

Remuneration Committee:

- 88 per cent of the total sample and 98 per cent of the top 50 have a remuneration committee, indicating that boards are responding to shareholder/stakeholder concern over the rapid escalation in the value of CEO remuneration packages.

Nomination Committee:

- 30 per cent of the total sample and 52 per cent of the top 50 have a nomination committee, indicating that the high ratio of NEDs vs. EDs on Australian boards may indicate board comfort with the board selection process.

Board charter

In the context of Australian corporate governance, it is common for major publicly listed corporations to establish a board charter, defined by AICD as "a formal written statement of the roles and responsibilities of the board. The charter plays a major part in any performance evaluation of the board" (AICD, 2007b). The charter sets down the role of the board of directors specifying those roles resolved for the board, such as to set strategic direction, and roles to be delegated. The AICD have embraced the Corporate Governance Charter™ (Kiel and Nicholson, 2003, p. 4) and incorporated this model into their principal Company Directors Course. The model charter is developed through four divisions:

- Defining governance roles
- Improving board process
- Key board functions
- Continuing development

Areas under debate

As the Australian corporate governance system continues to evolve, many issues surface and are the subject of ongoing debate. The following are of current interest.

CEO remuneration

An alignment of interests: "The bottom line for most shareholders is that executive pay should bear some relationship to their own returns. It sounds reasonable enough, and it's relatively easy to arrange when a company's profits are rising. But what about when they're not?" (Nesbit, 2008).

   The CEO remuneration debate pivots largely around structuring a competitive remuneration package in a thin talent market. The need is to provide an acceptable level of transparency for shareholders fuelled by a shift in stakeholders' expectations amid news of large renewal contracts and payouts, especially those received by failed CEOs. Changing legislation adds to the mounting pressures facing company boards. Under the CLERP 9 non-binding votes on executive remuneration reform publicly listed companies are required to publish in their annual reports the remuneration for the five most highly paid officers and then subject these remuneration packages to a non-binding vote by shareholders. While boards are under no obligation to follow the outcome of increasingly negative shareholder responses, the anger voiced in recent shareholder voting indicates that going forward boards may do so at their peril.

Continuous disclosure

The corporate excesses of the 1980s spawned the introduction of a continuous disclosure regime in Australia. Continuous disclosure requirements are covered under the Corporations Act 2001, the ASX Listing Rule 3.1 and the ASX Corporate Governance Principles. Although there is broad support for this system, issues including the following remain a source of concern in Australian boardrooms:

- When is information so certain as to require disclosure?
- When does it become price sensitive?
- How companies are required to respond to market rumours?

Failure to comply with the continuous disclosure requirements is an offence under s 674 of the Corporations Act and can create a civil or criminal liability. Directors may also contravene their duty of care and diligence under s 180(1) of the act by not complying with continuous disclosure obligations under the listing rules and s 674.

Director liability

In May 2008, the Federal Minister for Superannuation and Corporate Law announced the launch, in conjunction with the AICD, of a survey of 600 directors of S&P/ASX-200 companies to seek views on how current laws affect decision making by directors. "Examining directors' liability and a range of other issues that relate to the role of directors is a key part of the Government's agenda to enhance corporate governance. Getting the balance right so that our directors make an entrepreneurial contribution is critical and this survey will give us important evidence to inform the policy debate." Indicative outcomes from this survey (AICD/Treasury, 2008) include the following:

- 78 per cent rated "medium" to "high" on: What degree of risk do you feel for being found personally liable (under any law) for decisions you or your board(s) of directors have made in good faith?
- 78 per cent rated "occasionally" to "frequently" on: Has the risk of personal liability (under any law) caused you or a board of directors on which you sit to take an overly cautious approach to business decision-making?
- "Continuous disclosure" and "Derivatives liability" laws rated the "highest" on: Which specific laws caused this overly cautious approach to business decision making?

ASIC have also indicated that they are responding to concern in the business community that able and experienced women and men are shying away from the listed company environment because of higher personal liability risks and that the potential of reputation damage is too much risk for a person to accept a board position. ASIC has stated that it recognises "that it may be time for a stock-take in this area of personal liability – to assess the balance between ensuring our boards take risks (so that our economy keeps growing) and protecting shareholders and creditors and consumers when individual liability may be an appropriate measure, either for compensation or deterrence."

Institutional investors

Institutional shareholders hold more than 80 per cent of the issued shares of Australian listed companies and overseas institutional investors hold more than 50 per cent of these shares. These institutional shareholders have a general responsibility to ensure that investments are managed in the financial interests of the ultimate beneficiaries who have placed their funds with these investors (AICD, 2003).

Institutional investors include institutions through which investors collectively invest, such as superannuation funds and managed funds that hold monies in trust for individuals, but also major principal investors such as insurance companies. Institutional investors have large-scale investors with massive funds at their disposal with potential to exert considerable influence over a company's operation, such as membership of boards and indirectly decisions of directors. In addition, they are able to invest in the long term, and therefore better positioned to place corporate responsibility ahead short-term profit. When and how institutional investors activate this responsibility in Australia's relatively small equities markets is at the forefront of governance debate and imposes constant pressure on directors.

Shareholder and director primacy

Shareholder primacy requires that directors must act in the best interests of their shareholders; however, boards are under growing pressure to take a more holistic view and examine the perspective of shareholders interest in the context of employees, customers and other stakeholders. Environmental and other socio-economic issues are also increasing pressure on boards to invest for the long term with potential short-term profit impact.

In 2006, an Australian Parliamentary Joint Committee on *Corporate Responsibility: Managing Risk and Creating Value* (Chapman, 2006, p. 46) was established to consider "the extent to which the current legal framework governing directors' duties encourages or discourages directors from having regard for the interests of stakeholders other than shareholders." It received a number of "restrictive" interpretations to the existing framework including "directors claim that they are unable to undertake activities based on corporate responsibility, because such activities may not be directly 'in the best interests of the corporation'." The committee concluded that directors who take this approach to the current law are misinterpreting the law, and that the current directors' duties were intended to provide protection for shareholders, not to create a safe harbour for corporate irresponsibility. The committee also came to the view that "this interpretation is relatively uncommon in corporate Australia. Most directors appear ready to accept that the current directors' duties allow them some leeway for corporate responsibility. The question for them is under what circumstances they should put corporate responsibility ahead of immediate profit generation." The answer for each company will depend on the competitive pressures, strategic position and community expectations of each individual company. The committee also stated that it considered that an interpretation of the current legislation based on "enlightened self-interest" is the best way forward for

Australian corporations arguing that "there is nothing in the current legislation which genuinely constrains directors who wish to contribute to the long term development of their corporations by taking account of the interests of stakeholders other than shareholders" (Chapman, 2006, p. 63).

Under the Corporations Act, the director's general duty is to act "in the best interests of the corporation," not the best interests of the shareholders (Berger, 2005). This contrasts with US law, which holds the interests of the shareholder as primary, which Bainbridge argues is "flawed both as a positive and as a normative account of corporate governance." He contends that director primacy should be ascendant given "vesting decision-making authority in a centralized entity distinct from the shareholders – i.e., the board – is what makes the large public corporation feasible" (Bainbridge, 2008, p. 233).

Sustainability and reporting

Aligned with the shareholder primacy debate, corporate sustainability calls for strategies and practices that aim to meet the needs of stakeholders today while seeking to protect, support and enhance the human and natural resources that will be needed in the future. This position seeks Australian boards to respond through

- a reduction in their corporations environmental impacts and risks and
- to engage in and report these actions with transparency and accountability beyond the traditional focus of financial performance.

2005 data from top 100 companies across multiple jurisdictions provided to the above-mentioned Parliamentary Joint Committee (Chapman, 2006, p. 15) indicate that Australia is lagging internationally in sustainability reporting:

- Japan: 81 per cent
- UK: 71 per cent
- Average (16 countries): 41 per cent
- Australia: 23 per cent

Risk management

The revised ASX Principle 7 sets out the oversight role of directors and the activities of management and moves from a focus on disclosure to encouraging management to adopt more substantive risk management activities. Recommendation 7.1 states that "companies should establish policies for the oversight and management of *material business risks* and disclose a summary of those policies." This mandates board high-level oversight and review to determine the types and levels of risk that are acceptable to the organisation, and review and assess policies on risk oversight, management and internal control. Management is responsible for detailed analysis and to identify all material business risks, and establish policies for oversight and management of material business risks. This outcome directs focus solely on the management of "material business risks" described as "the most significant areas of uncertainty or exposure, at a whole-of company level, that could have an impact on the achievement of company objectives" (ASX, 2008a).

Disclosure of non-financial risks appears generally silent: leaving open how boards may move to consider these broader risks.

Performance vs. conformance?

Corporate directors are eager to spend more time developing long-term strategy. But this may be easier said than done, they argue, they lack the knowledge, expertise, and substantive interaction with management that could help them contribute to developing long-term strategy.

Boards that greatly influence the creation of corporate value work differently: they focus on long-term strategy, have deep expertise and access to many levels of managers, and emerge with management in substantive debates about long-term strategy. (Chen and Osofsky, 2008)

Involvement in setting the overarching strategic direction of the organisation is of particular interest to Australian NEDs (Cottrell, 2007), an involvement conditioned by board members' interests, experience, past decisions taken, public pressure and corporate reputation (Kemp, 2006), which with ongoing global change is often more profound than is commonly understood. This function demands a new mindset – a mindset positioned as "cultural transformation" that needs a future-oriented approach (Ratcliffe, 2006). The issue of board involvement in strategy has been, and remains, front-of-mind and far from being resolved as indicated by the following statements:

The board's job is to create the future, not mind the shop.... The board's job is to govern the organisation; management's job is to run the organisation. (Carver, 1991)

Regarding the board focus...a greater emphasis has to be placed on performance rather than mainly on conformance (compliance). Clearly, the challenge is to 'see the future first', to become proactive in strategy evaluation, development and implementation. Boards are not satisfied with the role they are playing in strategy development. What they want and need is to get more engaged in the process. (Barrett, 2001)

"Strategic direction" in this context is defined by the AICD (2007a) as "a term describing the process of defining and evaluating a plausible future for the company, rather than 'strategic planning' – the term given to the process of determining 'how to' get there."

Leadership

Boards "will truly be leaders, not by invading territory best left to management but controlling the big-picture, the long term, and the value laden," and are best described as "ownership one step down rather than management one step up" (Carver, 2006, p. 6). Although boards sit at the apex of the organisation, it is not uncommon for the strategy literature to relate only to a management hierarchy resolving that boards play a marginal role, if any (Mintzberg, 1994; De Wit and Meyer, 1998, 2005), or participate only to influence the "forming" function and purpose: defined as "the organization's fundamental reasons for existence: a perpetual guiding star on the horizon, not to be confused with specific goals or business strategies" (Hubbard et al., 2007). To fulfil this primary reserved role, boards require a conceptual approach, via a dialectic of shared understanding, embracing a culture of strategic thinking so empowering directors with the framework to promote the setting of strategic direction (Garratt, 1995).

More than ever, boards of directors are being held accountable for the organisations they govern. Moreover, in turbulent and ever changing environment, "the escalating ineffectiveness of more traditional approaches...calls for an entrepreneurial approach to enhance the firm's performance, its capacity for adaptation, and its chances of long term survival," arguing that "a new type of leader is needed" (Tarabishy, 2003). This leadership is arguably beyond even the most competent of CEOs to deal with, they will be out of their depth – "Nothing has wrecked more companies and resulted in more executive terminations than the inability to anticipate both the near and long term future. And nothing has been more misguided than elevating gut instinct to the level of infallibility" (Buchen, 2005).

In this environment "leadership" of the organisation is in question and requires to be reframed – beyond the traditional areas of control – to an extended leadership – combining anticipatory leadership with participatory management offered through the attributes of a pro-active independent chairman acting in harmony with a decisively selected CEO, supported in a collegiate of knowledgeable directors and senior managers. The Australian board governance model aspires to such lofty heights. In stark contrast to the US preference for role duality through the combined CEO/chairman role across its leading publicly listed corporations (Kiel and Nicholson, 2003; Monks, 2008), Australia has reframed the Anglo-American governance model in terms of "clear" separation of the roles of chairman and CEO and positioned "boards likely to more determine the vision of the organization and take a commanding role in driving the strategy" (Kakabadse and Kakabadse, 2008). The US and UK inspired compromise of a "lead" or "senior" independent director has not found room in Australia save for some small growing enterprises where the founder/blockholder holds the dual lead roles.

Conclusion

Whilst Australian boards operate in the solitude of an island continent located down-under in the southern hemisphere, they are part of a global cohort of boards aspiring to one desire but recognising the many realities and unique requirements to governance for their respective jurisdictions and corporations. Locally or globally "one-size-does-not-fit-all" and each board will vie for the scarce resources needed to meet the variety of the ever changing global environment and move to establish a governance model that supports corporate sustainability and social responsibility.

References

ACCC (2008), "For General Information on the ACCC," available at www.accc.gov.au/content/index.phtml/itemid/54137 (accessed 25 October 2008).

The Age (2008), "Bush Backs Free-Market Principles at G20," *The Age*, 16 November 2008, available at http://news.theage.com.au/world/bush-backs-freemarket-principles-at-g20–20081116–67z2.html (accessed 2 December 2008).

AICD (2003), "CEO Report – AICD Monitors International Issues," www.companydirectors.com.au/media/company+director/2003/september/ceo+report+-+aicd+monitors+international+issues+aicd+review.htm (accessed 18 August 2008).

AICD (2006), "The Greaves Case and the Responsibilities and Liabilities of a Chairman," available at www.companydirectors.com.au/policy/policies+and+papers/2006/greaves+case+-+responsibiliites+and+liabilities.htm (accessed 18 August 2008).

AICD (2007a), "Role of Non-Executive Directors," available at www.companydirectors.com.au/Policy/FAQs/Roles+Duties+And+Responsibilities/?LM (accessed 15 May 2008).

AICD (2007b), "The Language of Directorship," available at www.companydirectors.com.au/bookshop/e-books/the+language+of+directorship.htm (accessed 6 December 2008).

AICD/Treasury (2008), "Survey of Company Directors," available at www.treasury.gov.au/content/company_directors_survey/surveysummary.html (accessed 20 December 2008).

ASX "Australian Securities Exchange: Share Ownership", available at ww.asx.com.au/about/asx/history/share_ownership.htm (accessed 16 October 2008).

ASX (2007), "Corporate Governance Principles and Recommendations, 2nd Edition," ASX Corporate Governance Council, available at www.asx.com.au/about/corporate_governance/revised_corporate_governance_principles_recommendations.htm (accessed 6 December 2008).

ASX (2008a), "ASX Corporate Governance Council Revised Supplementary Guidance to Principle 7," ASX Corporate Governance Council, available at www.asx.com.au/supervision/pdf/09_asx_cgc_revised_supplementary_guidance_to_principle_7.pdf (accessed 4 December 2008).

ASX (2008b), "Equities for Institutional Investors," available at www.asx.com.au/professionals/institutional/equities.htm (accessed 26 November 2008).

Australian Services Roundtable (2008), see www.servicesaustralia.org.au.

Bainbridge, S. M. (2008), *The New Corporate Governance in Theory and Practice*, Oxford University Press, USA.

Barrett, P. (2001), "Corporate Governance – More Than Good Management," Proceedings of the CPA South Australia Annual Congress 2001 – Riding the Next Wave, Adelaide.

Berger, C. (2005), "The Myth of Shareholder Primacy," accessed at www.onlineopinion. com.au/view.asp?article=3436&page=0

Bosch, H. (1995), *The Director at Risk: Accountability in the Boardroom*, Pitman, South Melbourne.

Buchen, I. H. (2005), "The Futures Agenda of the Future CEO," *Foresight*, 7, 3–7.

Cadbury, A. (1992), *Report of the Committee on the Financial Aspects of Corporate Governance*, Gee and Co. Ltd, London.

Carver, J. (1991), *Boards That Make a Difference*, Jossey-Bass, San Francisco.

Carver, J. (2006), *Boards That Make a Difference: A New Design for Leadership in Nonprofit and Public Organizations*, 3rd Ed, Jossey-Bass, San Francisco.

Chapman, G. (Chairman) (2006), *Parliamentary Joint Committee on Corporations and Financial Services: Corporate Responsibility – Managing Risk and Creating Value*, Commonwealth of Australia, Canberra.

Cheffins, B. R. (2001), "Comparative Corporate Governance and the Australian Experience: A Research Agenda," available at SSRN: http://ssrn.com/abstract=268935 (accessed 20 August 2007).

Chen, A. & Osofsky, J. (2008), "Making the Board More Strategic: A Mckinsey Global Survey," *The Mckinsey Quarterly*, February, 1(10), 1–10.

Corporations Act (2001), "Corporations Act 2001," Commonwealth of Australia, available at www.austlii.edu.au/au/legis/cth/consol_act/ca2001172/ (accessed 13 November 2008). A note to this section states that "this subsection only operates in relation to duties under this section and their equivalent duties at common law or in equity (including the duty of care that arises under the common law principles governing liability for negligence) – it does not operate in relation to duties under any other provision of this act or under any other laws."

Cottrell, J. (2007), "Confronting Short-Termism – Embedding a Forward Thinking Boardroom Culture Based on the Provision of Strategic Direction," *Keeping Good Companies*, 59, 495–9.

De Wit, B. & Meyer, R. (1998), *Strategy: Process, Content, Context: An International Perspective*, Thomson Learning, London.

De Wit, B. & Meyer, R. (Eds) (2005), *Strategy Synthesis: Resolving Strategy Paradoxes to Create Competitive Advantage*, Thomson, London.

DFAT, "Department of Foreign Affairs and Trade: Overview," available at www.dfat. gov.au/aib/overview.html (accessed 25 October 2008).

Dignam, A. & Galanis, M. (2004), "Australia Inside-Out: The Corporate Governance System of the Australian Listed Market," *Melbourne University Law Review*, 28(31), 623.

Dunlop, J. (1972), "The Relationship between Management and Board," *The Australian Director*, 1, 13–19.

FRC (2008), "About the Financial Reporting Council," available at www.frc.gov.au/ about/ (accessed 25 October 2008). The FRC is responsible for providing broad oversight of the process for setting accounting and auditing standards as well as monitoring the effectiveness of auditor independence requirements in Australia and giving the minister reports and advice on these matters.

Garratt, B. (Ed.) (1995), *Developing Strategic Thought: Rediscovering The Art of Direction Giving*, McGraw-Hill, London.

Gross, B. (2008), "PIMCO Investment Outlook, December 2008," available at www. pimco.com (accessed 4 December 2008).

Hall, J. (2001), "The 21st Century Board – Leading the Change," Proceedings of the AICD Tasmania Division AGM, Tasmania, Australian Institute of Company Directors.

HIH (2003a), "Report of the HIH Royal Commission, Part Three: Directions for the Future, Chapter 6 Corporate Governance," available at www.hihroyalcom.gov.au/finalreport/chapter%206.html (accessed 25 October 2008).

HIH (2003b), "Report of the HIH Royal Commission, Part Three: Directions for the Future, Chapter 6.6 Corporate Governance: An Epilogue," available at www.hihroyalcom.gov.au/finalreport/chapter%206.html (accessed 25 October 2008).

Hubbard, G., Delyth, S., Heap, S. & Cocks, G. (2007), *The First XI: Winning Organisations in Australia*, Wiley, Milton.

Kakabadse, A. P. & Kakabadse, N. (2008), *Leading the Board: The Six Disciplines of World Class Chairmen*, Palgrave Macmillan, New York.

Kalokerinos, J. (2007), "Developments in the Role of the Chair in the Private and Public Sectors," *Corporate Governance ARC Project*, University of Canberra.

Kemp, S. (2006), "In the Driver's Seat or Rubber Stamp? The Role of the Board in Providing Strategic Guidance in Australian Boardrooms," *Management Decision*, 44, 56–73.

Kiel, G. C. & Nicholson, G. J. (2003), *Boards That Work*, McGraw-Hill, Australia.

Kirby, M. The Hon Justice (1998), "The Company Director: Past, Present and Future," Luncheon Address – The Australian Institute of Company Directors, Tasmanian Division, 31 March, Hobart, available at www.hcourt.gov.au/speeches/kirbyj/kirbyj_company.htm

Korn/Ferry (2007), *Board of Directors Study in Australia and New Zealand*, Korn/Ferry International in Association with Egan Associates, Sydney, Australia.

Leblanc, R. & Gillies, J. (2005), *Inside the Boardroom: How Boards Really Work and the Coming Revolution in Corporate Governance*, Wiley, New York.

Lipton, M. (2008), "Shareholder Activism and the 'Eclipse of the Public Corporation': Is the Current Wave of Activism Causing another Tectonic Shift in the American Corporate World?" *Corporate Governance Advisor*, 16, 1–7.

Mcdermott, M. (2005), "Company Law in Australia: Principles and Applications," Speech to the High Court of Australia – Foreword by the Hon Justice Michael Kirby, available at www.hcourt.gov.au/speeches/kirbyj/kirbyj_18mar05.html

Mintzberg, H. (1994), "The Fall and Rise of Strategic Planning," *Harvard Business Review*, January–February, 107–14.

Monks, R. & Minnow, N. (2008), *Corporate Governance*, Blackwell, Oxford.

Moody's (2008), "Investors Should Focus on Quality of Corporate Governance," Moody's Investors Service, available at www.researchrecap.com/index.php/2008/12/01/investors-should-focus-on-quality-of-corporate-governance/ (accessed 6 December 2008).

NACD (2008), "Key Agreed Principles – 2008," available at www.icgn.org/organisation/documents/ALL-NACD_KeyPrincipals_Board_Copy.pdf (accessed 4 December 2008).

Nesbit, M. (2008), "Executive Pay," *New Directions, AICD*, available at www.companydirectors.com.au/nr/exeres/1233a0c9-7ae2-44e0-9866-4be38b99d645.htm (accessed 6 August 2008).

Pumphrey (2004), "Leadership Trends in Australia – Corporate Governance Challenges Board Composition," *Leadership Capital Series*, Heidrick & Struggles International, Sydney, Australia.

Ratcliffe, J. S. (2006), "Challenges for Corporate Foresight: Towards Strategic Prospective through Scenario Thinking," *Foresight*, 8, 39–54.

Schein, E. H. (1997), *Organizational Culture and Leadership*, Jossey-Bass, San Francisco.

Spencer Stuart (2008), *Spencer Stuart Board Index*, Spencer Stuart, Canada.

Sykes, T. (1994), *The Bold Riders: Behind Australia's Corporate Collapses*, Allen & Unwin, St Leonards.

Sykes, T. (1998), *Two Centuries of Panic: A History of Corporate Collapses in Australia*, Allen & Unwin, St Leonards.

Tarabishy, A., Fernald, L. W. Jr., & Solomom, G. T. (2003), "Understanding Entrepreneurial Leadership in Today's Dynamic Markets," *Small Business Advancement*, University of Central Arkansas, Conway, AR.

4
The Chinese Boardroom: Roles, Dynamics and Relationships

Nada Kakabadse, Andrew Kakabadse and Chen Yang

Introduction

Since embarking on its comprehensive programme of economic and political reform, China has experienced extraordinary wealth and growth. By 2007, some 20 Chinese companies were ranked as the world's largest companies according to the Fortune Global 500 list (Lodge, 2007), giving a clear signal that Napoleon's "sleeping dragon" has woken and will be soon spitting fire. Concurrently, the governance structures (*gongsi zhili*) of Chinese enterprises have also undergone a significant transformation, whilst maintaining long established political and cultural features, namely active government ownership and strong family networks. In fact, the heart of Chinese economic reform is the redesign of corporate governance whilst simultaneously defending the essence of the "Chinese nature." It can be said that the government-led reform of corporate governance has been a major aspect of China's economic transition. In response to the State Council's withdrawal from direct intervention in the economy and change of role to one of acting as a regulatory authority (Qian and Wu, 2000; Ngok and Zhu, 2007), the emerging corporate governance paradigm is fashioned from the Anglo-America model of a market-determined legalistic framework (Tam, 2002). Despite that, China continues to adopt a quasi two-tier board structure, loosely designed on the German system, consisting of a board of executive directors and a supervisory board (Clarke and Du, 1998).

Cognisant of the formal change of government purpose but of the reality of its influence, the strength of kinship ties and the effect of the corporate reform movement, China is geared towards realising greater economic and social liberalisation. Within such a context, this chapter explores the role and contribution of the Chinese chairperson and his/her effect on boardroom dynamics and performance within "state-owned enterprises" (SOEs) and/or "state-controlled enterprises" (SCEs). SOEs are enterprises where the controlling shares are owned by the state (*guoyou gu*) and/or state-legal person (*guoyou faren gu*), and the remaining shares are owned by other institutional and individual strategic investors including pension funds, security funds, investment trusts and in theory qualified foreign institutional investors (QFIIs) and other public investors.

There exist over 150,000 SOEs controlled by different levels of government in China, of which only 158 are large sized under the direct control of the State Asset Management Committee (SAMC; SASAC, 2007a). In order to better understand the context within which Chinese chairman operate, we first provide a brief overview of the market conditions that have been instrumental in shaping Chinese enterprises and adopted governance mechanisms. From there on, the study results of the impact of SOE chairman on board dynamics, board role and board performance are reported (Elloumi and Gueyie, 2001; Weir and Laing, 2001; Kakabadse et al., 2006). Discussion and analysis of these findings draws on existing literature (Lorsch and MacIver, 1989) and concludes that board involvement in the functioning of the organisation is critical in order to minimise crises effects and, as such, much relies on the chairman to nurture an atmosphere of openness and dialogue, and inclusive working practice.

Growth miracle

By the late 1970s, China had embarked on its economic reform. The then State Council initiated five major rounds of institutional restructuring of central government, from 1982 to 2003. The aim was to strengthen the role of government under the leadership of the Chinese Communist Party (CCP) to better enable the transition to a market economy in response to the increasing pressure for economic globalisation (Zhang, 2002; Ngok and Zhu, 2007). In 1992, the CCP formally recognised that a market-based economy was the ultimate aim of economic reform, formally endorsing the concept of private property rights (Zhang, 2002). After joining the WTO in 2001, considerable administrative change was pursued in China in order to "overcome the inappropriate situation in the system of government" (Wang, 2003, p. 549). The aim was to "transfer the government's role from micro-management to macro-regulation, strengthening the management of state assets, improving the macro-economic control regime, integrating the domestic and foreign trade regime, reinforcing the market regulatory system, and enforcing the food and production safety regulation regimes" (Ngok and Zhu, 2007, p. 231). Previous CCP concern with equality and the system of "rice bowl" employment minimising differences between those in different professions and balancing rewards between executives and workers at around 4: 1, gave way to Kang Xiaoping's new principle of "each according to his work" (Easterby-Smith et al., 1995). Further, since the opening of the Shanghai Stock Exchange (SHSE) and Shenzhen Stock Exchange (SZSE) in December 1990 and July 1991 respectively, China's stock market has expanded rapidly. By 2005, 1365 companies were listed (829 on the SHSE and 536 on the SZSE) with a total market capitalization of about $4248.7 billion. As a result, by 2005, China became the fourth largest economy in the world overtaking Britain in terms of gross domestic product (GDP; Xu, 2007).

The Communist government promotion of economic expansionism ushered the era of "statist capitalism" and in doing so, the fundamental restructuring of SOEs in order to build a "modern enterprise system." The push was on to transform SOEs into corporate entities. Under Chinese company law, to be listed and thus raise capital directly from the public, the enterprise has to adopt the legal structure of a joint stock company (*gufen youxian gonsgsi*; Clarke, 2006). As a result, more than 80 per cent of the SOEs were legally repositioned as Western corporations (Chen, 2005).

Although Chinese government policy towards foreign investment shifted dramatically, offering for the first time significant domestic market access to firms that brought in advanced technology, the package of measures, including SOE corporatisation, did not facilitate full privatisation. In 2004, around 64 per cent of all issued stock for companies (including state-owned shares and legal person shares) listed on the SHSE and SZSE were non-tradable with only 26 per cent available as public shares (Li and Zhang, 2007). However, due to globalisation pressure, the prevalence of non-tradable shares (NTS), typically held by central and local governments, was also poised to change (Tucker, 2006). In 2005, the Chinese Securities Regulatory Commission (CSRC) announced a new initiative, the "Administrative measures on the split share structure reform of listed companies," aimed to convert non-tradable shares into tradable ones (Qiang, 2003). In fact, state shares being held by government agencies such as the State Asset Bureau, with legal person shares were owned by domestic institutions. Only A shares could be publicly traded. According to Wang and Chin (2004, p. 543),

> shares of a typical firm are split into state shares, legal-entity shares, and tradable shares, with the restriction that state and legal-entity shares cannot be traded publicly. State shares are those owned by the central or local government. Legal-entity shares are those held by domestic legal entities (institutions) such as listed companies, SOEs, banks, etc. Tradable shares are the only class of shares that can be traded on domestic stock exchanges, and are further classified into tradable A- and B-shares. Tradable A-shares are ordinary shares available exclusively to Chinese citizens and institutions. B-shares were designated for overseas investors prior to opening the market to domestic investors in February 2001.

Through the CSRC initiative, 96 per cent of listed SOEs were trading all their shares by December 2006. Accompanying the boost to the stock market through the conversion of non-tradable to tradable shares, new and revised accounting standards for business enterprises, "the New Accounting Standards," were introduced.

The energetic pursuit of these reforms, including the privatisations of SOEs, emphasises China's move towards free enterprise (Chen et al., 2006). Yet underlying the enormity of change, the state still attempts to retain control of market exposed organisations, although that is reduced to around 24 per cent of all shares.

Despite the evident need for reform, foreign observers perceive that the marketisation strategy has not been successful as the performance of the majority of listed companies is viewed as having declined, mostly due to flawed governance structures and inadequate performance incentives resulting from continued state ownership and interference (Green, 2004). The Chinese government encouraging companies to improve their corporate governance through stricter and more detailed disclosure requirements (CSRC, 2006a; Cheung, 2007) has not been able to overcome the suspicion held by Western interests that social concerns predominate over shareholder value maximisation. Property rights still remain unclear, due to a deliberate opaque policy pursued by the Chinese government. Therefore, who owns what and how Chinese assets can be exploited remain vexed questions.

As the Chinese marketisation reform movement has still some way to go and with every intent on the part of government to proceed to turn China into a free market, a study of "board performance" and chairman role and contribution was considered necessary in order to assess the "reality" of boardroom contribution to effective governance implementation. The assumption made by the researchers is that so much of China's economic reforms depend on boards appropriately preparing the organisations under their stewardship to be "globally market ready." In doing so, it is considered that strong leadership of the boards is essential to improve the competence of large-sized Chinese companies to compete in the global market.

The study

Considering the paucity of study of Chinese board and chairman role and contribution, an exploratory qualitative study was pursued in order to identify the critical performance dimensions relevant to both. Mace (1986) emphasised the usefulness of a qualitative approach in studying the role and responsibilities of boards of directors in medium and large US firms, arguing that any other approach would result in misleading and fallacious conclusion. Similarly, Lorsch and MacIver (1989) adopted qualitative methods in their attempt to understand boardroom dynamics. Also Stiles (2001) argued that because research on board directors is an emerging field, no prior classifications should be placed on the gathering of data and so chose to concentrate on interview data as the primary means of field observation.

Qualitative study focuses on the "richness" and holism of the data gathered, and acts as the basis for revealing complexity (Miles and Huberman, 1994). Qualitative data allow for "thick descriptions" that are vivid, nested in a real context, and have that ring of truth which will have a strong impact on the reader (Miles and Huberman, 1994, p. 10).

One the basis that sample selection for qualitative research is required to be purposeful and strategic (Gilchrist, 1992, p. 57) taking account of the conditions under which particular findings appear (Glaser and Strauss, 1967), we concentrated on SOEs that are deemed to be of strategic importance to the Chinese economy. Particularly attention was given to those under the direct control of the State Asset Management Committee (SASAC, 2007a). Distinction was drawn between the different classes of enterprise ownership according to status of registration (*China Statistical Yearbook*, 2006, p. 505). For example, there exist 25,339 SOEs, 141,772 collective owned enterprises, 756 state joint-ownership enterprises, 1064 joint state-collective enterprises and 2083 state sole funded corporations amongst others (*China Statistical Yearbook*, 2006, p. 505). However, at the time of the study, only 158 large-sized SOE plcs existed under the direct control of the SAMC (SASAC, 2007a). The study therefore focused on large-sized SOE plcs.

Our sample consisted of 17 board members from seven boards of SAMC-controlled SOE plcs, whose interests lay in the finance and energy sectors. The headquarters of these organisations were either in Shanghai or in Beijing. Negating access to board members was demanding and took months to organise. Two of the authors had grown a network of graduate alumni and senior Chinese executives over a number of years, and whose members agreed to provide access to top Chinese directors. Semi-structured, open-ended interviews were conducted with the intention of allowing the study participants to reveal their experiences concerning their participation on Chinese boards. The length of interview varied from 1.5 h to 6.5 h, with the average interview lasting about 2.5 h. Interviews were conducted both in English and in Chinese, depending on the study participants' language skill and choice. Considering that one of the inquirers is bilingual and a native Chinese speaker, choice of language for interviews was easily accommodated. Most of the study participants were uneasy with the use of a tape recorder, so context was captured through shorthand and later transcribed. No formal confidentiality agreement was signed as assurance of confidentiality was considered as sufficient by the study participants.

The interview transcripts were read independently with the aim of identifying recurring narratives, particularly focusing on director's role and ways of working. Hunt and Benford (1994, p. 16) argue, "interpreting is a continuous monitoring process that takes place before, during and after a research performance" which highlights the fact that qualitative data analysis is itself a process of construction. Interviews have the advantage for accessing respondents' interpretations of the social world, and thus offer an "insider's perspective" (Jensen, 1989; Norburn and Grinyer, 1974).

Findings

Seven themes recurred through the 17 narratives, namely governance, board roles and purpose, board size and composition, Chairman/CEO relationship, director nomination, ways of working and ethical dilemmas.

Governance

> Two parallel systems govern state owned companies in the finance and banking industry and other SEOs of strategic importance – the Party system and the State administrative system. For example in Shanghai, the Municipal Party System provides balance between the two systems. (Vice-Chairman, Board 2)

> According to corporate law, introduced in 1994, it is compulsory to set up a board for all "Guoyou Konggu SOEs (SOE plcs)". However, there are no such requirements for boards of Guoyou Duzi SOEs (SOE Ltd), since most of these companies adopt "zong jingli fuzezhi" (CEO/general manager is responsible), where the CEO/General Manager makes the strategic decisions and takes full responsibility for the company. (CEO, Board 4)

A contrast of governance mechanisms is identified, that is, two forms of state involvement – the local communist party and state administration in the form of the SAMC. The former is more concerned with meeting communal stakeholder concerns and building stakeholder relationships and the latter with enhancing company performance. Reconciling what are purported as a contrasting set of demands imposed by bodies external to the enterprise is viewed as impossible to achieve through one governance mechanism. In fact, the SOE plc is represented as adopting western governance through the introduction of western-type boards, observant of modern day governance codes and requirements (Tables 4.1 and 4.2). The counter measure is that of the SOE Ltd enterprise whose governance practice is determined by one individual, the CEO/general manager. Certainly, the mix of governance mechanisms and demands extend way beyond the requirements for enterprises based in the Anglo-American or Continental European economies (Li and Zhang, 2007).

> China adopts a 'mixed' governance structure, borrowing from both the US and German model. There is a supervisory board in a Chinese Plc, but the supervisory board does not hold substantial authority like the German counterpart.(Independent Director, Board 4)

> In mid-1990s, the Chinese Security Regulation Committee (CSRC) approved the first group of 10 security and fund companies, which were set up in China. These companies were headed by scholar-CEOs, who had overseas education and adopted the 'standard' American corporate governance structure. These companies received support from the government and were hailed as the model for the future for the newly

Table 4.1 Municipal Party Committee – balance between two systems

Municipal Party Committee	
Party system	**State administrative system**
Led by Provincial Municipal Finance Party Committee (*jinrong dang gongwei*)	Led by Provincial State Asset Management Committee (SAMC)
In charge of	In charge of
(1) balance of stakeholder relationships	(1) management of companies
(2) CSR	(2) performance of companies
(3) risk and conflict management	(3) focus on shareholder return
Balance between two systems	

Source: Complied by authors.

Table 4.2 SOEs

SOE plc	**SOE Ltd**
Adopts the modern enterprise mechanism (*xiandai qiye zhidu*)	CEO/General Manager responsible
	Responsible to State Asset Management Committee
Follow the corporate governance code and relevant regulations	State Asset Management Committee makes certain strategic decisions

Source: Complied by authors.

emergent financial sector in China. However, rampant corruption and misconduct of funds was reported by the financial media in China in 2001. Exposed were problems of internal control and a vacuum of accountability. As most scholar CEOs did not have practical experiences, but were appointed according to their status, they failed to cope. The governing bodies realised that the 'standard corporate governance' model did not fit the circumstances of transitional China. So, a share structure reform for fund companies was introduced.. It became compulsory for fund and trust companies to have accountable large shareholders, holding at least 50% of shares. This reform worked as the performance of companies improved, and corruption was curbed. (CEO, Board 2)

China is all about relationships. You can have as many or as few governance systems as you want. They are not going to make that much difference to the way China does things. (Party Member, Board 3)

Although the study participants argued that professional inexperience and the "unthinking" utilisation of western models led to the number of failures, some critics (Gong, 1997) purport that a new form of corruption has emerged, driven by cadre entrepreneurship (*xiahai*). Party and government cadre have entered the market, relying on their close financial and personal contacts with government institutions. That proximity has enabled them to earn considerable sums of money over a short period. Cadre patronage of government officials is considered to have led to "*gong hui*" corruption (Gong, 1997; He, 2000; Fan, 2002). This situation is further fuelled through the introduction of contrasting approaches to governance responsibility (the party and state administration system) and governance accountability (Western-type boards and total focus on the CEO).

Board roles

The study participants identified two critical board roles, strategy determination and decision making.

Strategy determination

Participants highlighted that the development of strategy is the prime purpose of the board. Moreover, it is reported that Chinese boards fully engage in determining the strategy of the firm.

> The board sets up the strategy, estimates the budget, presents the call for new products or product portfolio, and compares our performance with other rival's. (Executive Director, Board 2)

> We set up what we call a 'strategic committee', which is composed of some of the board of directors and the CEO. We also conduct seminars and workshops. Further we meet with the top and middle managers to formulate strategy.(Chairman, Board 5)

The board is viewed as an active body that plays a crucial role in determining strategy, in most cases through cooperation with management. This is achieved through a series of committees, requiring the participation of board members and full time management. In that sense, Chinese boards are reported as more representing the unitary Anglo-American board, rather than the German two-tier enterprise.

Decision making

> Chairman and CEO are in charge of business strategy. However some decisions such as the expansion of company branches must be approved by the China Securities Regulation Committee (CSRC). The company follows CSRC policy guidelines on branch development. Our current size of investment in Chinese stock exchanges is 3.7 billion RMB and 80% of these investments were not processed through the board. (Independent Director, Board 1)

Decisions concerned with investment of less than 20% of the company's net assets are the responsibility of the board. If the size of investment goes over 20%, it is the shareholder assembly that makes the decision. For minor investment projects, the CEO/General Manager working meeting can make the decision, but that depends on the project. Smaller and minor projects can be proposed by the regional company and implemented once headquarters approve the plan. International Projects are approved by the board. In reality the board has limited knowledge and information with regard to projects ("dongshi bu dongshi"), so the CEO, or, senior managers, who have more knowledge make the decision and the board acts passively as a 'rubber stamp'. (Chairman, Board 4)

The study participants emphasised that the responsibility for decision making and implementation is shared between the board and management. Critically, the CEO/general manager and the chairman agree on the allocation of tasks and responsibilities between board and management. Additionally, some of the respondents argue that the responsibility of the board is to allocate the "right talent" to strategically important positions. However, critics have countered and assert that a critical function of the board is the allocation of politically "right" people to important positions, regardless of the individual's level of expertise (Zheng, 2007).

Board size and composition

Two critical issues emerged from interviews, analysis and description of various board roles and size of board.

Board composition

According to the corporate governance code of plcs listed on Chinese stock exchanges, one third of board members should be independent. The independent board director (IBD) is not appointed by the Party. The company invites professionals to join the board as an IBD, in accordance with relevant laws and codes. It is compulsory to have IBD's opinion with regard to any decision relevant to the largest shareholder. (Independent Director, Board 3)

The board is composed of representatives of major shareholders and is thus mainly concerned with investment return. In most Chinese plcs, independent board members are not really independent. As a result, I think that problems associated with internal control are more prevalent in Chinese companies. (Independent Director, Board 2)

Independent board members in Chinese PLCs only take passive actions, to prevent bad/negative things happening. They play a defensive role. If 2/3 of independent board members refuse to sign, the decisions cannot be passed. (Executive Director, Board 5)

The role and contribution of the independent director attracted extensive discussion in interview. The study participants emphasised that independent directors are not allowed to occupy any executive position in the listed companies on whose board they sit (CSRC, 2004). In addition, they cannot enter into any business or other relationship with that company or major shareholders in order to ensure that they are not distracted from acting independently or objectively (CSRC, 2004). In addition, independent directors are prohibited from directly or indirectly holding more than 1 per cent of the designated listed company's total shares (CSRC, 2004). The majority of independent directors in our sample were university educated, exhibiting expertise in economics, law and professional services.

Yet despite safeguards, the majority of the study respondents indicated that independent directors are strongly influenced by the relationships and interactions on their boards. Although independent directors are positioned to influence board decisions, at best they are viewed as taking a "passive" role (Executive Director, Board 5), preventing decisions from being made, rather than directly influencing the decision-making process. Certainly, the judgement of the majority of respondents is not favourably inclined towards independent directors acting independently. However, a minority of the study participants make some favourable comment.

> In addition to the Chairman and CEO, independent members play a key role on the board. Our three independent board members chair three committees, Health, Safety and Environment Committee (HSEC), Personnel Development and Compensation Committee (PDCC) and Auditing Committee (AC). (Vice-Chairman, Board 4)

Favourable comment forwards independent directors highlighted either a particular contribution being made by a named individual director or that the independent director held a particular role on the board, or a subcommittee of the board (Vice-Chairman, Board 4). Only through either being an "exceptional individual" or through discharging a clear and focused responsibility is the independent director considered as sufficiently separate from majority opinion on the board. Yet even the most talented independent director, acting according to their own judgement and conscience across a range of boardroom issues, is unlikely to continuously act independently. The outstanding individual was reported as taking a particular stand on one or possibly two issues, but not positioning themselves as offering an independent perspective across a range of issues.

Also, considerable attention was given to the roles of CEO and Chairman.

> Although we tend to collectively to share board responsibilities, the Chairman's title symbolizes the highest respect in terms of status. It

also invokes the image of our most famous chairman, who was a visionary statesman, strategist, philosopher, warrior, poet and calligrapher. In short, this title sets an expectation of the highest standard of responsibility. Highly respected Chairman enhances the value of the company. (Party Representative, Board 3)

The chairman has a very important role as he follows up on the entire firm's business such as employee' errors, customers' problems, new regulation from government agencies, etc. Consequently, the board chairman has a strong connection with the managing director. However, all share responsibility for their own and each others actions. (CEO, Board 2)

Governments in both developed and developing economies are not immune to policy errors. Policy errors occur when government fails to recognise the size of the gap between new ways and existing institutional capabilities. The Chinese government is very careful in adopting new policies, which at the time may appear a slow process for a fast changing business world. My role as the Chairman of this enterprise, together with others in my position, is to advise the provincial party on industry and business needs as well as on the impact that new polices have. Development is a joint effort, so we all share responsibility in this. (Chairman and Party Member, Board 2)

Although the Chairman was described as having the most visible and respected role, the study participants also reported that it is rare that he/she, or any one individual on the board for that matter, will be held responsible for any particular board action. Rather, the emphasis is on collective action and responsibility across all levels of the firm's hierarchy. According to the law, the chairman is not held individually to account for any single act, as that is shared by the whole board. Confucian governance, namely creative decision making based on rank, order, hierarchy harmony and reconciliation, dominates the Chinese boardroom. Thus, negotiation is routine and entails intensive interaction with several individuals who share responsibility and accountability for board decisions and actions. This collectivistic approach in areas such as financial budgeting is particularly noted (Ueno and Sekaran, 1992; Earley, 1993) and is considered a way of life in the Chinese business culture.

The Confucian concern for stability and harmony sets the parameters for the desired attributes of a successful chairman, which the study participants highlight as being non emotional, reassuring, concerned for people, always in control but not intimidating, self-made, preferably well educated and interestingly more respected if the individual has an agricultural background, this final point being a leftover from the Mao period of "back to basics!"

Size of board

Size of board and orientation of board members equally dominated conversation.

> Last year we had 19 board members. Now we only have 11. This is a typical case of internal decision and control. The Chairman felt that there was a lot of hassle in decision making with the larger board. So the two largest shareholders met and decided to reduce the size of the board. (CEO, and Party Member, Board 6)

> There are two types of directors/senior managers with SOEs – cadre oriented and market oriented. The former are appointed and promoted by the party/state and develop their career within the system. The latter grow out of business ventures. In the future, hopefully, the professional managers will become the mainstream of senior managers within SOEs. Most senior managers are not board members but they may take part in board meetings. (Independent Director, Board 7)

The CSRC (2006b) stipulates that supervisory boards should consist of between 5 and 19 members, of which one third or preferably a half be independent directors. Independent directors tend to be recruited from prestigious investment banks, or from consultancies and audit practices, with most having a background in economics. In our sample, the average SOE board size was that of 16 directors, including the chairman. However, certain boards were reported as having recently reduced their size to only nine members. Although efficiency of decision making and taking, and board member communication improve through smaller group size (Pfeffer, 1972; Pearce and Zahra, 1992), Firstenber and Malkiel (1980, p. 26) remind us of the importance of network ties in forging business links in China. Our study participants, who placed strong emphasis on the maintenance of networks ("guanxi") with business people and government, support this view. The strength of the network was seen as providing access to scarce resources such as land, labour, raw materials, import and other licences, insider information and endorsements. Thus, network ties were reported as still predominating over concerns of board performance efficiency (Becht et al., 2002). On this basis, a number of the respondents considered that larger boards offered far better network accessibility. Thus, overall there was little appetite to reduce the size of the boards amongst the majority of our study participants. Of course, network dependence and obligation calls into question the "true independence" of the IBD and places board size and configuration as being of secondary concern.

Only few participants mentioned the role of the institutional investor/government representative. Even then, the opinion offered was that the role played by institutional investors on boards is more social and holds little significance for board performance effectiveness.

The representatives of the government's institution are less effective as they are not professionals and not close to the market. (Executive Director, Board 3)

The Chairman /CEO relationship

As the Chinese seek harmony, there are three possible scenarios:

- "ni si wo huo" (you die I live): two sides can not reconcile the conflict, either chairman gets rid of CEO, or, a more dominant CEO gets rid of the chairman.

- The conflict between two sides is overt and the company is divided into two 'gangs'. However, both sides intend to reconcile the conflicts to reach a long-term co-existence.

- "Xin zhao bu xun" (heart knows no talk): The conflict between two sides is covert; two sides pretend to be in harmony but play games accordingly.

The third scenario is the most popular in Chinese companies. (CEO, Board 7)

We adopt 'group leadership'. Most decisions are reached through discussion between the Chairman, CEO and the board. In the future, we may combine the Chairman and CEO to be held by one person. It is difficult to tell which form is better. For some industries, split roles may be better. For us there is a rationale to merge the two roles into one. We are listed on the NYSE. We have two boards, supervisory and management to constrain each other. (Deputy Chairman, Board 6)

Despite talk of tension, between chairman and CEO, the majority of the study participants emphasised the strong relationship between the board, the chairman and top management. Although the board does not meet frequently (average 6 to 12 times per year), the interaction between the chairman and top management continues on almost a daily basis. Common practice is that the CEO and/or managing director invites counsel from the chairman on every important decision.

It should also be stated that power struggles are not uncommon on Chinese boards. However, as CEO board 7 indicated, they are conducted covertly and handled offline. Not losing face and outward displays of harmony are reported as paramount requirements.

Director nomination

Top posts such as chairman, directors and top managers are nominated or elected by the party's organization and the government's personnel department, which the board then approves. In each boardroom, at least one member has to be a party representative, who may or may not have the role of chairman or CEO. Under this selection model, managers of state shareholding companies more often pursue political relationships with government officials rather than be concerned with performance improvement. (Board Director, Board 2)

The shareholder assembly appoints the chairman. The government as the largest shareholder nominates the chairman. As we are of national strategic importance, 88% of our shares are state owned non-tradable shares. (Chairman, Party Member, Board 8)

'In terms of the appointment of chairman and CEO, the party/state system is still at the helm. "Dang guan ganbu", or the party manages/supervises the cadre. This remains the norm in most large sized SOEs. However the party/state system no longer engages in the direct management of the company, but controls three key issues – appoints the No. 1 ("yi ba shou") Chairman and CEO of the company; sets profit/performance targets; allocates total remuneration. For most SOEs, the party committee merely organises leisure activities. However, in the near future, the party/state system hopefully will fully retreat from plcs. (CEO, Party Member, Board 9)

Board membership is decided through negotiation between the largest shareholder and the other two larger shareholders. The chairman comes from the company attached to the largest shareholder. Municipal Party Committee also appoint their representatives as board members. (CEO, Board 8)

The study participants affirm SASAC's founding role, that of separating government administration from enterprise management, and of separating ownership from management control (SASAC, 2007b). SASAC's role is to act as investor on behalf of the state, supervise and manage state-owned assets and guide the reform and restructuring of SOEs (SASAC, 2007b). In doing so, the SASAC appoints and removes the top executives of enterprises (under the supervision of the central government), evaluates their performances and rewards, and penalises and supervises the management of local state-owned assets (SASAC, 2007b). Considering that board appointments are often politically determined and assigned to those with party connections, personal connections based on the principle of *guanxi* are strong determinants of job placement and performance.

Although Chinese company law stipulates that the CEO and the supervisory board have to be elected by the shareholders' meeting (Gu, 2006), the state as the controlling shareholder is legally responsible for the appointment of candidates to these positions. As the study participants emphasised, party involvement plays a critical role in employee relations and in the operation of the firm (Lin, 2001). The governance of China's listed SOEs is that of "insider control (*neibu ren kongzhi*)," determined by the party and government officials.

Critics view insider control as open collusion, resulting in tax evasion and corruption amongst SOE managers (Tam, 2002). Close links between business and government favours appointments based on connections rather than on merit (Fan, 2002; Lin, 2004). However, the Irish experience of the "flexible developmental state," exhibits many characteristics of liberal pluralism and shows that it is possible for government to cultivate harmonious consensus through networked relationships in developing industry along corporate lines (O'Rriain, 2000; O'Higgins, 2002).

Ways of working

The commercial legal system is still in its development and there are many grey areas in which new enterprises operate.... No, I am not saying that we are behaving unethically but rather that business is more advanced than the legal system and that technically in order to do business we often have to venture into the grey area as there is no clear letter of the law. But that is business. (Chairman, Board 1)

Board effectiveness depends not only on directors' quality of relationship but also on their individual and corporate networks (guanxi). The wider the guanxi and the more personal relationships board has and can call on, the less likely board will be surprised by new initiatives. Guanxi networks are guided by unwritten traditional rites ('li') of 'face trading' (obligation) that allows board members to relay heavily on the social responsibilities that come with a well-maintained guanxi relationship and achieve results that are in harmony with society. No rule or law to date has proven as effective. (Executive Director, Board 2)

Traditionally we regard the law ('fa') as inefficient, arbitrary and a cumbersome mechanism for deciding what can and cannot be. This does not mean that we behave unethically. On the contrary, we follow traditional customs and rites ('li') of proper conduct that cover the whole range of relationships aiming for harmony and balance. (Chairman, Board 7)

Strongly emphasised by the study participants is that social relationships are the glue that holds Chinese society together (Mills, 1956; Useem, 1984, Westphal and Zajac, 1996). In fact, the maintenance of relationships is considered as so embedded in China that Chinese society has traditionally relied on a well-functioning social network (*guanxi*). From this perspective, economic action is rooted in social relations, as economic behaviour stems from social behaviour (Granovetter, 1985). In fact, Benson (1975) postulates that social networks are a political economy concerned with the distribution of scarce resources. Yet, as already alluded to, embeddedness of social relationships at board level also encompasses "collusion," involving restricting competition (in effect price fixing), "cooption" or the absorption of potentially disruptive elements into an organization's decision-making structure and/or "resource dependence" (Pfeffer and Salancik, 1978) where the control of other firms' resources through the expertise and influence of directors is useful to the host firm (Useem, 1984).

Bruton et al. (1999) found that Chinese business culture has a high tolerance for information asymmetry between the firm's insiders and external investors as well as outside board members. Therefore, strong emphasis is placed on the maintenance of networks (*"guanxi"*) that favour harmony over information disclosure and shareholder rights (Bruton et al., 2004). Luo (2000) argues that the main reason why large-scale networks (*guanxi*) exist stems from poorly determined legal and administrative frameworks. Tsang (1998) views *guanxi* as a resource that can be called on when needed but which also poses a liability when a favour is owed. The emergent view is that *guanxi* is an enduring feature of Chinese boards. The study participants consider that *guanxi* is used efficiently and thereby creates value for both the board and the relevant parties involved.

Ethical concerns

Our corporate governance system is based on three principles, conscientiousness, prudence and the taking of full responsibility. However, occasionally one encounters unethical but not immoral practice, because in China, market regulations are neither sufficient nor regularly updated. Market reforms have always taken place long before amendments to the law. Chinese law and regulations only provide principles for legal behaviour and activity. Thus the practice and enforcement of law and regulation is dependent on peoples interpretation. 'Unethical' practices often occur in the grey area where the 'market steps ahead of the law', which means, that certain business practices have not been legal but vitally important for the business development of the company. That is very different to 'legal but immoral' cases, which are not popular in China. (Deputy Chairman, Board 6)

Board members encounter three types of dilemma

- A market developed far ahead of the amendment of the law. If we strictly followed the law, we would lose development opportunities. Under such circumstances, many Chinese managers grab opportunity but that action may be illegal at the time.

- Dated laws and regulations. I don't think we should be constrained by impractical laws.

- Business action that is neither legal nor moral, and hence most people would not touch it.

Overall 'moral constraints' are more effective than 'legal constraints'. In the west, you think that if something is illegal it also must be immoral. In transitional China, this is not necessarily the case. (Executive Director, Board 7)

During 1980s and again in 2000, western boards were plighted by corrupt practices. There was Watergate, then Gulf Oil's illegal trust, the Equity Fund fraud, Lockheed Aircraft's bribe of the Japanese Prime Minister, the International Telephone payment to the Republican National Committee in order to settle antitrust suit with Hartford Insurance Company and more recently Enron, ImClone and World Com. Our recent scandals in Shanghai and Beijing have led to arrests, dismissal and suspension from the party of hundreds of officials. These developments and actions need to be understood from the Chinese perspective. They do not represent western style corruption cases as portrayed by the media, but rather that the State Counsel is cleaning up 'decaying' party members and their supporters. (Independent Director, Board 4)

As emphasised throughout this chapter, social and cultural practices are deeply rooted in the Chinese boardroom and often take precedence over legitimate decisions based on legal stipulation. The relationship between business and government takes precedence, particularly under circumstances of underdeveloped shareholder rights and restricted flows of information (Johnston, 1997). For outsiders, such orientation borders on corruption, but as the study participants emphasise, the critical concern for the Chinese is the maintenance of social norms. To add to the study participants' case, Yu (2002) found that the Chinese, in general, feel that government's reliance on law *("fa")* to reinforce its authority indicates its inability to rule by established custom *("li")*. Historically, the Chinese have a distaste for ruling through law as laws change with the change of government. For example, the first emperor of the Qin Dynasty (Quin Shi Huang-di, 259–210 BC) adopted harsh laws to unify China in order to form a centralised empire. Chairman, Mao Zedong, instituted socialist laws that operated within the boundaries of policy directives and socio-political programmes such as the "Great Leap Forward" and the "Cultural Revolution" during the period 1966–76, under the guidance of Party policy principles (Yu, 2002). Although recognising the need to do so, reverting to legal stipulation is not favoured. The study participants express collaborative action based on a shared appreciation of the challenges being faced as the desired pathway forward.

Conclusion

Although China boasts a rich history of 5000 years of civilisation, it has only limited experience of modern day corporate structures. Qualitative study through open-ended questions surfaced that Chinese corporate governance is evolving and is characterised by a strong insider system of social networks *(ganuxi)*, but a weak legal system. The emerging view of the study participants is that the "unique" Chinese model of governance will emerge integrating legal requirements with social custom, and together exercise control over the enterprise. It is likely that Chinese corporate governance will undergo a similar process of adjustment as did Japanese enterprises in the 1960s and 1970s. Not just the case of the Japanese, but history in general teaches us that economic development leads to a transformation of ideology, ways of thinking and a redefinition of community and national values (Fu, 1997). In 2002, the Chinese authorities acknowledged that their unprecedented economic growth had brought about an opening of foreign relationship and capital investments stimulating scientific, technological and economic advance which will accelerate China's transformation process. In May 2007, the regulators gave Chinese investors their first opportunity to invest in foreign equities according to a strict quota in order to prevent massive outflow of capital and subsequent panic on international stock exchanges (*The Week*, 2007).

However, accompanying growth are undesired environmental and social issues (CSRC, 2002). The emerging conclusion from this study is that sixth-century BC Confucian philosophy valuing harmony within society over material wealth is giving way to a rapid accumulation of wealth on par with western economies. The traditional ethico-moral ideology of China symbolised by conservatism and a closed character (Liu, 1997) is being subsumed by individual entrepreneurs with extensive social networks and exorbitant wealth creation appetites. As custom rather than the law has determined practice in China, it is little wonder that when custom is in turbulent flux as much due to focusing on economic gain, questionable ethics and a mistrust of the law are the outcome.

Until judicial consideration and application reflects the most dominant force in China, namely marketisation, reliance on custom is likely to be little more than a face saving mechanism. In the short to medium term, so-called corruption and "unethical" practice is likely to increase. Only when jurisprudence is given greater attention will China be able to say it has effectively entered the global market and by that time party influence, nationally and locally, is likely to have reduced substantially.

References

Becht, M., Bolton, P. and Roell, A. (2002), "Corporate governance and control," *ECGI Working Paper Series in Finance No. 02/2002*, The European Corporate Governance Institute (ECGI), Copenhagen Business School, Copenhagen.

Benson, J.K. (1975), "The interorganizational networks as a political economy," *Administrative Science Quarterly*, Vol. 20, pp. 229–48.

Bruton, G., Ahlstrom, D. and Yeh, K. (2004), "Understanding venture capital in East Asia: the impact of institutions on the industry today and tomorrow," *Journal of World Business*, Vol. 39, No. 1, pp. 72–88.

Bruton, G., Dattani, M., Fung, M., Chow, C. and Ahlstrom, D. (1999), "Private equity in China: differences and similarities with the Western model," *Journal of Private Equity*, Vol. 2, No. 2, pp. 7–14.

Chen, G.M., Firth, M., Gao, D.N. and Rui, O.M. (2006), "Ownership structure, corporate governance, and fraud: evidence from China," *Journal of Corporate Finance*, Vol. 12, No. 3, pp. 424–48.

Chen, J. (2005), *Corporate Governance in China*, Routledge Curzon, London and New York.

Cheung, Y.-L.S. (2007), "How does the grabbing hand grab? Tunneling assets from Chinese listed companies to the state," *Asian Roundtable on Corporate Governance*, OECD, Singapore, 27–28 June.

China Statistical Yearbook (2006), 5th edition, China Statistics Press, Beijing.

Clarke, D.C. (2006), "The independent director in Chinese corporate governance," *Delaware Journal of Corporate Law*, Vol. 36, No. 1, pp. 125–228.

Clarke, T. and Du, Y. (1998), "Corporate governance in China: explosive growth and new patterns of ownership," *Long Range Planning*, Vol. 31, No. 2, pp. 239–51.

CSRC (Chinas' Security Regulation Commission) (2002), "The collection of laws and regulations of securities and futures of the People's Republic of China," http://211.154.210.238/en/homepage/index_en.jsp (accessed 20 October 2007).

CSRC (China Securities Regulatory Commission) (2004), "China's securities and futures markets," *Report*, CSRC, Beijing.

CSRC (China Securities Regulatory Commission) (2005), "Administrative measures on the split share structure reform of listed companies," http://211.154.210.238/en/jsp/detail.jspinfoid=1129278662100&type=CMS.STD (accessed 20 March 2008).

CSRC (China Securities Regulatory Commission) (2006a), *Revised Securities Law*, http://211.154.210.238/en/homepage/index_en.jsp (accessed 10 January 2006).

CSRC (China Securities Regulatory Commission) (2006b), "China overhauls takeover code of listed companies," *China Law & Practice*, CSRC, 18 October.

Earley, C. (1993), "East meets West meets Mideast: further explorations of collectivism and individualistic work groups," *Academy of Management Journal*, Vol. 36, No. 2, pp. 319–48.

Easterby-Smith, M., Malina, D. and Yuan, L. (1995), "How culture-sensitive is HRM? A comparative analysis of practice in Chinese and UK companies," *International Journal of Human Resource Management*, Vol. 6, No. 1, pp. 31–59.

Elloumi, F. and Gueyie, J.P. (2001), "Financial distress and corporate governance: an empirical analysis," *Corporate Governance: International Journal of Business in Society*, Vol. 1, No. 1, pp. 15–23.

Fan, Y. (2002), "Questioning guanxi: definition, classification and implications," *International Business Review*, Vol. 11, pp. 543–61.

Firstenber, P.B. and Malkiel, B.G. (1980), "Why corporate boards need independent directors," *Management Review*, Vol. 69, No. 4, pp. 26–38.

Fu, J.Z. (1997), "Economic development and moral reformation," *Economic Ethics and Chinese Culture*, Chinese Philosophy Studies, XIV, Cultural Heritage and Contemporary Change, Series 3, Vol. 14, http://www.crvp.org/book/series03/III-11/chapter_xviii.htm (accessed 10 January 2005).

Gilchrist, V.J. (1992), "Key informant interviews," in B.F. Crabtree and W.L. Miller (Eds), *Doing Qualitative Research: Multiple Strategies. Research Methods for Primary Care,* Vol. 3, Sage, Newbury Park, CA.

Glaser, B.G. and Strauss, A.L. (1967), *The Discovery of Grounded Theory: Strategies for Qualitative Research,* Aldine Publishing Company, New York.

Gong, T. (1997), "Forms and characteristics of China's corruption in the 1990s: change with continuity," *Communist and Post-Communist Studies,* Vol. 30, pp. 277–88.

Granovetter, M. (1985), "Economic action and social structure: the problem of embeddedness," *American Journal of Sociology* , Vol. 91, pp. 481–510.

Green, S. (2004), *The Development of China's Stock Market 1984–2002, Equity, Politics and Market Imitations,* Rutledge, Curzon.

Gu, M. (2006), *Chinese Company Law: A Comparative Introduction – Change of Corporate Governance Structure of Funds in China,* Hong Kong University Press, Hong Kong.

He, Z. (2000), "Corruption and anti-corruption in China," *Economics in Transition,* Vol. 13, pp. 211–38.

Hunt, S.A. and Benford, R.D. (1994), "Identity talk in the peace and justice movement," *Journal of Contemporary Ethnography,* Vol. 22, pp. 488–517.

Jensen, M. (1989), "Qualitative methods in physical therapy research: a form of disciplined inquiry," *Physical Therapy,* Vol. 69, pp. 492–500.

Johnston, M. (1997), "What can be done about entrenched corruption," *World Bank Working Paper Series,* World Bank, New York.

Kakabadse, A., Kakabadse, N. and Barratt, R. (2006), "Chairman and chief executive officer (CEO): that sacred and secret relationship," *Journal of Management Development,* Vol. 25, No. 2, pp. 134–50.

Li, P. and Zhang, X. (2007), "Has China's the non-tradable shares improved listed companies' performance? A DEA evaluation of China's listed companies," Central University of Finance and Economics, Beijing, http://efmaefm.org/Symposium2007/pu.pdf (accessed 20 October 2007).

Liu, F.T. (1997), "Moral predicament and reconstruction in contemporary China: a comment on pragmatism as a moral theory and it influence in China," *Economic Ethics and Chinese Culture, Cultural Heritage and Contemporary Change,* Series 3, Vol. 14, http://www.crvp.org/book/series03/III-11/chapter_xviii.htm (accessed 10 January 2005).

Lin, C. (2001), "Corporatisation and corporate governance in China's economic transition," *Economics of Planning,* Vol. 34, No. 1, pp. 5–35.

Lin, T.W. (2004), "Corporate governance in China: recent developments, key problems and solutions," *Journal of Accounting and Corporate Governance,* Vol. 1, No. 1, pp. 1–23.

Lodge, S. (2007), "Emerging winners," *World Business,* May, pp. 14–5.

Lorsch, J. and MacIver, E. (1989), *Pawns or Potentates,* Harvard Business School Press, Boston, MA.

Luo, Y. (2000), *Guanxi and Business,* World Scientific, Singapore.

Mace, M. (1986), *Directors: Myth and Reality,* Harvard Business School Press, Boston.

Mills, C.W. (1956), *The Power Elite,* Oxford University Press, New York.

Miles, M.B. and Huberman, A.M. (1994), *Qualitative Data Analysis,* 2nd edition, Sage, Newbury Park, CA, pp. 10–2.

Norburn, D. and Grinyer, P. (1974), "Directors without direction," *Journal of General Management,* Vol. 1, No. 2, pp. 37–48.

Ngok, K. and Zhu, G. (2007), "Marketization, globalisation and distractive reforms in China: a zigzag road to promising future," *International Review of Administrative Science,* Vol. 73, No. 2, pp. 217–33.

O'Higgins, E.R. (2002), "Government and the creation of the Celtic tiger: can management maintain the momentum?' *Academy of Management Executive*, Vol. 16, No. 3, pp. 104–20.

O'Rriain, M. (2000), "The flexible developmental state: globalization, information technology and the Celtic tiger," *Politics and Society*, Vol. 28, No. 2, pp. 157–93.

Pearce, J.A. and Zahra, S. (1992), "Board composition from a strategic contingency perspective," *Journal of Management Studies*, Vol. 29, No. 4, pp. 411–38.

Pfeffer, J. (1972), "Size, composition and function of hospital boards of directors: a study of organization – environment linkage," *Administrative Science Quarterly*, Vol. 17, No. 2, pp. 218–28.

Pfeffer, J. and Salancik G.R. (1978). *The External Control of Organization: A Resource Dependence Perspective*, Harper Row, New York.

Qian, Y. and Wu, J. (2000), "China's transition to a market economy: how far across the river?" *Centre for Research on Economic Development and Policy reform Working Paper Series No. 69*, Stanford University, Stanford, CA.

Qiang, Q. (2003), "Corporate governance and state-owned shares in China listed companies," *Journal of Asian Economics*, Vol. 14, pp. 771–83.

SASAC (2007a), State-owned Assets Supervision and Administration Commission of the State Council, *SASAC Register*, http://www.sasac.gov.cn/zyqy/qyml/default.htm (accessed 15 June 2007).

SASAC (2007b), "Welcome to the Website of the State-owned Assets Supervision and Administration Commission of the State Council (SASAC)," http://www.sasac.gov.cn/eng/zrzc.htm (accessed 15 June 2007).

Stiles, P. (2001), "The board's role in strategy,' in Corporate Governance Forum of Japan (Eds), *Corporate Governance: Reform of UK Companies*, Commercial Law Centre, Tokyo, pp. 156–75.

Tam, O.K. (2002), "Ethical issues in evolution of corporate governance in China," *Journal of Business Ethics*, Vol. 37, pp. 303–20.

The Week (2007), "Will we all be burnt in the Chinese stir-fry?" Issue 614, 19 May, p. 47.

Tsang, E. (1998), "Can guanxi be a source of sustained competitive advantage for doing business in China?" *Academy of Management Executive*, Vol. 12, No. 2, pp. 64–73.

Tucker, P. (2006), "Macro, asset price and financial system uncertainty," *Roy Bridge Memorial Lecture*, 11 December, London.

Ueno, S. and Sekaran, U. (1992), "The influence of culture on budget control practices in the USA and Japan: an empirical study," *Journal of International Business Studies*, Vol. 23, No. 2, pp. 659–74.

Useem, M. (1984), *The Inner Circle*, Oxford University Press, New York.

Wang, Z. (2003), " 'Guanyu guowuyuan jigou gaige fangan de shouming' (The explanatory note of the programme for restructuring the State Cancel)," Report delivered at the *1st Session of the 9th National People's Congress*, 6 March, Beijing, China.

Wang, C. and Chin, S. (2004), "Profitability of return and volume based investment strategies in China's stock market," *Pacific Basin Finance Journal*, Vol. 12, pp. 541–64.

Weir, C.M. and Laing, D. (2001), "Governance structures, director independence and corporate performance in the UK," *European Business Review*, Vol. 13, pp. 86–94.

Westphal, J.D. and Zajac, E.J. (1996), "Director reputation, CEO-board power and the dynamics of board outside directors," *Administrative Science Quarterly*, Vol. 41, pp. 2–19.

Xu, B. (2007), "China's GDP grows 10.7% in 2006, fastest in 11 years," *China Daily*, January 26, p. 1, http://www.chinadaily.com.cn/china/2007-01/26/content_793128.htm (retrieved 12 June 2007).

Yu, P.K. (2002), "The second coming of intellectual property rights in China," *Occasional Paper Series in Intellectual Property*, Vol. 11, Benjamin N. Cardozo School of Law, Yeshiva University, New York.

Zhang, T. (2002), "Urban development and a socialist pro-growth coalition in Shanghai," *Urban Affairs Review*, Vol. 37, pp. 475–99.

Zheng, L. (2007), "Political embeddedness as a double-edged sword; firms in China's stock market," Stanford University.

5
Workings of the Board: Case of the International Joint Venture "Arman," Kazakhstan

Elina Oseichuk, Nada Kakabadse and Andrew Kakabadse

Introduction

Considerations of responsible corporate practice have evolved over considerable periods of time, often in response to corporate failure or crisis. In so doing, developed countries have established complex laws, regulations and institutions, leading to a culture of compliance concerning the management of the firm. In parallel, globalisation and the need to be responsive to continuous change have increased the likelihood of acquisition, merger and joint venture occurring as a dominant form of organisation design (Iskander and Chamlou, 2000).

Similarly, the developing world has also faced its own challenges in the area of corporate responsibility. Economic crises in East Asia, Russia and other regions have demonstrated how macroeconomic problems can be exacerbated by a failure of corporate responsibility stemming from weak legal and regulatory systems, inconsistent accounting and auditing standards, poor banking practices, unregulated capital markets and ineffective boards of directors (Iskander and Chamlou, 2000).

As the need for good governance in developed and developing countries is evident and the ultimate mechanism for governance application is the board, the study presented in this chapter reports the results of an inquiry into the inner workings of the board of directors of the International Joint Venture "Arman" (IJV "Arman"), Kazakhstan, particularly concerning board structure and composition, the roles and duties of directors, as well as how directors balance divergent issues, which conflict with responsible corporate practice. In the study, account was taken of the contextual sensitivities of the transitional economy of the Republic of Kazakhstan where the requirements and demands of the partners were often not aligned. The research question upon which this study is drawn was, "how does the Board of Directors of the International Oil and Gas Joint Venture 'Arman' balance conflicting agendas whilst contributing to responsible corporate practice?"

Two conceptual platforms influenced the design of this study, namely the policy governance model (Carver, 1997) and role theory (Kahn et al., 1964; Hales, 1987; Zahra and Pearce, 1989, 1992; Fondas and Stewart, 1994). The policy governance model (Carver, 1997) was used as the philosophical framework to assess how a group of executives charged with seeing that the organisation under their authority achieves its aims whilst avoiding unacceptable circumstances and actions. Role theory (Kahn et al., 1964; Hales, 1987; Zahra and Pearce, 1989, 1992; Fondas and Stewart, 1994), on the other hand, provided the theoretical framework for examining the reconciliation or not of role-determined demands that varied according to the degree of homogeneity and complementarily with the other roles on the board.

International Joint Ventures (IJVs)

Since the 1970s, corporations have increasingly relied on IJVs for the execution of their international strategy. The IJV structure allows companies to rapidly and economically complement their own resources with those of other firms (Hambrick et al., 2001). The rapid proliferation of IJVs has been seen by some as an "explosion of cooperation" (Harrigan, 1988). Within the international context, such alliances can facilitate quick entry into new geographic markets, provide access to specialised or low-wage labour, allow for a meshing of complementary technologies, support learning from partners and facilitate other cross-border advantages (Barkema et al., 1997; Inkpen and Beamish, 1997).

However, there is a growing body of literature that also draws attention to the challenge of making IJVs work effectively in transitional economies (Mjoen and Tallman, 1997). These study findings consistently emphasise differences between the perceptions of partners from developed and developing countries in determining the effective performance of IJVs (Beamish, 1993).

Emerging economies pose considerable challenge to IJV performance effectiveness due to the rapidity of change in developing markets that heightens uncertainty. Emerging markets are more likely to put foreign and local partners at odds with each other rather than encouraging the complementarity typical of developed economies (Luo, 1997). One reason is that parent company control over directors is more direct than that exercised by widely scattered shareholders or even institutional investors. Parent companies have a vested interest to ensure that their concerns are appropriately represented on the joint venture board (Carver, 2000).

Although central to the workings of the fledgling enterprise, few studies have examined IJV board conflict (Mohr and Puck, 2003). One popular mechanism for examining board-related conflict is that of role conflict which Pandey and Kumar (1997, p. 191) define as "a state of mind or experience or perception of the role incumbent arising out of the simultaneous occurrence of two or more role expectations such that compliance with one would make compliance with the other(s) more difficult or even impossible." Shenkar and Zeira (1992) provided one of the first studies of IJV role conflict by examining the organisational and personal antecedents of IJV management. Such exploration was followed by analysis of the relationship between role conflict and the performance of IJVs, particularly through the efforts of Gong et al. (2001).

Mohr and Puck (2003) perceive role conflict as a multidimensional phenomenon comprising three different categories, inter-role, intra-role (both intra-sender and inter-sender conflict) and person-role conflict. Mohr and Puck (2003) suggest that inter-sender conflict is a major problem for the managers of IJVs due to the existence of two or more partners with legitimate, though potentially incompatible, expectations towards the IJV enterprise. Role conflict may arise both because of differing role expectations in the external environment as well as due to internal forces being forced upon by the often-conflicting agendas of the participants in the joint venture (Das, 2001).

Critical therefore, according to Lee et al. (2003), is to arrange for an adequate governance structure to better ensure the success of the IJV. Based on a survey of around 700 Sino-foreign joint ventures, Lee et al. (2003) found that the occurrence of an asymmetric governance structure is significantly associated with the differential resource contributions from the collaborative partners and the vertical structural linkage between the foreign partner and the venture. Luo et al. (2001) highlight that different control expectations between the partners lead to tensions on the IJV board, whilst Geringer and Hebert (1989) show that levels of parental satisfaction may or may not coincide with acceptable accounting measures.

However, complementarity of governance structure and application is determined by the individuals who sit on IJV boards (Pearce, 2000). Osborn and Hagedoorn's (1997, p. 271) review of the alliance literature led them to conclude that "the potentially important role of individuals in operating alliances remains virtually unexplored." In turn, Pearce (2000) argues that although the decision to create a shared-management structure often reflects both the strategic compatibility of the parent organisations and the personal relationships of their top executives, the IJV assigned managers may not share those attitudes or understandings. The full extent of the differences between the appointed executives is only likely to emerge once fully embroiled with the IJV (Salk, 1996). Indeed, study has shown that the amount and depth of difference between the appointed executives can surprise those who created the joint venture (Kanter, 1994). Thus Pearce (2000) emphasises that the effectiveness of top management inside a joint venture is significantly determined by the nature of relations between the executives appointed from different parent companies.

Pearce (2000) further identifies a growing sense of "us" versus "them" factionalism between executives from different parent companies, and a heightened propensity to use power in a manipulative way, undermining openness of communication and information exchange.

Not that board tension is a feature of IJV boards. According to Forbes and Milliken (1999), boards of directors are episodic and interdependent groups, vulnerable to the interaction difficulties that prevent groups from achieving their full potential. Thus, the effectiveness of boards is considerably dependent on socio-psychological processes, particularly pertaining to group participation and interaction, information exchange, and critical discussion (Butler, 1981; Milliken and Vollrath, 1991). Additionally, cultural and background differences as well as language barriers inhibit IJV's directors from improving communication, discussion and participation in the board's activities.

In turn, Forbes and Milliken (1999) emphasise that the board's ability to continue working together, as evidenced by board cohesiveness, is partly influenced by board members' degree of attraction to each other. In studies of workgroups, researchers have found that when group members are more attracted to one another, they realise higher levels of member satisfaction (Katz and Kahn, 1978; Summers et al., 1988) and higher levels of commitment to the group (Zaccaro and Dobbins, 1989).

Another distinctive feature of board of directors is that of cognitive conflict between the members of the group (Forbes and Milliken, 1999). Jehn (1995, p. 258) defined cognitive conflict as "disagreements about the content of the tasks being performed, including differences in viewpoints, ideas and opinions." Because the issues facing boards are complex and ambiguous, directors are liable to characterise issues differently and are likely to hold different opinions about what should be the appropriate response to those issues (Dutton and Jackson, 1987). Further, cognitive conflict can arouse negative emotions (Nemeth and Staw, 1989) that reduce interpersonal attraction amongst members. Findings by Jehn (1995) and Schweiger et al. (1986) demonstrate that members of groups with high levels of cognitive conflict experience less satisfaction with that group, a finding which holds distinct relevance to boards (Mace, 1986).

Kazakhstan

Having provided an overview of the nature of boards and IJV boards in particular, attention now focuses on the demography of Kazakhstan. By land mass, Kazakhstan is the ninth largest country in the world. Located in central Asia, Kazakhstan was an important meeting point on the Great Silk Road where Buddhism, Nestorianism, Christianity, Zoroastrianism and Islam met

(George, 2001) enriching the cultural milieu of the current 15.1 million Kazakhstan population with a heterogeneity of some 132 nationalities (George, 2001; Groman, 2005; Walker, 2007). Rich in culture and paternalistic tradition, Kazakhstan has survived 300 years of Tsarism and 75 years of Soviet government. It is described by some as an oriental autocracy (George, 2001) or eastern hierarchy as found in Japan and Singapore, where the head of the family is still the person responsible for the whole family. The configurational model of Kazakhstan is captured as that of "father leadership," epitomised by a clear hierarchy, roles, discipline and obedience (Low, 2006; Kim and Low (2007a; 2007b).

According to the CIA (2004), Kazakhstan is the largest of the former Soviet republics in terms of territory, possessing enormous fossil fuel reserves as well as plentiful supplies of other minerals and metals (Kaiser and Kubekpayeva, 2006). It is also a livestock and grain producer. The dismantling of the USSR in December 1991 and the collapse in demand for Kazakhstan's traditional heavy industry products resulted in a short-term contraction of the economy, with the steepest annual decline occurring in 1994. By 1995, the government program of economic reform and privatisation quickened, resulting over the next years in a substantial shifting of assets to the private sector. Kazakhstan enjoyed double-digit growth in 2000–01 and a solid 9.5 per cent in 2002, thanks largely to its booming energy sector, but also to economic reform, plentiful harvests and inward foreign investment. The opening of the Caspian Consortium pipeline in 2001, linking western Kazakhstan's Tengiz oilfield to the Black Sea, substantially raised oil export capacity. Since then, the country has embarked upon an industrial policy designed to diversify the economy away from an overdependence on oil by developing light industry. The policy shift from energy also aimed to reduce the influence of foreign investment and foreign personnel one reason being that the government has engaged in several disputes with foreign oil companies over the terms of production agreements. In fact, the tension continues to this day.

Yet despite economic improvement, Kazakhstan has one of the lowest social performance indicators in Europe and Central Asia, including access to safe drinking water and incidence of tuberculosis (World Bank, 2004). In addition, environmental degradation, including the receding of the Aral Sea, poses a major challenge for the country. Although income per capita reached US$1510 in 2002, substantial inequalities remain. Preliminary calculations in 2001 based on the Government's minimum level of subsistence revealed an overall poverty rate of 38 per cent.

Still, economic development proceeds. The Asian Development Bank (2004) reported that during the previous 3 years' foreign direct investment had, on average, exceeded 10 per cent of GDP, with the bulk of that investment still in the oil sector and largely based on bilateral deals with the Government.

Within such a context, the International Oil and Gas Joint Venture, "Arman," named after the Arman oil fields in western Kazakhstan, was established in June 1994 in Mangistau province, one of poorest provinces of Kazakhstan. The Arman field is estimated to hold recoverable reserves of 3.65 million metric tons of oil and some 74 million cubic meters of gas (Kaiser and Kubekpayeva, 2006). Arman was positioned as an extraction and sales oil enterprise. At the time of its initiation no consideration was given to fundamental differences in corporate governance systems used by the parent companies. Originally, Arman was created as an equal partnership between one American company and two Kazakhstani organisations. The American company was a public company with stock traded on the U.S. New York Stock Exchange. The Kazakhstani partners were a state-owned subsidiary of a major Kazakhstani governmental enterprise, MangistauMunaiGas, and the State Holding Company Zharkyn (IJV "Arman," 1994; Kaiser and Kubekpayeva, 2006). Later on, the Kazakh partners were collapsed into one local organisation.

One of the stated roles of Arman's board was a regular review of the performance, development and production of the Arman oilfield. At the beginning of each fiscal year, the board would approve the annual budget for the IJV. In subsequent board meetings, the performance of the IJV was reviewed and the management called upon to justify their performance.

The study

The primary data collection methods included semi-structured interviews (May, 1997) and contextual observation (Yin, 1994). The semi-structured interviews were pursued through face-to-face encounters and telephone discussion as well as electronic correspondence (Sapsford and Jupp, 1996; Miles and Huberman, 1994). Those individuals interviewed were selected on the basis of being the board directors and managers of the IJV "Arman," and included

A. Western members of the IJV "Arman" board of directors;
B. local members of the IJV "Arman" board of directors;
C. Western management of the IJV "Arman";
D. local management of the IJV "Arman";
E. third parties associated with the IJV "Arman" board activities, that is, contractors, regulatory agencies, and so on.

The total number of interviews was 14. Face-to-face and telephone interviews were recorded in order to preserve the original format and content of discussion. Each interview was transcribed and then read independently by two of the three authors in order to both challenge and reach shared agreement on interview content and meaning (Nothdurft, 1987).

Further, contextual observation was adopted allowing the researchers to "pick out what is relevant for analysis and piece it together to create tendencies, sequences, patterns and orders" (Ericson et al., 1991, p. 55). The observation method employed was of a less-structured nature (Sapsford and Jupp, 1996, p. 61), but was intended to capture the perspectives of social actors, their ideas, attitudes, motives and intentions, and the way they interpreted their social world. Less-structured observation aims to qualitatively describe human behaviour in order to illuminate social meaning and shared culture. Data derived from contextual observation were combined with information from interview and, where appropriate, documentary sources to produce an in-depth and rounded picture of the culture of the IJV board group, placing the perspective of the group members at its centre and reflecting the complexity of their social world.

The method of data analysis employed was qualitative thick description (Blaikie, 2000, pp. 251–2), which allowed for an understanding of the participants' "interpretations of what is going on and for the researcher to produce analysis and explanations which do justice to the milieu in which his or her observations and interviews are conducted."

Triangulation, namely comparing data from different sources (Silverman, 2000), was employed in order to check the validity of the respondents' answers. The transcripts of the interviews were subjected to thematic qualitative analysis (Denzin and Lincoln, 1998), where the themes, issues and recurring motifs within them were isolated and interpreted, leading to pattern matching.

The study participants were categorised as representatives of specific groups and were given their respective code numbers. Interviews and questions were categorised as well. All these variants were coded which is highlighted in Table 5.1.

Table 5.1 Coding of the participant groups

No.	Variant	Code
1.	Western members of the IJV "Arman" Board of Directors	WBD
2.	Local members of the IJV "Arman" Board of Directors	LBD
3.	Western Management of the IJV "Arman"	WM
4.	Local Management of the IJV "Arman"	LM
5.	Third parties associated with the IJV "Arman" Board activities, that is, contractors, regulatory agencies, and so on	TP
6.	Interview response	Int
7.	Questionnaire response	Q

Source: Compiled by the authors.

Results

The following themes were identified: corporate governance, board composition, directors' role, board responsibilities, board performance, group dynamics and board effectiveness.

Corporate governance in the IJV "Arman"

The majority of the respondents expressed the view that the purpose of the IJV "Arman" was to make profit for both of the parent companies and to also develop the assets of the enterprise. However, several individuals also shared the opinion that there were several other purposes for IJV collaboration. The venture, in their view, was to open new possibilities for the western partner, the local staff, the community and economy

> Jointly, between the western company and the local company, to develop an oilfield in such a way that would make money for both companies and develop the oil industry, improve Kazakhstan's personnel training and provide exposure to western technologies. (WBD-1 Int)

> Oil production and marketing. (TP-4 Int)

The two comments indicate that there was a difference of view concerning the purpose of the IJV. If the only purpose were to make profit, then the venture would be governed by the financial targets set, and would be accountable to the parent companies on that basis. Having a wider purpose demands achieving additional aims, thus bringing into question of whether a shared view exists concerning the governance of the enterprise.

The contrasting spread of interpretation of the purpose of the IJV "Arman" did not only exist at board level but also exist among the creators of the venture, the community, and most important, the management of the enterprise.

Yet despite differences of views concerning board purpose, once the participants were asked about the benefits that "Arman" brought, almost all of them mentioned yields in both, economic and social aspects.

> Successful development of Arman, will produce an economic stimulus for western Kazakhstan, and profits for the partnership. (WM-1 Q)

> ...for the western partner – to develop relationship with the local authorities for a future bigger project. (LM-1 Q)

> Not only bring money and training to local employees, but, also, meaningful employment for Kazakhstan's citizens, filling high skills jobs with Kazakhstan employees, raising the Kazakhstan oil industry to higher standards. (WBD-4 Q)

The interviewees also indicated their concerns, namely each partner's vision of success. The western partner, according to the local participants' views, was clearly using "Arman" for realising profit, penetrating the local market, building expertise in the local business environment and strengthening their presence in the country through a trained staff and a local infrastructure of Western quality. As for the local partner, according to the Western participants, their vision was to have "Arman" reach a dividend paying position, to bring investment into the local economy and to train local personnel. However, some indicated that the hiring and training of local personnel also created problems for the IJV "Arman."

> The Kazakh partner has many different drivers, including profit, employment for friends and relatives of officials, personal gain for board members, and profit from providing services to the IJVA. (WM-1 Int)

The hiring and training of locals were viewed as a source of conflict in the boardroom. An additional tension was the sale of oil to different markets. In the foundation documents (IJV "Arman," 1994), it was specifically stated that the IJV "Arman" would be provided with specific quotas to sell the oil it produces to international markets. This guarantee was subsequently not honoured by the government of Kazakhstan.

> The JV quickly established that they could operate successfully in Kazakhstan. However, there were difficulties in the marketing area. The JV was not allowed access to the pipeline system in Kazakhstan and was not allowed to sell their oil in the international market as provided for in the JV contract. This had a severe negative impact on the overall economics of the venture, and caused the relationships between the partners to deteriorate. (WM-1 Int)

Another source of conflict identified was the regulatory and bureaucratic systems in Kazakhstan and the costs associated with becoming fully compliant with local regulations.

> The naivety of the western partner was there to see, particularly concerning the regulatory environment. (WBD-1 Int)

The issues affecting the governance of the IJV have been captured as contrasting considerations concerning internal, IJV Arman and external broader stakeholder interest motivations (Figure 5.1).

Stakeholder considerations were the common reference point for governmental enterprises in Kazakhstan. In contrast, the western partner was more driven by shareholder motivation. Consequently, the members of the board being the representatives of the parent companies were subjected to

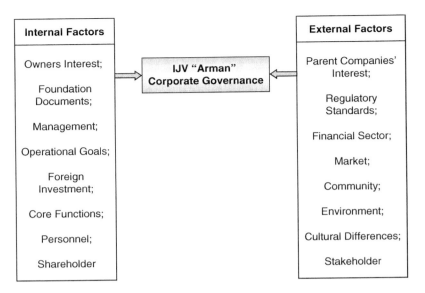

Figure 5.1 Corporate governance factors
Source: Compiled by the authors.

contradictory demands in terms of corporate governance, which adversely affected the inner working of the board.

Board composition

All of the study respondents considered the composition of the "Arman" board as fairly representing the parent companies' interests:

> Two from the foreign side and two from the Kazakh side. (LBD-2 Int)

> Each participant of the JV had the opportunity to appoint a specified number of members to the Board. (WM-3 Int)

> The JV was a 50/50 venture with half of the Directors being from the foreign side and half from the local side. (E-1 Int)

In terms of board and managerial expertise, only one respondent mentioned that the "Arman" board was composed of directors who were experts and carried a reputation of being "the best in their field." When asked what was meant by the criteria of "being the best," the response was

> They were perceived by their parent companies as being the best in business skills, negotiating skills, able to work on boards and to accomplish the board's goals. (WBD-1 Int)

The local representatives noted a contrasting set of criteria for selection as board members:

Potential international operation experience with further chance for career growth. Creation of new operating company from zero – a challenge. Financial and other benefits. (LM-3 Int)

From the western company board members' point of view, the independence of the Arman board was called into question. The reason identified was the notion of board membership being used as a vehicle for obtaining personal benefit. As a result, the long-term success of the JV was questioned.

The selection criteria adopted for appointment to the board emphasised that this was the exclusive responsibility of each of the respective parent companies. The majority of the study participants confirmed that there were no shared principals concerning the selection process.

However, when asked to account for the qualities of the chosen members, some respondents stated the following:

The criteria for appointment was not always merit, but often amounted to political favouritism. (WM-2 Q)

The Management of each Parent company appointed its members. Foreign Party: knowledge/experience in international oil negotiations; ability to represent foreign interests, and business approaches. Management: High professionalism. Local Party: experience in oil development and partially tribalistic. Management: tribalistic. (TP-3 Q)

These statements indicate another important factor, local considerations. Representing local values and the demands of the local community were identified as important a consideration as oil expertises and management skills and board experience.

In addition to member selection, the stability and sustainability of the board were called into question. Some thought that the board was ineffective due to constant change of members, whilst others thought that as a less than significant issue:

There were no constant changes in foreign membership. Also the frequent change of local members did not impact the business as all real operations were under foreign supervision and control. (TP-3 Q)

With the constant change on the board, it was difficult to build trusting relationships. (WM-2 Q)

No. The ongoing operations of the IJV "Arman" were the responsibility of management. (LM-3 Q)

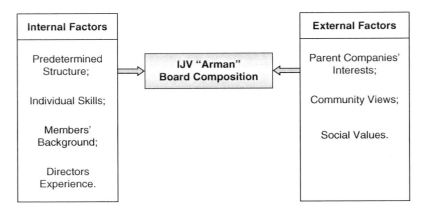

Figure 5.2   Board composition factors
Source: Compiled by the authors.

> Inconsistencies were noted and newer directors were unfamiliar with the field and the operations. (WBD-3 Q)

The responses concerning board composition of "Arman," have been divided into internal and external factors (Figure 5.2).

The two contrasting sets of factors placed considerable pressure on the "Arman" directors. Responding to local practices was questioned by the Western directors unaccustomed to the political and social values of Kazakhstan. Consequently, the members of the "Arman" board, who were representatives of their parent companies, were subjected to meeting the parent company's interests, which at times contrasted with the spirit and intended purpose of the IJV.

Board member roles and responsibilities

Questions concerning the clarity and nature of the roles and responsibilities of the members of the "Arman" board surfaced two different opinions. Some of the study participants highlighted that there was no clear definition of roles and responsibilities. Others referred to the provisions specified in the Foundation Documents of the JV.

> Chairman – local Director, Deputy Chairman – foreign Director, no other individual roles defined. (LBD-1 Int)

> There were no defined roles for individual board members, other than to represent their respective side of the Joint Venture. (M-1 Int)

With no predetermined, clear definition of roles and responsibilities, the directors did not discuss individual roles, nor discussed who should be assigned with which responsibility. Neither did the Arman board members receive any instruction from their respective parent companies before appointment to the board. The study participants stated that the board directors discussed tactics rather than their specific role as a director:

> Internally by each Party and yes, jointly by both Parties only to the extent of their duties. (LBD-2 Q)

> The leaders of the respective sides controlled the activities of the board of directors. The other members were basically advisory and less influential. However, in many cases they were appointed for a purpose and given specific assignments. (WBD-2 Q)

The study participants stated that had the parent companies assigned specific roles based on directors' skills and experiences, the "Arman" board as a whole would have considerably benefited. The decision-making process would also have considerably improved, rather than board members facing the same divergent opinions and divisions from meeting to meeting:

> Chairman and Deputy Chairman – leading roles, two other Directors – their respective assistants. It would have helped a great deal to have had this clarity. (LBD-1 Int)

> In general, the Directors had technical backgrounds (i.e. Engineering and Geology) and later, it became apparent more business/financial expertise might have been useful. (LM- 2 Int)

> …I don't think their backgrounds effected the way they were playing their roles. It was more in understanding what role they had to play. (WBD-1 Int)

However, opinions varied concerning whether the Arman board in particular and the JV in general would have benefited from greater role clarity.

> In most boards, the objective of the board members is to maximize the success of the venture. In this case, the board members were trying to maximize the success of their side—which in many cases did not make the JV successful. (WM-1 Int)

> I didn't think the fact that Arman was an international JV had any bearing on the roles of the directors. Directors are going to try and serve the JV to the benefit of their respective parties and hopefully to the benefit of the JV as a whole. (LBD-2 Int)

Considering the limited size of the resource, the fact that Arman was an International JV may have focused more attention on the venture than was necessary. (TP-2 Int)

Overall, the study respondents considered that greater role clarity was secondary to serving the particular interests of each parent company and particularly to having international experience:

The western members being familiar with international finance and state of the art technology gave them an advantage. (TP-1 Q)

Yes, there was definitely an advantage on the western side in this regard. However, this proved to be fertile training ground for the local members in foreign business practices. (WM-3 Q)

Although the local representatives recognised their disadvantage in terms of international expertise, the handling of complex local cultural issues was described as needing to have local knowledge.

The western members of the IJV "Arman" had a much better understanding of how to manage a business for profit. However, the Kazakh members had a much better understanding of how to operate in Kazakhstan. The Kazakh members also controlled much of the infrastructure around the Arman field, which gave them a significant advantage. (LBD-2 Q)

The expertise of the Western board members was not employed to prevent or resolve certain local issues. In fact, certain western directors admitted their naivety and lack of understanding of the local environment:

Rather than trying to drive things by the book, we should've been a little bit more careful working through the system as it existed and helped the Kazakhstani members find where we were going, rather then beat on them the Agreement as the only rule. It created problems. (WBD-4 Q)

Neither of the parent companies had a board evaluation or a development process in place. Yet, certain board members indicated that they would have benefited from such a process:

You are put on the Board, and you go to a meeting and you try to figure it out as you go. What are they (the board) supposed to do? Are they there to run the business, or to be advisory to the management...? (WBD-1 Int)

Understanding one's responsibilities as a Board member, understanding of the foundation documents which really laid out the purpose of the Board, the roles, the responsibilities of the members. Cultural understanding. For Kazakhstanies, knowing that the western party would come to the table with the understanding of the Agreement and try to do everything by the Agreement, should probably have made them read the Agreement beforehand. As for us, understanding that the Kazakhstanies would rely more on the system that they are used to, would probably have helped us in understanding cultural differences. (WBD-1 Int)

Some kind of training, induction, guide or preliminary introduction would be very important. And for somebody who did not serve on the Board before, there should be some discussion on what could be the difficulties of putting the two systems together. (WBD-1 Int)

The comments concerning board members' roles and responsibilities have been clustered under two headings, the influence of internal and external factors (Figure 5.3).

At times, the tension between the two sets of directors was considerable. Each fulfilling their duty according to the "agenda" of each parent company contrasted sharply with each director's individual expertise. In addition, through having no appropriate induction or evaluation process, the tension between the directors just continued.

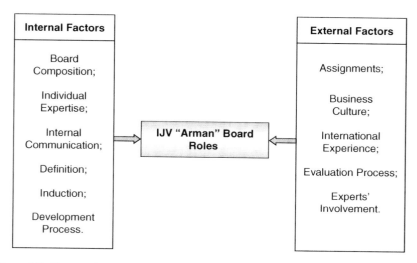

Figure 5.3 Factors determining directors' roles
Source: Compiled by the authors.

Responsibilities of the Arman board

The majority of respondents outlined the key responsibilities of the board as focusing on operational and financial oversight, whilst paying attention to government relations. As already emphasised, individual director's responsibilities were viewed as representing the parent company:

> I view the Board as the one body not running the day-to-day business. That's the management's team responsibility. The Board's responsibilities are to set the strategy and direction. Some specific responsibilities are to approve the annual Work Plan and Budget, maybe talk about some staffing issues on the Board, but beyond that, not much more. (WBD-1 Int)

> Foreign members are mainly in charge of strategy and operation. Local members for reporting to local government and explanation of the government policy to the foreign members. (LBD-4 Int)

> The primary responsibility of the directors is related to the formulation of an operational plan and the appropriation of a budget to support it. Secondly, they must acquire the senior staff/contractors to implement operations. (WM-2 Int)

However, local management offered a different perspective, namely that the local partner was responsible for strategy and implementation. In contrast, western management thought that the local partner was responsible for community relations.

This divergence of opinion was attributed to the lack of briefing on the responsibilities of directors in particular, and of the board as a whole:

> I personally never experienced such a briefing. (WBD-3 Int)

> I am not aware of any briefings as such. (LBD-1 Int)

Yet, despite differences of views, all of the respondents agreed that ultimately, the directors were primarily responsible for representing parent company interests:

> The ultimate duty of the Directors is to represent the interests of their parent company. (WBD-3 Q)

> Report to the Parent Companies and the local Government about the other side's requirements and convince to meet them or fight them. (LBD-1 Q)

> We did some of that, but never looked at that as a specific responsibility. We were always interfacing between the Joint Venture and

the regulatory environment, always inter-relating with the largest construction companies, and the community. I think, there was a degree of being an agent, but it was never considered as a special responsibility. (WBD-4 Q)

As can be seen, the general agreement over the controlling and monitoring role of the board contradicted its strategic role. The study respondents attributed such differences to the lack of clarity concerning the purpose of the JV and to the differences of vision of turning IJV Arman into the parent companies. The respondents considered that both sides shared the vision of a profitable venture, but the local side was viewed as focusing more on community development and training, and technology transfer.

> ... neither party was naïve. I believe that both parties at least understood the main concept of the agreement but each had an agenda. To the western parent, IJV "Arman", was an opportunity to gain experience and contacts for doing business in Kazakhstan and the former Soviet Union. To the local parent, it was, "what have you done for me lately". They wanted short-term result; jobs/wages and the associated taxes they collected; training and expertise in all aspects of production and management; donations to local organizations and charities. (LBD-3 Q)

The western parent concentrated on profitability and growth, and the local parent was concerned with local employment, training and taxation, in addition to the profitability and growth of the Joint Venture. Some local representatives were concerned with the social contributions of the IJV more than even the profitability of the IJV itself. (WBD-3 Q)

All of the respondents agreed that such divisions were recognised from the foundation stage:

> While the foreign side wanted to be good corporate citizens, their appetite was more tempered than the local side. I believe both sides were aware of the other's expectations. (TP-1 Q)

> I believe that it was clear from the start that there was a lack of alignment, but there was hope that a compromise was possible for both sides to reach most of their objectives. (WM-1 Q)

> Both Parties believed that they had the same vision, though the local parent company was not sufficiently experienced in joint operations to have long-term expectations. (LBD-4 Q)

Despite the awareness of the needs, intentions and activity of the "other side," the study respondents reported that it was particularly difficult to balance and discuss the areas of difference:

> I believe I knew the needs of the representatives of the other side. However, at times there was a good bit of secrecy, which made their needs less clear. (WBD-3 Int)

> I expected that there would be some conflicts with regard to the divergent needs, but, in reality, there were more than I expected. I believe that we should've told each other in advance that, understanding the parent companies' needs, we should be prepared for compromise. We should always have had a plan which would reflect deviations from the preconceived plan considering the needs of the other partner or the IJV itself. Understanding the necessity for compromise, we could have adjusted our expectations. (WBD-1 Int)

All of the participants considered it difficult to balance the divergent demands of their parent companies, the needs of the JV and local community and government requirements:

> Sometimes impossible. For example the agricultural loans to the community and the demands of the parent company to provide supplies to the local refinery. The only resolution was a concession. (LBD-1 Int)

> Two things. One, balancing was always an issue. Two, the more depth was applied to the analysis of the foundation documents, the better. Because there is a way to manage the Venture if it is organised to minimise the conflicts in the future. (WBD-1 Int)

Feeling the pressure of balancing these divergent agendas, the directors reported themselves as being "pushed" to make a choice between the priorities of the IJV "Arman" and their respective parent company. Although, a wide range of opinions was expressed concerning the long-term prosperity of the IJV, or that of achieving quick dividends for the parent company, the majority of the local participants indicated that the parent company was always their priority. In contrast, the Western members tended to underline the importance of the JV. Yet, some of the study participants attempted to find a compromise between the two priorities:

> Both! I know this is not the answer you wanted.... But it was really a difficult issue. Because the western parent company was driven by results, profitability, budgets, where as the Joint Venture needed other things. We needed to compromise on the employment issues, the equipment we used. It was a balancing act because the optimisation of the Joint Venture

did not always match up with the direct desire of the parent company. It was always a struggle. (WBD-1 Int)

Irrespective of whether the IJV and the parent companies' needs were prioritised, several of the study participants noted that the local members mixed their professional priorities with their personal interests:

> I think the local directors were also interested in personal gain. (WM-3 Int)

> I believe that the Kazakh side of the Board did not want the JV to fail, but they were more interested in their own interests, and their parent company's interests. (WM-1 Int)

The balance of divergent issues on the Arman board is captured as a contrast of internal and external factors (Figure 5.4).

Group dynamics

Aside from the divergent strategy and policy issues, the study respondents emphasised that the nature of the conflicts on the Arman board was also caused by operational, financial or staffing issues. The IJV "Arman" lending money to the government to support agricultural projects, and later not being able to recover the debt, disputes over staffing vacancies, and gaining approval for drilling contractors, typified the tactical nature of the JV's

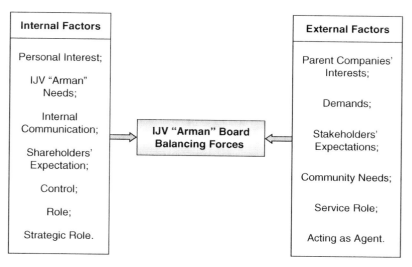

Figure 5.4 Balancing the issues facing the board
Source: Compiled by the authors.

board continuous disputes. Also there were conflicts between the original local parent companies as well as differences between Arman's interests and those of relevant stakeholders:

> Initially there were 2 parent companies that owned interests on the local side. While one was more powerful than the other, this was a source of conflict. The primary source of conflict proved to be financial issues dealing with community needs and the lack of income to the local partners. (WBD-3 Int)

> There were three messages: The western parent had a message, the local parent had a message and the Joint Venture was in the middle. (WBD-1 Int)

When the study respondents were asked how they attempted to resolve these conflicts, most responded that they tried to find compromise:

> Reached consensus. Concession of the foreign Party. (LW-1 Int)

> We were always able to come to a compromise after some active discussions. (WM-1 Int)

Reaching a compromise was reported as time and effort consuming. Due to the diverse nature of the group, particularly in pushing parent companies' interests, little effort was considered to be made to identify a process for conflict resolution.

> Yes, when the Board was working well together, a good deal of discussion took place (generally behind the scenes) addressing difficult situations and how to work through those issues. Unfortunately, there were times when this did not work effectively. (WBD-3 Int)

Yet despite the tension, the majority of respondents described the conflicts in the boardroom as constructive and healthy.

> Depending on the issue and the way how we were trying to resolve it. I think, overtime they became healthier. Remember, after all the trouble we had over the drilling contractor issue, what we did gave us (both parent companies), the boost of confidence in being able to work though these issues. The next time we went to the compromise solution quicker. It depended if one of the parties would dig in their heels. Sometime, they were really destructive. (WBD-1 Q)

> I felt the conflicts were healthy. They did not result in personal attacks or adversarial relationships. They mostly were driven by differences in goals and culture. (WM-1 Q)

Inevitably, the levels of satisfaction and willingness to continue as board directors varied considerably.

> 10 years – many groups, some of them were very satisfying and some very frustrating. (LBD-1 Q)

> In some ways it was very rewarding and satisfying when the job was done and the conflicts were resolved. Looking back and feeling the frustrations, I would probably give it a middle mark. With that said, I would still be willing to continue, because it was worthwhile. (WBD-1 Q)

> Very satisfying – I found my time spent as a director challenging but very fulfilling. I enjoyed the cultural interaction and the satisfaction of accomplishment. (WBD-3 Q)

Those that expressed satisfaction with being an Arman board director attributed their positive response to the effort they devoted to achieving positive interaction between themselves and their board colleagues. It was pointed out that a significant amount of time was spent outside the boardroom developing personal relationships between particular board directors. The ones not satisfied with their work on the board were distinguished by their limited informal interaction outside formal board meetings:

> Every time at dinners after the BOD meetings (that is two times a year). (LBD-1 Q)

> We did meet informally, but on very limited occasions. A lot of times we were trying to meet ahead of time to resolve the difficult issues. (WBD-1 Q)

What exacerbated the situation was change of board members, often at the instruction of either parent company. With changes on both sides, board relationships became even more strained. Trust between directors quickly deteriorated to suspicion.

> In the very early stages, there was trust. Then it grew to suspicion, then back to trust though sharing difficulties. I think, it is both now. When people work there longer, they develop trust. When new people came onto the Board, there was that suspicion again. Fighting started over issues that were already previously fought over. It could have been better. (WBD-1 Int)

The responses of the participants concerning group dynamics and conflict resolution are grouped into two clusters, inadequate internal communication and attitudes of directors (Figure 5.5).

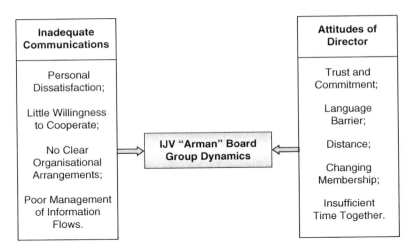

Figure 5.5   Group dynamics
Source: Compiled by the authors.

Overall, the lack of partners' positive attitude towards each other or their projects, the lack of satisfaction with the dynamics of the board, the inevitable language barriers, frequency of new board entrants and having no clear organisational arrangements for board member succession all contributed to the poor functioning of the board. Only individual directors' willingness to build better personal relationships eased the tensions on the Arman board.

Board effectiveness

The majority of the respondents concluded that combatant group dynamics undermined board effectiveness. Yet, the critical concern regarding board performance focused on the foundation documents determining board governance.

Most of the study participants underlined the importance of clearly understanding the Arman IJV foundation documents. Some of the respondents claimed that the foundation documents should have been taken more seriously. Others felt that the documents themselves were not clear and that in itself led to tensions on the Arman board:

Yes, though sometimes the directors have different interpretations. (LBD-4 Int)

No and some areas were subject to interpretation and not just concerning two languages…(WM-3 Int)

While not everyone was familiar with the documents, the documents were referred to on a regular basis and provided the catalyst for resolution for many issues. (WBD-3 Int)

In addition to the lack of understanding of the governing documents, the lack of clarity in understanding the regulatory environment was considered as impacting on the governance of the IJV. Many of the study respondents felt that "Arman" was simply one example of the reality of how IJVs function, and in that sense not unusual:

> Very much so. Unstable as well inconsistently applied legislation, tax and customs laws. All were a constant burden on the operations of the IJVA. (LM-3 Int)

> Yes, however, the regulatory environment was evolving which provided a challenge to all JVs and foreign companies in Kazakhstan. (TP-1 Int)

> Yes, this significantly increased costs and slowed progress. I would estimate that greater than 50% of the administrative cost of the JV was spent on regulatory approvals. This is compared to less than 10% in most countries worldwide. In addition, the JV attempted to import a lot of new technologies that were not commonly used in Kazakhstan. That also made regulatory approvals more difficult. This regulatory burden will discourage smaller foreign companies from doing business in Kazakhstan. (WM-1 Int)

Other challenges to board effectiveness were identified by the participants. Restricted support from the local government, poor preparation by the board members for meetings and limited involvement of the local party in strategic discussions all contributed to poor board performance. Also noted was that more attention should have been paid to the economic viability of the venture.

Yet despite the frustrations, the IJV "Arman" was still seen positively and described as a learning experience, assisting with the growth and independence of Kazakhstan, despite the constantly evolving regulatory and business pressures.

> IJV "Arman" was a pioneer of international joint ventures in Kazakhstan. In a lot of ways it was a test site for new rules, regulations, requirements and responsibilities. I think, "Arman" grew a lot, became one of the strongest companies in Kazakhstan's oil industry and is taken as an example of success. (WBD-1 Int)

> Literally, as a child has grown from an infant to a functioning adult, the JV Arman has gone from a few hotel rooms with few assets to a functioning member of the international economy. With employees and contractors utilizing services in many different counties to produce and market its product. (LBD-2 Int)

Using the experience and knowledge that the members of the Board acquired over the years of working with the IJV "Arman," further probing concentrated on what could be done to promote a more effective board. Most of the study respondents agreed that an induction process for new directors, as well as more clearly presented governance documents, would have aided realising board effectiveness. Additionally, spending more time preparing for meetings, clarifying the role and responsibilities of the director and familiarising the group with the historical and current issues within and outside of the company were further recommendations identified by the study respondents for enhancing board effectiveness.

> It is important to develop mutual trust and respect among the directors. If that can be done, any conflict can be resolved. Trust and respect can be developed by open discussion of goals and objectives, and by meeting commitments. The best that can be done is to create an environment where there is motivation to resolve conflicts in a cooperative manner. (WM-1 Int)

> The foundation documents cannot be re-written. That should be understood by both parties. But it would be a good idea to have something in place that would describe what we are doing, how we are doing it, what the responsibilities are, what areas are not the responsibilities of the Board. Something to bring reality into perspective. And some commitment from the parent companies to leave people to serve on the Board a lot longer. Those two issues would really be important. (WBD-1 Int)

All respondents considered that the experience of board membership of the IJV "Arman" provided an opportunity to capture learning for other IJVs in Kazakhstan, particularly over issues of staffing, regulatory approval, profit distribution and cultural differences:

> IJV "Arman", being one of the first international joint ventures, generated a lot of good learning, which can be applied elsewhere. The majority of the western investors are coming from the USA, Canada or European Union. Culturally they are different, but their corporate culture keeps them on one side of the line. The local partners, coming from a Soviet Union culture, are on the other line. The learning "Arman" went through could be adopted for other IJVs. One of the critical learnings is understanding of the foundation documents. (WBD-1 Int)

> I just recently was responsible for a joint venture developing a field in China. This venture is currently recognized as the most successful oil venture in China. It is important to take time to understand the people, their culture, ideals, and their goals. We all want to be respected and valued. Respect is the international language that connects us all. (WM-1 Int)

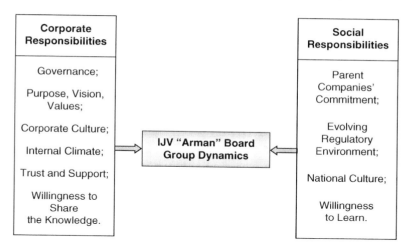

Figure 5.6 Board effectiveness
Source: Compiled by the authors.

Those factors considered to have influenced board effectiveness, both positively and negatively in terms of corporate versus social responsibilities, are captured in Figure 5.6.

The emerging conclusion is that board effectiveness would have been enhanced if there had been a better appreciation of the nature of the corporate and social responsibilities facing the Arman directors. The board members considered that they had learned the hard way to balance the requirements of an evolving regulatory environment and weigh that against the corporate culture of the parent companies and the needs of the IJV "Arman." However, the study participants admitted that all of these factors were symptoms of the need to share knowledge and display a willingness to learn. That above all else was reported as key to enhancing board effectiveness.

Discussion

According to Child and Faulkner (1998, p. 277), emerging markets are clearly attractive for companies from developed economies. Cooperation with local companies provides for them a strong entry route into that market. However, such environments often lack well-developed legal systems and market infrastructures. Local institutions are immature in comparison to those from highly industrialised countries, and so correspondingly are their business practices.

Such differences are clearly demonstrated through the study of the IJV "Arman" and its board of directors. The magnitude of difference spanning, the background of the Board members, the vision laid out by the parent companies, the needs of the JV itself and the requirements of the environment all affected the inner workings of the board. Despite these complexities, Child and Faulkner (1998) consider that the objectives of prospective partners from developed and emerging economies are, nevertheless, often reasonably compatible, at least in the short to medium term. Initially, there is usually a strategic fit between the foreign partner's wish to develop the local market and the local partner's desire to acquire particular competitiveness, achieve financial survival and to share in market expansion.

Critical therefore is the governance of the IJV. According to Luo et al. (2001), parent companies transact from different vantage points, not only with each other but also with the jointly formed IJV entity. Different tolerances of uncertainty and different decision-making styles contribute to an asymmetry in transactions, suggesting different configurations of control–performance relations between foreign and local parents. Moreover, differences of institutional configuration and familiarity (or the lack of it) with the host environment between foreign and local firms lead to variations in searching for and obtaining accurate information. The IJV "Arman" was simply one example of asymmetry of transaction and poor performance control.

Several participants in the study noted that certain directors were pursuing personal interests. As most local partner firms in emerging economies are state-owned, local parent managers have an idiosyncratic incentive structure to reward compared to foreign parent managers. This further increases the asymmetry of transactions and bounded rationality between foreign and local managers. As IJV controls are contingent on bounded rationality and the strategic goals inherent in such rationality (Hennart, 1988), the asymmetry in the control–performance alignment between foreign and host parents is accordingly magnified.

Another dimension of governance, reflected in this study, is captured by Luo et al. (2001) who suggest that asymmetry in control–performance relations between foreign and local parents is amplified when the host government intervenes in the operations of the IJV. The source of the host government's bargaining power against foreign companies is the ability to control market access and the distribution or withholding of investment incentives. The reason is the benefits local businesses realise from host government protection. In emerging economies, such protection becomes even more apparent due to the government ownership of many local enterprises (Nee, 1992). In this environment, control over JV activities becomes more critical for foreign parents in order to mitigate threats imposed by local governmental interference.

Studies have already established that the inner workings of boards of directors of IJVs are more challenging than those of the unitary companies (Child and Faulkner, 1998), principally due to maintaining active cooperation between two or more partner companies. Parent company expectations and pressures; multiple demands on resources; differing motivations; unlike cultures with associated differences in values, ethics, and practices; complicated and unclear network boundaries; limited communication; obscured information flow; greater necessity to establish personal connections with the opposite side all undermine board performance (Hofstede, 1980; Salk and Shenkar, 2001).

Therefore, for IJV's more than other enterprises, quality of board of decisions is significantly determined by the openness between the directors and their willingness to build consensus and emerge with a shared vision for its future (Amason, 1996; Priem et al., 1995; Pearce, 2000).

Therefore, boards of IJVs find themselves taking into account a greater number of variables, such as governmental regulators, community organisations and an unfamiliar national environment (Child and Faulkner, 1998). It was clearly demonstrated that the board of directors of the IJV "Arman" was stretched in balancing corporate and social responsibility requirements. As Child and Faulkner (1998, pp. 181–2) outline, the importance of overseeing external relationships and internal relationships within the IJV are strong determents of IJV success. The case study of IJV Arman confirmed that partner attitudes, especially concerning trust and commitment and clear organisational arrangements, and the management of information flows, deeply influence board performance.

Directors committed to building closer relationships, using trust and positive attitude as their "glue," promote better understanding of each others' expectations and demands, and thereby position the activities of the board towards an improved balancing of divergent agendas (Lewicki and Bunker, 1996).

More and McGrath (1996) attribute alliance success to effective relationship management. This is especially the case with directors of IJVs who find themselves in unfamiliar territory where they have no clear frames of reference. Different assumptions, attitudes and expectations about the alliance as well as private fears about their role are further complicated by cultural differences, communications barriers, suspicions concerning partner motives and latent divergence in the partner companies.

In order to overcome such differences, Doz (1988) found that partners in the most successful alliances engage in a series of iterative and interactive learning cycles, which help to better appreciate each director's capabilities. Doz and Hamel (1998) suggest that companies should look at the early phase of an alliance as an opportunity to improve, learn, refine and build trust and that this is likely to be more important than rushing to implement specific joint tasks. Working together on a small project at the beginning enables the partners to better understand and work out their differences, refine expectations and to test assumptions about their ability to contribute to the "value creation logic" of the partnership.

The case study of IJV Arman strongly suggests that IJV board directors should continually be on the lookout for opportunities to enhance trust and to nurture partnership. Such findings are in keeping with Parkhes (1998) recommendation that partners should recognise each other's concerns and run the alliance in a way that serves the interests of both.

References

ADB (Asian Development Bank) (2004) Kazakhstan Overview Report. http://www. adb.org/Kazakhstan/default.asp (17.08.04).

Amason, A. (1996) Distinguishing the Effects of Functional and Dysfunctional Conflict on Strategy Decision Making: Resolving a Paradox for Top Management Teams, *Academy of Management Journal,* Vol. 39, pp. 123–48. Cited in Pearce R.J. (2000) The General Manager's Perspective On How Factionalism Can Impact the Behaviors and Effectiveness of Top Managers Inside a Shared Management Joint Venture, *Journal of Management & Governance,* Vol. 4, No. 3, pp. 189–207.

Barkema, H.G., Shenkar, O., Vermeulen, F., Bell, J.H. (1997) Working Abroad, Working with Others: How Firms Learn to Operate International Joint Ventures, *Academy of Management Journal,* Vol. 40, No. 2, pp. 426–42.

Beamish, P.W. (1993) The Characteristics of Joint Ventures in the People's Republic of China, *Journal of International Marketing,* Vol. 1, No. 2, pp. 29–48.

Blaikie, N. (2000) *Designing Social Research,* USA: Polity Press/Blackwell.

Butler, R. (1981) Innovations in Organisations: Appropriateness of Perspectives from Small Group Studies for Strategy Formulation, *Human Relations,* Vol. 34, pp. 763–88. Cited in Forbes, D.P. and Milliken, F.J. (1999) Cognition and Corporate Governance: Understanding Boards of Directors as Strategic Decision-Making Groups, *Academy of Management, Review,* Vol. 24, No. 3, pp. 489–506.

Carver, J. (1997) *Boards That Make a Difference: A New Design for Leadership in Nonprofit and Public Organizations* (2nd ed.). San Francisco: Jossey-Bass.

Carver, J. (2000) The Opportunity for Re-inventing Corporate Governance in Joint Venture Companies, *Corporate Governance: An International Review,* Vol. 8, No. 1, pp. 75–86.

Child, J. and Faulkner, D. (1998) *Strategies of Cooperation. Managing Alliances, Networks, and Joint Ventures,* Oxford: Oxford University Press.

CIA (2004) *World Fact Book.* http://www.cia.gov/cia/publications/factbook/print/ kz.html (15.07.04).

Das, T.K. (2001) Training for Changing Managerial Role Behaviour: Experience in a Developing Country, *The Journal of Management Development,* Vol. 20, No. 7, pp. 579–603.

Denzin, N.K. and Lincoln, Y.S. (1998) *Collecting and Interpreting Qualitative Materials,* Thousand Oaks, CA: Sage.

Doz, Y. (1988) Technology Partnerships between Larger and Smaller Firms: Some Critical Issues, *International Studies of Management and Organisation* (Winter), pp. 31–57. Cited in Kelly, M.J., Schaan, J.-L. and Joncas, H. (2002) Managing Alliance Relationships: Key Challenges in the Early Stages of Collaboration, *R&D Management,* Vol. 32, No. 1, pp. 11–22.

Doz, Y. and Hamel, G. (1998) *Alliance Advantage: The Art of Creating Value through Partnering*, Boston: Harvard Business School Press. Cited in Kelly, M.J., Schaan, J.-L. and Joncas, H. (2002) Managing Alliance Relationships: Key Challenges in the Early Stages of Collaboration, *R&D Management*, Vol. 32, No. 1, pp. 11–22.

Dutton, J. and Jackson, S. (1987) Categorizing Strategic Issues: Links to Organisational Action, *Academy of Management Review*, Vol. 12, pp. 76–90. Cited in Forbes, D.P. and Milliken, F.J. (1999) Cognition and Corporate Governance: Understanding Boards of Directors as Strategic Decision-Making Groups, *Academy of Management, Review*, Vol. 24, No. 3, pp. 489–506.

Ericson, R., Baranek, P. and Chan, J. (1991) *Representing Order: Crime, Law and Justice in the News Media*, Milton Keynes, UK: Open University Press.

Fondas, N. and Stewart, R. (1994) Enactment in Managerial Jobs: a Role Analysis, *Journal of Management Studies*, Vol. 31, No. 1, pp. 83–103. Cited in Das, T.K. (2001) Training for Changing Managerial Role Behaviour: Experience in a Developing Country, *The Journal of Management Development*, Vol. 20, No. 7, pp. 579–603.

Forbes, D.P. and Milliken, F.J. (1999) Cognition and Corporate Governance: Understanding Boards of Directors as Strategic Decision-Making Groups, *Academy of Management, Review*, Vol. 24, No. 3, pp. 489–506.

George, A. (2001) *Journey into Kazakhstan: The True Face of the Nazarbayev Regime*, Lanham, MD: University Press of America.

Geringer, J. M. and Hebert, L. (1989) Control and Performance of International Joint Ventures, *Journal of International Business Studies*, Vol. 20, No. 2, p. 235. Cited in Luo, Y., Shenkar, O. and Nyaw, M.-K. (2001) A Dual Parent Perspective On Control And Performance in International Joint Ventures: Lessons From a Developing Economy, *Journal of International Business*, Vol. 32, No. 1, pp. 41–58.

Gong, Y., Shenkar, O., Luo, Y., and Nyaw, M.-K. (2001) Role Conflict and Ambiguity of CEOs on International Joint Ventures: A Transaction Cost Perspective, *Journal of Applied Psychology*, Vol. 86, No. 4, pp. 764–73. Cited in Mohr, A.T. and Puck, J.F. (2003) Inter-sender Role Conflicts, General Manager Satisfaction and Joint Venture Performance in Indian–German Joint Ventures, Bradford University School of Management, Working Paper No. 03/19.

Groman, S. (2005) The Urgency of Kazakhstan to Grow – Thanks to Immigrants, May 9, http://www.languages-study.com/demography/kazakhstan.html (accessed: 20.05.2005).

Hales, C.P. (1987) The Manager's Work in Context: A Pilot Investigation of the Relationship between Managerial Role Demands and Role Performance, *Personnel Review*, Vol. 16, No. 5, pp. 26–34.

Hambrick, C.D., Li, J., Xin, K. and Tsui, A.S. (2001) *Compositional Gaps and Downward Spirals in International Joint Venture Management Groups*, New York: Columbia Business School, Columbia University.

Harrigan, K.R. (1988) Joint Ventures and Competitive Strategy, *Strategic Management Journal*, Vol. 9, No. 2, pp. 141–58.

Hennart, J. 1988. A Transaction Costs Theory of Equity Joint Ventures. *Strategic Management Journal*, Vol. 9, No. 3: p. 361374. Cited in Luo, Y., Shenkar, O. and Nyaw, M.-K. (2001) A Dual Parent Perspective On Control and Performance in International Joint Ventures: Lessons from a Developing Economy, *Journal of International Business*, Vol. 32, No. 1, pp. 41–59.

Hofstede, G. (1980) *Culture's Consequences*, Beverly Hills, CA: Sage. Cited in Pearce R.J. (2000) The General Manager's Perspective on How Factionalism Can Impact the Behaviors and Effectiveness of Top Managers Inside a Shared Management Joint Venture, *Journal of Management & Governance*, Vol. 4, No. 3, pp. 189–207.

IJV "Arman" (1994) Agreement and Charter of the Joint Venture Arman, IJV "Arman".

Inkpen A., Beamish P.W. (1997) Knowledge, Bargaining Power and International Joint Venture Instability. *Academy of Management Review*, Vol. 22, No. 1, pp. 177–202.

Iskander, M.R. and Chamlou, N. (2000) *Corporate Governance: A Framework for Implementation*, Washington, DC: The World Bank.

Jehn, K. (1995) A Multi-method Examination of the Benefits and Detriments of Intragroup Conflict, *Administrative Science Quarterly*, Vol. 40, pp. 256–82. Cited in Forbes, D.P. and Milliken, F.J. (1999) Cognition and Corporate Governance: Understanding Boards of Directors as Strategic Decision-Making Groups, *Academy of Management, Review*, Vol. 24, No. 3, pp. 489–506.

Kahn, R.L., Wolfe, D.M., Quinn, R.P. and Snoek, J.D. (1964) *Organizational Stress: Studies in Role Conflict and Ambiguity*, New York: Wiley. Cited in Das, T.K. (2001) Training for Changing Managerial Role Behaviour: Experience in a Developing Country, *The Journal of Management Development*, Vol. 20, No. 7, pp. 579–603.

Kaiser, M.J. and Kubekpayeva, A. (2006) Economic and Operational Assessment of the Arman Field in Kazakhstan, *Natural Resources Research*, Vol. 15, No. 4, pp. 241–54.

Kanter, R. (1994) Collaborative Advantage: The Art of Alliance, *Harvard Business Review*, July–August, pp. 96–108. Cited in Pearce, R.J. (2000) The General Manager's Perspective on How Factionalism Can Impact the Behaviors and Effectiveness of Top Managers Inside a Shared Managements Joint Venture *Journal of Management & Governance*, Vol. 4, No. 3, pp. 189–207.

Katz, D. and Kahn, R. (1978) *The Social Psychology of Organisations*, New York: Wiley. Cited in Forbes, D.P. and Milliken, F.J. (1999) Cognition and Corporate Governance: Understanding Boards of Directors as Strategic Decision-Making Groups, *Academy of Management, Review*, Vol. 24, No. 3, pp. 489–506.

Kim, P. and Low, C. (2007a) The Value of Diversity: the Kazakhstan Perspective, *Journal of Management Development*, Vol. 26, No. 7, pp. 683–99.

Kim, P. and Low, C. (2007b) Father Leadership and Small Business Management: the Kazakhstan Perspective, *Journal of Management Development*, Vol. 26 No. 8, pp. 723–36.

Lee, J.-R., Chen, W.-R. and Kao, C. (2003) Determinants and Performance Impact of Asymmetric Governance Structures in International Joint Ventures: An Empirical Investigation, *Journal of Business Research*, Vol. 56, No. 10, pp. 815–818.

Lewicki, R.J. and Bunker, B.B. (1996) Developing and Maintaining Trust in Work Relationships in R.M. Kramer and T.R. Tyler (eds.) *Trust in Organisations: Frontiers in Theory and Research*, Thousand Oaks, CA: Sage, pp. 114–39. Cited in Kelly, M.J., Schaan, J.-L. & Joncas, H. (2002) Managing Alliance Relationships: Key Challenges in the Early Stages of Collaboration, *R&D Management*, Vol. 32, No. 1, pp. 11–22.

Low, K.C.P. (2006) Father Leadership – The Singapore Case Study, *Management Decision*, Vol. 44, No. 2, pp. 89–104.

Luo, Y. (1997) Partner Selection and Venturing Success: The Case of Joint Ventures in China, *Organization Science*, Vol. 8, No. 6, pp. 630–45.

Luo, Y., Shenkar, O. and Nyaw, M.-K. (2001) A Dual Parent Perspective on Control and Performance in International Joint Ventures: Lessons from a Developing Economy, *Journal of International Business*, Vol. 32, No. 1, pp. 41–59.

Mace, M. (1986) *Directors: Myth and Reality* (2nd ed.). Boston: Harvard Business School Press. Cited in Forbes, D.P. and Milliken, F.J. (1999) Cognition and Corporate Governance: Understanding Boards of Directors as Strategic Decision-Making Groups, *Academy of Management, Review*, Vol. 24, No. 3, pp. 489–506.

May, T. (1997) *Social Research. Issues, Methods and Process* (2nd ed.). Buckingham, Philadelphia: Open University Press.

Miles, M. B., & Huberman, A. M. (1994). *Qualitative Data Analysis* (2nd ed.).Thousand Oaks, CA: Sage.

Milliken, F. and Vollrath, D. (1991) Strategic Decision-Making Tasks and Group Effectiveness: Insights from Theory and Research on Small Group Performance *Human Relations*, Vol. 44, pp. 1–25. Cited in Forbes, D.P. and Milliken, F.J. (1999) Cognition and Corporate Governance: Understanding Boards of Directors as Strategic Decision-Making Groups, *Academy of Management, Review*, Vol. 24, No. 3, pp. 489–506.

Mjoen, H., Tallman, S. (1997) Control and Performance in International Joint Ventures, *Organization Science*, Vol. 8, No. 3, pp. 257–74.

Mohr, A.T. and Puck, J.F. (2003) Inter-sender Role Conflicts, General Manager Satisfaction and Joint Venture Performance in Indian–German Joint Ventures, Bradford University School of Management, Working Paper No. 03/19.

More, E. and McGrath, G. M. (1996) Cooperative Corporate Strategies in Australia's Telecommunication Sector – The Nature of Strategic Alliances, Department of Industry, Science and Tourism. Cited in Kelly, M.J., Schaan, J.-L. & Joncas, H. (2002) Managing Alliance Relationships: Key Challenges in the Early Stages of Collaboration, *R&D Management*, Vol. 32, No. 1, pp. 11–22.

Nee, V. (1992) Organizational Dynamics of Market Transition: Hybrid Forms, Property Rights, and Mixed Economy in China, *Administrative Science Quarterly*, Vol. 37, No. 1, pp. 1–27. Cited in Luo, Y., Shenkar, O. and Nyaw, M.-K. (2001) A Dual Parent Perspective on Control and Performance in International Joint Ventures: Lessons from a Developing Economy, *Journal of International Business*, Vol. 32, No. 1, pp. 41–59.

Nemeth, C. and Staw, B. (1989) The Tradeoffs of Social Control and Innovation in Groups and Organisations, *Advances in Experimental Social Psychology*, Vol. 22, pp. 175–210. Cited in Forbes, D.P. and Milliken, F.J. (1999) Cognition and Corporate Governance: Understanding Boards of Directors as Strategic Decision-Making Groups, *Academy of Management, Review*, Vol. 24, No. 3, pp. 489–506.

Nothdurft, W. (1987) Gesprächsanalyse subjektiver Konfliktorganisationen: Ein Natürliches Design zur Rekonstruktion Individuellem Konfliktverständnisses. In Aster, R., Merkens, H., Repp, M. (eds.) *Telnehmende Beobachtung: Werkstattberichte und Methodologische Reflexionen*, pp. 71–83, Franfurt: Campus. Cited in Flick, U. (1999) *An Introduction to Qualitative Research*, London: Sage.

Osborn, R. and Hagedoorn, J. (1997) The Institutionalisation and Evolutionary Dynamics of Interorganizational Alliances and Networks, *Academy of Management Journal*, Vol. 40, pp. 261–78. Cited in Pearce, R. J. (2000) The General Manager's Perspective on How Factionalism Can Impact the Behaviors and Effectiveness of Top Managers Inside a Shared Managements Joint Venture, *Journal of Management & Governance*, Vol. 4, No. 3, pp. 189–207.

Pandey, S. and Kumar, E.S. (1997) Development of a Measure of Role Conflict, *The International Journal of Role Conflict*, Vol. 8, No. 3, pp. 187–215. Cited in Mohr, A.T. and Puck, J.F. (2003) Inter-sender Role Conflicts, General Manager Satisfaction and Joint Venture Performance in Indian–German Joint Ventures, Bradford University School of Management, Working Paper No. 03/19.

Parkhes, A. (1998) Building Trust in International Alliances, *Journal of World Business*, Vol. 33, No, 4, pp. 417–37. Cited in Kelly, M.J., Schaan, J.-L. & Joncas, H. (2002) Managing Alliance Relationships: Key Challenges in the Early Stages of Collaboration, *R&D Management*, Vol. 32, No. 1, pp. 11–22.

Pearce R.J. (2000) The General Manager's Perspective on How Factionalism Can Impact the Behaviors and Effectiveness of Top Managers Inside a Shared Management Joint Venture, *Journal of Management & Governance*, Vol. 4, No. 3, pp. 189–207.

Priem, R., Harrison, D. and Muir, N. (1995) Structured Conflict and Consensus Outcomes in Group Decision Making, *Journal of Management*, Vol. 21, pp. 691–710. Cited in Pearce R.J. (2000) The General Manager's Perspective on How Factionalism Can Impact the Behaviors and Effectiveness of Top Managers Inside a Shared Management Joint Venture, *Journal of Management & Governance*, Vol. 4, No. 3, pp. 189–207.

Salk, J. (1996) Partners and Other Strangers: Cultural Boundaries and Cross-cultural Encounters in International Joint Venture Teams, *International Studies of Management and Organisation*, Vol. 26, pp. 48–72. Cited in Pearce, R. J. (2000) The General Manager's Perspective on How Factionalism Can Impact the Behaviors and Effectiveness of Top Managers Inside a Shared Managements Joint Venture *Journal of Management & Governance*, Vol. 4, No. 3, pp. 189–207.

Salk, J.E. and Shenkar, O. (2001) Social Identities in an International Joint Venture: An Exploratory Case Study, *Organisation Science*, Vol. 12, No. 2, pp. 161–78. Cited in Pearce R.J. (2000) The General Manager's Perspective on How Factionalism Can Impact the Behaviors and Effectiveness of Top Managers Inside a Shared Management Joint Venture, *Journal of Management & Governance*, Vol. 4, No. 3, pp. 189–207.

Sapsford, R. and Jupp, V. (eds.) (1996) *Data Collection and Analysis*, London: Sage.

Schweiger, D., Sandberg, W., and Ragan. J. (1986) Group Approaches for Improving Strategic Decision Making: A Comparative Analysis of Dialectical Inquiry, Devil's Advocacy and Consensus, *Academy of Management Journal*, Vol. 28, pp. 51–71. Cited in Forbes, D.P. and Milliken, F.J. (1999) Cognition and Corporate Governance: Understanding Boards of Directors as Strategic Decision-Making Groups, *Academy of Management, Review*, Vol. 24, No. 3, pp. 489–506.

Shenkar, O. and Zeira, Y. (1992) Role Conflict and Role Ambiguity of Chief Executive Officers in International Joint Ventures, *Journal of International Business Studies*, Vol. 23, No. 1, pp. 55–75. Cited in Luo, Y. (2002) Partnering with Foreign Firms: How Do Chinese Managers View the Governance and Importance of Contracts?, *Asia Pacific Journal of Management*, Vol. 19, No. 1, pp. 127–41.

Silverman, D. (2000) *Doing Qualitative Research. A Practical Handbook*, London: Sage.

Summers, I., Coffelt, T., and Horton, R. (1988) Work Group Cohesion, *Psychological Reports*, Vol. 63, pp. 627–36. Cited in Forbes, D.P. and Milliken, F.J. (1999) Cognition and Corporate Governance: Understanding Boards of Directors as Strategic Decision-Making Groups, *Academy of Management, Review*, Vol. 24, No. 3, pp. 489–506.

Walker, S. (2007) One Man's Grand Ambition Gives Veneer of Bailing to an Ancient Land, *The Independent*, October 19, pp. 36–7.

World Bank Group (2004).http://lnweb18.worldbank.org/ECA/eca.nsf/ExtECADocby Unid/5D05C09A58C08DB285256D82004B242D?Opendocument (19.09.04).

Yin, R.K. (1994) *Case Study Research: Design and Methods* (2nd ed.). Thousand Oaks, CA: Sage. Cited in Bickman, L. and Rog (eds.) (1998) *Handbook of Applied Social Research Methods*, London: Sage.

Zaccaro, S. and Dobbins, G. (1989) Contrasting Group and Organisational Commitment: Evidence for Differences among Multilevel Attachments, *Journal of Organizational Behaviour*, Vol. 10, pp. 267–73. Cited in Forbes, D.P. and Milliken, F.J. (1999) Cognition and Corporate Governance: Understanding Boards of Directors as Strategic Decision-Making Groups, *Academy of Management, Review*, Vol. 24, No. 3, pp. 489–506.

Zahra, S.A. and Pearce, J.A. II. (1989) Boards of Directors and Corporate Financial Performance: a Review and Integrative Model, *Journal of Management*, Vol. 15, pp. 291–344. Cited in Gopinath, C., Siciliano, J.I., and Murray, R.L. (1994) Changing Role of the Board of Directors: In search of a New Strategic Identity, *The Mid-Atlantic Journal of Business,* Vol. 30, No. 2, pp. 175–86.

Zahra, S.A. and Pearce, J.A. (1992) Board Composition from a Strategic Contingency Perspective, *Journal of Management Studies,* Vol. 29, No. 4, July, pp. 411–38. Cited in Daily, C.M. (1995) An Empirical Examination of the Relationship between CEOs and Directors, *Journal of Business Strategy,* Vol. 12, No. 1, pp. 50–68.

6
Turkish Chairmen: Contrasting the Art of Dialogue against the Discipline for Governance

Andrew Kakabadse, Nada Kakabadse and Orhan Yavuz

Introduction

With its unique geo-political location at the crossroads of Europe and Asia, Turkey has undergone rapid expansion, whereby highly diversified business groups have come to hold a significant role in the development of the Turkish economy (Bugra, 1994). As a result of the transition from a planned economy to that of market liberalisation, the governance of Turkish companies has undergone a significant transformation. One area however that has not adjusted to the new global governance regime is that of family ties and networks, dominating the ownership and management of Turkish firms.

Against this backdrop and cognisant of the influence of kinship ties being interwoven into the corporate reform movement in Turkey itself geared towards Anglo-American governance application (COO; IIF Equity Advisory Group, 2005), this chapter explores the role and contribution of the Turkish Chairman and his/her effect on boardroom dynamics and performance within the context of "Emergent Turkish Family Holdings (ETFH)." In particular, our interest focuses on the boards of Turkish publicly listed enterprises.

In appreciating the context within which Turkish chairmen operate, we first provide a brief overview of Turkish market conditions, then an outline of the configuration of private business enterprises and the governance mechanisms within the country. In order to provide comparison with governance application internationally, particularly concerning the role of the chairman, an overview of Anglo-American and Continental European models of board and enterprise governance and structure is presented and contrasted against Turkish practice. Following such analysis, the results of a qualitative inquiry into the Turkish chairman role, contribution and influence on board performance are reported (Elloumi and Gueyie, 2001; Weir and Laing, 2001; Kakabadse et al., 2006). The reason for such particular focus is provided by Lorsch and MacIver (1989) who conclude that board involvement in the functioning of the organisation is primary to minimising crises effects and, in doing so, much relies on the chairman (or the chairman/CEO in the US context) to create inclusive working procedures and an atmosphere of openness and dialogue.

The study results captured highlight six themes, namely governance adoption and practice, board membership, board role, board structure, board dynamics and the skills and qualities of the Turkish board chairman. It is concluded that the business and relational skills of the Turkish chairman and board members are extensive, but their "neglect" of governance leaves the organisation, first, vulnerable in terms of an overdependence on one person, the owner/chairman, and second, undermining of corporate reputation, which is considered to adversely impact on attracting international partnerships and global investment to Turkey. The chapter concludes that nationally determined demographics influence the identity and configuration of the role of the chairman, thus calling into question whether the position of the chairman can be considered as a universalistic managerialist concept.

Turkish chairman: contextual overview

The modern Turkish Republic was founded as a unitary centralised state in 1923. A new economic order emerged, based on institutional values of secularism and statism with the aim of transitioning to a market economy driven by an indigenous business class (Robinson, 1963). By the 1950s, challenge to the single party political system gave way to liberal economic policies (Ahmad, 1977). Two distinct periods of liberal reform followed, the Planned Period (1960–1980) and the Liberalisation Period (post-1980s) (Karademir et al., 2005). Despite differences in terms of institutional frameworks and market mechanisms adopted, both periods share substantial economic and political commonalities such as improvements in regulatory discipline and in communication channels, unfortunately accompanied by a wide range of market failures as well as political and economic instability (Arnold and Quelch 1998; Khanna and Palepu, 2000). Protectionist economic policies fuelled the development of a flourishing domestic market and in particular an increase in the number of large scale and capital-intensive manufacturing enterprises (Keyder, 1987). For example, the number of privately owned firms grew from 48 per cent in 1963 to 67 per cent in 1975 (Keyder, 1987). Preference for the family-owned business group, organised in the form of a holding company, allowed deep relationships to be formed between the head of the family-owned conglomerate and government representatives for protecting critical business interests (Bugra, 1994). The closeness of such interlinkages varied according to personal alliances and political instability particularly in the form of military intervention (as in 1971), leaving the business sector vulnerable to idiosyncratic politically determined policy.

Such depth of uncertainty was brought to an end with the military intervention of 1980, which allowed an orthodox stabilisation program to be pursued under the auspices of International Monetary Fund (IMF). The IMF intervention reduced inflation, minimised the trade balance and also opened up the economy to international business (Inselbag and Gultekin, 1988; Baysan and Blitzer, 1991). In fact, the IMF was instrumental in facilitating a radical shift to export promotion strategies that brought further change in the private sector that at the time was accustomed to operating in a protected local market. Despite the traumas of adjusting to the rigours of the open market, overall, output growth and productivity increased in the private sector. Those companies that benefited most operated in low-skilled, low-cost labour intensive export industries such as textiles, clothing, food, leather products, non-metallic products and transportation equipment (Nas and Odekon, 1996).

Despite inattention to social responsibility concerns, and the collapse of manufacturing enterprises unable to adapt and the resulting unemployment that generated (Bugra, 1994), Turkey now has approximately 84,000 active stock ownership enterprises. The paradox of Turkish liberalism has certainly had its effect (Bugra, 1994). However, of these less than 400 are listed on the Istanbul Stock Exchange (ISE), itself only recently inaugurated at the end of 1985 (TOBB, 2004). The majority of enterprises not publicly listed mostly have over 250 shareholders, a surprising dispersal of ownership for essentially small- to medium-sized businesses (SMEs; IIF Equity Advisory Group, 2005).

Despite all changes, the family has remained the pillar of Turkish society where kinship and in-group relationships significantly influence the lives of Turkish people and, in turn, the pattern of business conduct (Kabasakal and Bodur, 2002). The dominant wealth creation vehicle of Turkey was and continues to be the family-owned enterprise, with approximately one-half of publicly listed companies being controlled by core family members, often through the use of group holding multiple voting rights (i.e., privileged shares) and/or board nomination rights (Gunduz and Tatoglu, 2003; IIF Equity Advisory Group, 2005). In fact, the greater proportion of the largest holding companies in Turkey are also family-owned business groups where executive and board roles of strategic importance are occupied exclusively by family members (Bugra, 1994, 2000 p. 209). On average, Istanbul Stock Exchange (ISE) listed corporate shares of the three largest shareholders account for more than 40 per cent of the total listing (Önder, 2003).

Thus characterised by maintaining a controlling shareholding of their affiliates, the family dominated holding company acts as a highly centralised vehicle shaping affiliate strategies as well as their governance structures, particularly the appointment of the chairman, board members and top executives (Bugra, 1994; Yurtoglu, 2000). Legally defined as the joint stock company, the purpose of the holding company is to hold and manage the stocks (shares) of the companies in the group (Yurtoglu, 2000).

In effect, more than 70 per cent of Turkish enterprises are directly or indirectly owned and controlled by families (IIF Equity Advisory Group, 2005; Kula, 2005). Further, 80 per cent of Turkish listed companies have at least one board member who is a member of the majority shareholding family and who, in turn, controls that majority of shares (Kula, 2005). Because a single shareholder can control more than 50 per cent of voting rights in 45 per cent of the companies listed on the ISE (TOBB, 2004) and irrespective of business performance, a number of highly publicised cases have suggested that minority shareholders have been disadvantaged. This is not unique to Turkey as families control a considerable proportion of large corporate groups around the world through pyramidal and cross-shareholdings mechanisms (La Porta et al., 1999).

However, Turkey in particular, has been criticised for not sufficiently protecting minority shareholders due to shortcomings in the legal and regulatory framework (Ararat and Ugur, 2003). Certain writers even claim that Turkish entrepreneurs are apologetic about their wealth and lack confidence in the legitimacy of their ventures (Bugra, 1994). The 2001 IMF rescue package for the Turkish economy introduced determined reform to governance practices as a precondition to loan support. Since then the World Bank, the Capital Market Boards of Turkey, The Turkish Foreign Investors Association, the Turkish Chamber of Commerce and the Turkish Treasury have been promoting the need for sound governance practices (Ertürk, 2003).

Structural contrasts with developed economies

Studies of family-owned businesses in western economies conclude that approximately 30 per cent of family members survive the second generation of family ownership with only 15 per cent surviving into the third generation (Morris et al., 1996, p. 68). That is not unusual, for examination of large corporations concludes that the average life span of Fortune 500 companies is 40–50 years, with certain exceptions as Shell, DuPont and Kodak whose life span has extended to over 75 years (De Geus, 2002). Even famous brands such as Disney, Wal-Mart and Sony have only a history of just over 50 years (Collins and Porras, 1998).

Therefore, what of managerialist accession? In Western enterprises, similar to family-owned SMEs, it is not uncommon for the founder(s) to have moved "upstream" to senior positions as that of the chairman. Similarly, long-standing, loyal employees have also migrated to senior positions, such as the CEO role, as has happened in the case of Dell, Microsoft and Staples. As the founders and employees have known each other for sometime and with the growth and maturing of the business, it became incumbent for purposes of effective leadership and governance that greater role clarity, focus and boundaries of and between key senior positions became established (Nadler et al., 2006). Michael Dell and Bill Gates, in their role of the chairman for example, have concentrated on technology innovation, namely the essence of the founding culture, whilst the CEO concentrates on running the company. Again, with family-owned enterprises, institutionalising the culture of the company founders is a challenging task for, as shown by Apple Computers, it failed to thrive without the hands-on presence of its co-founder, Steve Jobs (Khurana, 2002).

In terms of ownership, in the USA, the UK and Australia, the vast majority of shares are in the hands of agents of financial institutions rather than private persons (Table 6.1). Owing to the regulations of Anglo-American countries, financial institutions are not allowed to hold shares in publicly listed companies on their own behalf; they mainly act as agents (Van der Elst, 2000). Moreover, companies in Anglo-American economies tend to be larger than their Continental European counterparts so that the shares of an Anglo-American firm represent enormous capital. Equally, there exist a greater number of listed companies. A particularly dominant shareholder within Anglo-American economies is the pension fund, an institutional investor of substantial influence and considered by some to be able to determine the performance of their investments (Monks and Minow, 2003). Research shows otherwise! Despite the Warren Buffett dictum of "think like an owner," studies highlight that shareholder activism prompts only small changes in each target firms' governance structures and equally has negligible impact on share value and earnings (Karpoff, 2001).

In contrast, Continental European countries including that of Turkey have shareholder groups that hold significant percentages of shares that are publicly traded, but these groupings comprise a balance of financial institutions and private persons with the limited use of agents to manage their shareholding (Franks and Mayer, 1994; Vincke, 1997; Van der Elst, 1999). Even within Western economies, wealthy families through vertical pyramidal ownership chains, dual-class shares and cross shareholdings control a considerable proportion of their economy's corporations. Faccio and Lang (2002) found that the ten wealthiest families in each country, as a percentage of market cap, control 34 per cent of Portuguese, 30 per cent of Belgian, 29 per cent of French, 29 per cent of Switzerland's, 21 per cent of Italian but only 4 per cent of UK, enterprises. Claessens et al.'s (2000) study of 2980 publicly traded corporations in nine East-Asian countries found that, with the exception of Japan, the majority of listed companies were controlled by families, with the greatest concentration being in Hong Kong (71.5 per cent). Certain estimates proximate that 90 per cent of all businesses in the USA, including corporations, partnerships and sole proprietorships, are family controlled and even 175 of *Fortune 500* US companies are family controlled (Anderson and Reeb, 2003; Attig et al., 2003).

Family businesses in the USA contribute to 50 per cent of GNP, employ 60 per cent of the USA's work force and contribute to 78 per cent of all new job creation (Attig et al., 2003; Perman, 2006). In Canada, 56 per cent of the 1121 listed firms are owned by families active in the leadership of these corporations (Attig et al., 2003).

In contrast to the Anglo-Americans, but similar to the Turkish context, only a small proportion of Continental European firms are listed (Franks and Mayer, 1994). Further, where fewer companies are publicly traded and where people more directly invest their savings, strong personal relationships exist between the management of the company and its shareholders and, in many cases, these two functions are not separated (Van Hulle, 1998).

Arguing in favour of the family-owned enterprise, Fama and Jenson (1983, p. 7) postulate its propensity for lower agency costs as the family hold the advantage for more disciplined monitoring of management, "family members have many dimensions for exchange with one another over a long horizon and therefore have the advantage of overseeing and decoupling related decision agents." Moreover, since founding family members often have a large fraction of their wealth directly tied to the firm, family members hold strong cash-flow incentives to closely supervise the firm, thereby having distinct information advantage over business operations than outside investors (Jensen and Meckling, 1976). Such contention is supported by Anderson and Reeb's (2003) study of US firm evaluation with the family-owned enterprise being attributed higher valuation than its non-family counterpart.

Franks et al. (2003) argue that managerial autonomy arises because of shareholders' optimal governance decisions. Attending to the governance of long-term employment, business information sharing between management and owners and external variables such as labour market rigidity and product or service market competition all have a positive effect on the value of the firm. In effect, certain studies conclude that owner-operated firms outperform their professionally managed counterparts (Daily and Thompson, 1994; Yeh and Shu, 2001). Yet, there is a downside to the family control of the publicly listed firm. Family members may derive private benefit through control not shared with other shareholders (Shleifer and Vishny, 1997). Further, the family may remain in control of the firm despite their lack of capability to run both the board and the firm (Burkat et al., 2003; Shleifer and Vishny, 1997). Cognisant of that fact, attention has been given in Turkey to CEO development in terms of professional management practice culminating in greater influence over shareholding family members (Buğra, 1998). Despite such progress, senior managers are still close associates of the family enjoying extended tenure in the same company and act "more like the steward of a rural estate than the professional manager of an industrial corporation" (Buğra, 1994, p. 208).

Table 6.1 Contrasting models of governance of financial markets

Governance characteristics	Anglo-American ("shareholder" or "outsider system")	Continental Europe ("stakeholder" or "insider system")	Turkey ("relationship" or "insider system")
Share ownership structure	• Dispersed ownership: – Agents of financial institutions (over 50%); – Private persons (20–30%) • Relatively small number of intercorporate share holdings	• Integrated ownership: – Private companies (20–40%); – Financial institutions (10–30%); – Private persons (15–35%) • Substantial intercorporate shareholdings	• Concentrated family control, i.e., direct or indirect ownership of more than 80% of a company, retaining majority control • Substantial intercorporate shareholding (i.e, pyramidal and cross shareholding structures)
Number of domestic public companies	Large number of listed companies (e.g., 6307 in the USA; 1702 in the UK)	Relatively small number of listed companies (e.g., 648 in the Germany; 966 Euronext: comprising Amsterdam, Brussels and Paris stock exchanges)	Few companies (i.e, 400 out of 84,000 companies) are traded on the ISE with: – 25 most actively traded companies represent three quarters of the volume; and – Five largest business groups account for approximately 50% of the total market capitalisation
External mechanism for managerial control	Strong: • Liquid capital market facilitates frequent control rights	Weak: • Outside investors unable to exert much control	Weak: • Lack of external devices (n.b. strong internal devices) • No active market: – Limited openness, almost impossible to acquire a traded company without

	• Large shareholders exercise monitoring role (i.e., incentive for takeover for a badly managed company)		• the prior willingness to sell by the controlling owner; – No shareholder mechanism for disciplining poor performers
Personal contact between managers and shareholders	Weak	Strong	Strong
Size of the company as percentage of market	Large	Medium	SME
Corporate law	Highly advanced (since 1765)	Evolving	Embryonic
Corporate governance code	In the UK, since Cadbury (1992), regular reviews and updates	Since 1997 regular updates	Introduced formally in 2003 and updated in 2005
Board structure	Unitary board, with predominately external directors	Mostly two tier boards (i.e., supervisory and management)	Unitary board, with one third being non-executive directors
Role separation of the CEO/chairman	24% of S&P 500 (USA) 95% of FTSE 100 (UK)	100% in two tier board (e.g., German, Netherlands, Japan, Russia)	Only small percentage as CEO role is not mandatory (often reduced to managing director)
Practised	USA, UK, Australia, NZ, Canada, South Africa	German *Sozialpartner* (social partners); French's *verroullage* (state control); Japanese *kieretsu*; Korean *chaeabol*	Family business structure; Turkey, Portugal, Greece

Source: Compiled from Van der Elst (2000); Kakabadse and Kakabadse (2001); Ararat and Ugur (2003); Higgs (2003); The Wilshire Index (2004); Wong (2004); World Federation of Exchanges (2004); IIF Equity Advisory Group (2005); Kula (2005).

Boards

As emphasised markets as Japan and Germany, characterised by a relatively small number of quoted companies where ownership and control rights are traded infrequently, which by implication denotes an underdeveloped financial market, are identified as "insider based" (Charkham, 1995; Table 6.1). The result is a more immature form of governance. Therefore, for both legal and historical reasons, companies rely more on debt finance from banks (Charkham, 1995). The boards of "insider based" companies operate on a two-tier basis, namely an executive board and a supervisory board (Stapledon, 1996). Within the two-tier board structure, board roles are strictly delineated according to particular tasks and responsibilities. Supervisory board members hold non-executive director positions responsible for the supervision of executive management who are full time and responsible for determining and realising enterprise direction. Top management is represented by, and hold positions on, the executive board, a body held accountable by the supervisory board (Kakabadse et al., 2006). The CEO heads the executive board, holding greater power in terms of operational decisions than the chairman of the supervisory board and, in turn, is prominent within and outside the enterprise (van Hamel et al., 1998). The chairman of the supervisory board, a prestigious if not limited position, at least has the authority to fire the CEO (van Hamel et al., 1998). Minimum supervisory board size is regulated by company law. Actual board size is regulated through co-determination laws such as in Germany or agreements reached between management and relevant stakeholders as in the Netherlands. The determining factor is the number of employees. Shareholders elect the chairman of the supervisory board who, in the event of a tie on any issue, has the casting vote (Charkham, 1995; Proctor and Miles, 2002). The chairman elected could be an employee or the outgoing CEO. In effect, the German corporate code intends to promote a culture of open discussion on both the executive and supervisory boards, with the chairman of the supervisory board held responsible for promoting dialogue on both boards (Charkham, 1995; Proctor and Miles, 2002). Franks et al. (2003) argue in favour of the superior "quality" of corporate law in Germany in comparison to the UK and the USA based on balancing shareholder and employee interests against the singular promotion of shareholder value. However, the downside to two tier boards is the dilution of decision-making fluidity, requiring that all critical parties are involved and participate in debate before any key decisions are reached (Andert, 2005).

With the US enterprise, the governance division of responsibilities occurs between the positions of the CEO and chairman. A criticism of the US unitary role structure is that the boardroom is little more than a managerially based hierarchical outcrop, as the positions of the chairman and CEO are one for approximately over 76 per cent of US companies. Some consider role duality (chairman/CEO under one person) to undermine board member autonomy and promote hierarchical thinking despite the adoption of independent external (non-executive) directors (Andert, 2005, p. 20).

The UK's principle-based form of corporate governance promotes separation of these two key leadership roles. The CEO is responsible for running the business and accountable for internal operational functions. The chairman is responsible for all matters concerning the board (Andert, 2005, p. 20). The chairman's role in the UK is increasingly positioned as independent of line management, even to the point where the CEO can only become the chairman in another firm, supervising a CEO with whom the incumbent has no prior working relationship. Such separation is pursued in order to minimise the undermining of the chairman's independence (Weir and Laing, 2000). The UK relationship between the chairman and the CEO is identified as a complex set of dynamics based on individual beliefs, capabilities, expertise and experience. Whereas the CEO is viewed as the significant determinant for running the business, the chairman's conduct is considered to be key to the effectiveness of the board (Kakabadse et al., 2006). Although the role and contribution of the chairman varies according to each corporate context, research highlights that the relationship between the chairman and the CEO is of critical importance to the future of the business, requiring both to pursue a sustainable and productive style of interaction, irrespective of the diversity and magnitude of challenges that the organisation, its board and the two role incumbents face (Heracleous, 1999; Kakabadse et al., 2001; Roberts, 2002). The chairman's social and political skills in "massaging" often sensitive relationships and egos, by being able to mitigate and avoid interpersonal collision, are recognised as being of crucial importance for effective boardroom functioning (Kakabadse et al., 2001).

As already argued in Turkey, the concept of "corporate governance" has increasingly become an important subject for companies. The principal reason for this has been successive Turkish government's promotion of accessing funds from international markets. In order to be a credible international player, good governance is viewed as the key mechanism to ensure that past financial crises and corporate scandals do not recur. Thus, the effective functioning of the Turkish board is recognised as a necessary precondition for the growth of the Turkish economy.

Turkish boards are identified as unitary in structure and for listed companies comprise at least three members appointed for a maximum term of three years. Under Turkish corporate governance guidelines, board members are appointed and dismissed by and at the shareholders General Assembly (CCPG, 2005). The exceptions are state commercial enterprises, where the state, province or municipality is granted the right to delegate a representative to serve as the director of an enterprise in which the government agency holds shares (ECGI, 2003). State-owned enterprise board members can only be removed by the government agency that appointed them.

Further, foreign citizens can be elected as directors of publicly listed and state-owned enterprises (IIF Equity Advisory Group, 2005). Additionally, it is not uncommon for the founders' shares to carry the right to nominate directors (IIF Equity Advisory Group, 2005). However, the corporate governance guide of the Capital Market Board (CMB) requires that companies provide to all shareholders detailed information regarding new board nominees' relations with the host company and other companies, their personal and educational backgrounds, their assets and whether or not they meet the required criteria for director independence (CCPG, 2005). The guide does not prescribe any particular expertise and/or education-related criteria for board membership, except for certain types of companies, such as banks, insurance companies, brokerage companies, real estate investment partnerships, which themselves are subject to specific laws concerning professional conduct (ECGI, 2003).

Similarly, the commercial code obliges the board to publish the company's balance sheet (i.e., directors report) outlining the company's commercial, financial and economic status and actions in these areas, as well as, a dividend distribution proposal indicating the percentage of profit to be distributed to shareholders and the level of company reserve (Ongoren Law Office, 2005). Such information is distributed within the first quarter of the fiscal year and submitted to the General Assembly for approval (ECGI, 2003).

Additionally, capital markets law, corporate tax law, social security laws and the banks acts impose liabilities on directors of companies (IIF Equity Advisory Group, 2005). Under the commercial code (Ongoren Law Office, 2005), shareholders, creditors, third parties, bankruptcy administrators or trustees appointed in a bankruptcy and certain regulatory authorities (e.g., tax offices) are entitled, subject to circumstances, to file a lawsuit against the directors concerning their liabilities. However, considering that family members are also the major shareholders "running" the board, the likelihood of such lawsuit arising is limited, and hence the need for director and officer liability insurance is equally limited (IIF Equity Advisory Group, 2005).

In 2005, the Turkish corporate code guidelines of 2003 were revised adding important provision to the role of an independent board and making mandatory consolidated financial reporting. As such, the principle of comply or explain was adopted by the capital market board (CMB) requiring publicly held companies to state in their annual reports whether or not they have complied with the Guide. Equally the "one share, one vote" and the adoption of corporate social responsibility (CSR), as defined by the European Commission (OECD, 2002; IIF Equity Advisory Group, 2005), are additional pressures for compliance. In support of the move toward greater governance, the Turkish Industrialist and Businessman's Association (TÜSİAD) introduced the concept of the CEO in its corporate governance code, encouraging companies to appoint a CEO additional to the chairman of the board. The lexicon of chief executive officer (CEO), however, is not defined in Turkish commercial legislation leading to contrasting interpretations of the role, from the CEO being the head of the company to that of chief operating officer (COO; IIF Equity Advisory Group, 2005). In effect, the corporate reform movement in Turkey has adopted Anglo-American governance and, in particular, the UK's focus of role separation but in a society of networked, stakeholder relationships.

The study

Due to the relative poverty of inquiry concerning the chairman's role and effect on board performance, a qualitative study was pursued in order to understand each study participant's experience of the role of the chairman and the incumbent's impact on the workings and performance of family controlled Turkish listed company boards. Considerations of effectiveness of board performance and governance application were derived from the perceptions of individual chairmans and board members. Through so doing, comparison is also drawn from findings of other studies examining the chairman's role and impact (Kakabadse et al., 2006). Similarities and differences are highlighted keeping in mind contrasts of structural and cultural context.

Cognisant that the role and contribution of the chairman vary according to corporate context (Pettigrew and McNulty, 1998; Kakabadse et al., 2001, 2006), considerable sensitivity was afforded to eliciting similarities of "good" chairman practice, rather than leaning to western model "best practice" as a universal norm. Through open-ended, semi-structured interviews that triggered reflexive narratives, the chairmans of eight Turkish boards of listed companies shared their experience of their role. Further, ten other additional participants outlined their experience of being board members, either as a member or as attendee (e.g., directors, MD, CEO), particularly focusing their responses on the chairman's impact on boardroom dynamics.

Access difficulties have been and remain a source of constraint in studying "managerial elites" (Pettigrew and McNulty, 1998). Kahl (1957, p. 10) stated that "those who sit amongst the mighty do not invite sociologists to watch them make the decisions about how to control the behaviours of others." Thus, without local assistance it would have been impossible to conduct this study. A local, but very well networked, member of the informal "chairman's club" crucially facilitated access to eight boards of family controlled listed companies.

Certain interviews were conducted in English and others in Turkish. All interviews were tape-recorded, transcribed and the Turkish language interviews translated into English. The narratives' scripts were subsequently analysed and coded adopting a grounded theory approach, as emerging themes and frameworks were amended in the light of following transcriptions (Glaser and Strauss, 1965). To gain consistency across interviews, the framework of role theory (Katz and Kahn, 1966) was adopted in order to better appreciate each incumbent's role-related expectations, their interactions with and degree of influence over other board members and wider stakeholders and how such experiences helped them shape their board role. Katz and Khan's (1966) theoretical treatise of role theory emphasises that what individual jobholders do is shaped by significant others' expectations. To improve data accuracy and to verify the findings, the members of the research team separately carried out interviews but in some cases jointly participated (Eisenhardt, 1989). The transcripts were then independently read with the aim of identifying recurring narratives, particularly focusing on boardroom performance effects. It was considered by the researchers that narrative methods are useful in organisational studies seeking to understand practical "lived" knowledge and socially constructed organisational processes (Pentland, 1999; Ng and de Cock, 2002; Feldman, 2004). The view adopted by the researchers was that narrative analysis allows for contextually sensitive interpretations to be made concerning the conduct of participant's lives, thus enhancing awareness of the relationships and inter-relationships central to boardroom life (Bruner, 1990; Ochberg, 1994; Gergen and Gergen, 2003; Feldman, 2004). The process of analysing narratives may take a number of approaches from an examination of the narrative as a whole (Lieblich et al., 1998), through to identifying self-contained story formats (Boje, 1991), to a pattern of themes that recur in boardroom discourse (Riessman, 1993; Pentland, 1999). The third approach was adapted since it allowed for exposure to repeatedly used expressions capturing the specificity and diversity of experiences.

Results

Six themes recurred through the eighteen narratives, namely governance practice, board membership, board role, board structure, board dynamics and the skills and qualities required of the high-performing owner/chairman.   '

Governance practice

Despite codes and other legal and voluntary stipulations, the respondents highlighted that the practice of governance is idiosyncratically pursued, a finding confirmed in studies of other countries (Kakabadse et al., 2006).

> When I was a CEO, I had no problem with my chairman but that's mainly because the chairman had given me the authority to run the corporation...but now that I am a chairman, I have difficulties with the CEO. But by talking to him and discussing with him, both of us solved our

problems. This is heavily related to family background, education and a way of understanding. There's a common language that comes through discussing. But, if you simply try to have your own way, then it's not fair, it's not good for the shareholders. In this kind of climate, if you are overly assertive with the board of directors and at the same time with the executive managers of the company, then many feel that there is a problem between the chairman and CEO and they rapidly lose confidence. (Chairman, second-generation owner, Board 1)

Although the most important decisions are still taken by the dominant shareholder or by a limited number of relatives before the board meeting, at informal meetings or reunions, changes are on the way. As the firm grows and requires new competitive skills, the family is increasingly reliant on professional managers, like myself. The family learns how to delegate day-to-day operational decision and minor strategic decisions. The move from strategic planning to action becomes more complex as professional, non family member managers increasingly take decisions and become responsible for one or more operational units. (CEO, Non-Family Member, Professional Manager, Board 1)

The practice of governance emerged as more driven by the outcomes of conversations (formal or informal), a finding which contrasts with western company practice where greater emphasis is given to protocol, procedure and board members being individually accountable for their actions according to the appropriate corporate codes of the country (Kakabadse and Kakabadse, 2001; Pye, 2002). Yet, despite the sophistication of western governance codes, boardroom interactions have also been identified as constraining Anglo-American board members to fully participate in meetings (Kakabadse et al., 2006). The experience of feeling inhibited to fully examine relevant issues has been reported by UK and US board members (Kakabadse et al., 2006). That is not to say that Turkish board members do not face sensitive issues which they find difficult to address, but greater attention to discussion was reported as the key vehicle for governance application. Repeatedly raised was the considerable time and effort invested in nurturing workable relations with Turkish board members. As it is not uncommon for a number of family members to be represented on the board and for family members to hold different views concerning the shape and future of the business, maintaining harmony whilst allowing for critical analysis of issues makes dialogue an invaluable boardroom tool in the eyes of Turkish board members.

We had the board minutes; it's all written and then printed out for the next board meeting. But that is not what makes us effective. Our board decisions, whether as a result of expression of views or protracted discussion, are determined by information and analysis which is the heart of our governance. Documents and agendas are a pretext which can be changed. Discussion, well-sourced information and agreement are what make us successful. (Chairman, first-generation owner, Board 3)

Board membership

Membership of Anglo-American boards is more determined by the incumbent's track record experience, particularly in effectively exercising fiduciary duties and attending to regulatory obligations (Pass, 2004). The interactive and communicative skills, although recognised as important, have only recently been given attention as criteria for board membership (Kakabadse et al., 2006).

As far as Turkish board members are concerned, the skills of finance and strategic thinking are held as important, but held in higher esteem are the interpersonal/interactive skills of communication. Equally, the values and "character" of each board member were described by the study participants as distinctly critical considerations.

The desired skill set for board membership emerged as a combination of analytical skills, sound strategic judgement and sensitive communication and interactive skills. As many Turkish companies now have second- and third-generation family members working as managers and consequently, or separately, holding board positions, the delicacy of managing family relationships, particularly at times of inheritance, was described as critical to board functioning.

> Until 1990, the family company served 10 to 15 family members who were shareholders. But since the 1990s or early 2000, the family company has to serve 40 or 50 members of families, where most of them are shareholders. But shareholder doesn't always mean board member. Board members' positions are different. More important is that some family members are asking to work within the company on a monthly salary basis which is not easy when they have to work with the professionals. The few that ask to join the board are then carefully selected. That is sometime difficult sometimes to explain to those shareholders, but we need members that can contribute. (Chairman, second-generation owner, Board 4)

Additional to sensitivity of selection for board membership, loyalty emerged as a critical consideration. In a society dominated by networks and informal understandings, loyalty was described as the basis for relationship trust, with board membership being one example of reward for relational bonding.

> One area difficult to mix is family on the board and family appointed as managers. Many such managers are not the best, but for me to raise that

would damage my relationship with the family which I have known for a long time. (Independent Board Member, Board 7)

Further, despite the better education of second-generation owners in comparison to their first-generation counterparts, family members, as salaried employees, are seen, by some, as undesirable. The power imbalance of horizontally working alongside professional managers who feel themselves as powerless and vertically deriving power from family members, who sit on the board, is recognised as extensive and counterproductive.

On occasions I struggle with some family members who desire to work in salaried jobs. Some aren't able to perform as well as professionals because they have not got the skills needed. Conveying this message is very tricky and highly sensitive. (Board Member, controlling family, Board 6)

I try to get the chairmen in my network to discuss the appointment of family members to management roles according to skills and qualification. Very few want to make this an issue. No wonder! few have sufficient business ability. (Chairman, first-generation owner, Board 2)

As with family members, a key criterion for appointment to the role of NED is relational trust. The individual would be known and trusted by the family. However, on probing, the role, purpose and contribution of any one or more NED did not emerge as clear, but for the study respondents that was not seen as problematic. Chairmen in particular, but also the other board members, confessed to being comfortable with the individual and gaining value from the person and from their skills and experience at a more informal, tacit level. The descriptions offered of the role of the "external-to-the-family" NED were akin to a friend, confidant and personal counsellor.

People who sit on boards are educated and cultured. They have skills and experience and I and my board search for the necessary skills that will assist our discussions. We are also conscious of the individual and try to bring together the people we can work with. (Chairman, first-generation owner, Board 6)

The chairman of board 6 emphasised relational trust, admitting that as more important than the skills and experience of NEDs in a networked society as Turkey.

Board role

The study interviewees emphasised the critical importance of determining the strategic plan(s) of the enterprise. The board was described as the strategic meeting point where family members consider strategic alternatives and require management to provide quality intelligence concerning market developments, competitor behaviour and global trends in order to discuss options for the future. To enhance the quality of strategic input, the majority of respondents stipulated that key senior managers are required to attend board meetings. Thus, strategic determination, oversight of the company and even managerial representation determine board role and purpose.

> Small or large, in Turkey we have family businesses. The family is directly involved in the running of the business and also in taking a bird's eye view and overseeing the firm. Many of us hear corporate governance but what does it mean? – that is why the senior managers attend all board meetings. (Independent Board Member, Board 5)

> Whether listed or not, family businesses are family business. The professional manager is there to provide advice and suggest strategy but not to make strategy. Strategy and corporate governance are the business of the family. (Managing Director, non-family, professional manager, Board 5)

Board structure

Three key constituents determined the structural configuration of Turkish boards: the chairman, often the owner/majority shareholder; majority and minority family shareholder members and externally appointed non-executive directors (NEDs). Which family members would sit on the board was determined by the spread and volume of share ownership, seniority, individual capability, and ultimately the approval of the chairman and other influential family members.

Additional to the oversight role of the board, chairmen and other board members reported playing an active business role, thus directly exposing themselves to the challenges of a vibrant market.

> My position is also confusing. I am a chairman and I should not be interested in the daily activities of the enterprise. But there are some important activities, such as buying land, investments or establishing a new company outside Turkey or buying important investment equipment that I have to know all there is to know and be involved. I take part with our managers but in a very friendly manner. (Chairman, first-generation owner, Board 3)

Although intermingling board work with managerial responsibilities was reported as common practice, a minority of the respondents felt this to be an outdated and unwelcome practice.

> There is a dubious division between the responsibilities of professionals (management) and shareholders (family members) on Turkish boards.

Board members should not act as professionals but should let the professionals work without interference...but here that is very unusual. (Retired Chairman and majority shareholder, Board 7)

The retired chairman of board 7 reported a damaging overlap of responsibilities between the role of board member and that of professional management. In his view, the more relational trust is emphasised, the more board members will not draw clear distinction between the responsibilities and accountabilities of professional management and those of the board. Not determining role clarity allows for interference in the affairs of management. The retired chairman of board 7 also offered the opinion that although management is substantially more able than most Turkish board members, it is powerless to enforce clearer delineation.

Yet, irrespective of the differing viewpoints on the value of relational trust and board member involvement in the affairs of management, all of the study respondents agreed that extensive board tenure facilitated for more personable relationships be considered an advantage to board functioning. Knowing each other "counted" for a great deal and seen as a particular strength of the "Turkish way of doing things."

In terms of board member tenure and contribution, the two challenges faced by Anglo-American boards, namely those of "searching" for the appropriate board director and allowing time to meaningfully progress through the learning curve once appointed, emerged as more "naturally" addressed in the Turkish context. As highlighted, board candidates, family or otherwise, "need" to be known to the board and the extended family for some time before being invited onto the board. Such exposure was reported as allowing for an extensive scrutiny of skills, experience and personal orientation but in a more socially acceptable way. Through so doing, the prospective candidate would equally become familiar with the company and family, thus reducing the intensity and duration of learning needed to make an effective contribution to the board. Further, board members' informal extended length of tenure was considered to allow for greater intimacy of understanding of the business. With low board turnover, the challenge of steering new appointees through their learning curve was not considered problematic.

Further, despite acknowledgement of board subcommittees, little attention seemed to be given to committee contribution other than that of the audit committee.

We designed an audit committee and this committee functioned properly and one of our board members is the head. We have compensation and staffing committees and an IT and technology committee also headed by one of our board members. These committees are useful and add a great deal to board discussions. But I think we are unusual in Turkey. (Chairman, second-generation owner, Board 4)

The clarity displayed by the chairman of board 4 concerning the value to be gained from board structures was exceptional and not replicated by the other study respondents.

Of the minority of cases where board subcommittees were valued, their clarifying of issues and providing guidance for the main board were identified as being of considerable benefit. Once critical issues are brought to the attention of the main board members, they would be formally discussed and/or informally "sorted out" between the key family members.

> Our chairman is fond of board committees. They give a chance to non board members to have direct input to the company's strategy. Still, the 'real' decisions are made by the chairman with the 'inner' family. (CEO, professional manager, Board 4)

Board dynamics

As already shown, an emerging characteristic of Turkish board membership is that board directors extensively interact with each other and also with senior management in what has been described as "lively, engaging, formal and informal meetings." The respondents outlined flexibility and friendliness of communication partly determined by the interconnectedness and their strong loyalty ties to the family. Interconnectedness was reported as the cultural "milieu" of Turkish social life.

> We know each other well. That helps a great deal. I know we can be accused of 'fixing' things but that is not the case. It is our personal knowledge of each other and respect for each other that helps us sort out our problems. (Family Board Member and Shareholder, Board 8)

In contrast, external directors of USA- and UK-based boards may have social and/or professional ties with the CEO but rarely with the other board directors (Chatterjee and Harrison, 2001). The declared advantage of Anglo-American professional criteria for membership is that lack of intimacy with each other encourages open contribution. On the downside, due to lack of knowledge of each other, in what has been described as professional relationships, the propensity for consensus seeking behaviour, "groupthink," does emerge where consensus seeking is identified as a method of reducing stress levels within the group (Janis, 1971; Demb and Neubauer, 1992; Cohan, 2002). In order to mitigate the risk of social exclusion from the group if stressful or conflicting information is introduced, western board members have reported that information and ideas have been suppressed in favour of conformity (Janis, 1971; Cohan, 2002; Westphal and Khanna, 2003). Research has identified that ambiguous or complex information tends to be dismissed as unmanageable and rather than address issues, western board members report themselves as avoiding dealing with the problem, leaving them feeling highly frustrated (Katz, 1959; Cohan, 2002; Kakabadse et al., 2006). Such behaviour leads to "inhibition to challenge" (Kakabadse et al., 2006) or "pluralistic ignorance" (Harvey et al., 1998, p. 18) or a "situation which virtually all members of a group privately reject group norms, practices or policies or have concerns about them, but believe that virtually all group members accept them" (Miller et al., 2000, p. 103). The evidence to emerge from this study indicates that the plague of Anglo-American boards, namely not addressing known concerns, occurs less on Turkish boards, where major issues are often addressed outside, if within board meetings prove to be too challenging.

An additional aspect of effective board performance is that of reaching consensus (Kakabadse and Kakabadse, 2007). This point was strongly emphasised by the study respondents. Freedom of expression and offering alternative viewpoints was encouraged as long as that did not undermine reaching a shared view. The study respondents felt it critical to reach alignment between the interests of shareholders, irrespective of whether they are majority and minority shareholders, as more often than not, they are members of the same family. To facilitate communication, board meetings were reported as frequently held, many reported as once a week. However, a point emphasised throughout is that issues are as much addressed informally outside the board as at board meetings.

> We know each other. Why do I have to wait for a board meeting to sort things out? Most important is not breaking trust and keeping each other informed. That is what I do. I talk to all the board members, get their view and we decide. (Chairman, first-generation owner, Board 6)

Informality of approach was reported as advantageous to enhancing trust and respect. Thus, extensive investment in one-to-one and "clique" wide communications was described in interview. In this regard, extended tenure of board members was considered as particularly valuable. Many reported that personal intimacy enabled informal communication to take place between board members without causing undue suspicion from others not directly involved in any one or other conversation.

Owner chairmen

The chairman, usually the majority shareholder, was described by the study respondents as the true leader of the Turkish board and, in fact, the company. The chairman sets the tone and working norms of the board, including expectations about attendance at meetings, preparation for meetings, corporate values, boardroom culture, ethical standards and the spirit and culture of the company.

Chairmen were viewed as the "culture carriers," modelling and determining the behaviour of other board members. They act as leaders of the board and are expected to be so. As such, descriptions of the chairman parallel many of the characteristics attributed to the CEO of Anglo-American enterprises (Cascio, 2004). Similar to the Anglo-American CEO, the study respondents outlined that effective chairmen spend considerable time interacting with relevant others, such as board members, the management team, employees and external stakeholders. In keeping with the Coombes and Wong (2004) conclusion that sound knowledge of the industry, coupled with independence of mind and having already served on the particular board in question, Turkish chairmen exhibited the desired characteristics attributed to broad experience of membership of international boards.

Further, owing to the ownership structure of Turkish companies, several other individuals on the board with extensive shareholdings may also play an important leadership role. The previous chairman (retired) but who remains a board member was described as potentially providing a counterbalance to the present incumbent, similar to the lead independent director (LID) on US boards or the senior independent director (SID) of UK boards (Kakabadse and Kakabadse, 2007). Whilst the LID, SID and other directors experience pressure to maintain their loyalty to the "boss" (i.e., the CEO) (Fama and Jensen, 1983; Baysinger and Hoskisson, 1990; Schaffer, 2002), the loyalty of Turkish board members is to the family (i.e., the shareholders) and by implication to the current chairman. With such complexity of personal relationships, chairmen described why "delicacy of touch" is necessary on Turkish boards. Other board members concurred outlining effective chairmen of Turkish boards as exhibiting high contextual sensitivity and diplomacy.

> In Turkey we do things differently. It's not that we do better than western boards. It's just different. You are brought up with these ground rules and you learn from an early age how to address sensitive issues. It is part of the culture. I think you learn the art of dialogue from the family so when you come to the board it means that others have recognised that you have learned well. (Board Member, family shareholder, Board 8)

> In family firms, the chairman is used to handling sensitive issues as there are always concerns through which the chairman negotiates, these may be related to conflict of interests, succession, control, sibling rivalries, favouritism and who drives business decisions, which sometimes badly affect the family equilibrium and which, in turn, can create long-term family feuds. (Independent Board Member, Board 8)

Sensitivity to relationships is reported as matched with objective and analytically determined argument. Other studies reveal similar findings. "Best practice" chairmanship requires delving deep into objective argument, drawing on relevant information, and through such penetrative analysis, the chairman guides board members to identify appropriate ways forward

Kakabadse et al., 2006). Relational skills, supported by "penetrative analysis," are primary elements of effective chairmanship. Anglo-American chairmen reported as high performing described their need to stand back from detail in order to gain the "bigger picture view" and thus allow a mindset of penetrative analysis to emerge. Recognising the power of role modelling, western chairmen concurred that if they could show being able to stand back and be analytical and data driven, the other board members would be encouraged to do likewise (Kakabadse et al., 2006).

> You know the passions of each member and through listening to them step-by-step you will find solutions by guiding them to see the reality. One way is get more information so that you can lessen their concerns. Another is to help them interpret the information. Helping them how to think and analyse is important. It's not easy as it's not possible sometimes to paint the picture of the vision in front of everybody and make them see it through my own glasses. (Chairman, second-generation owner, Board 8)

Turkish chairmen emerged as powerful at penetrative analysis (i.e., argument interrogation). Objectivity of mind with sensitivity of approach was observed on a number of occasions. However, standing back was more problematic. Due to internal and external relationship exposure, the duties of the chairman were described as stretching. From attending to considerable detail to determining and driving forward the vision, as well as running board meetings and attending to community and social responsibilities, time for reflection was viewed as a "luxury." Current first- and second-generation chairmen reported such an extensive portfolio as manageable. It was considered that the next generation of chairmen would face considerable difficulty in "juggling" with the same extensive workload. Despite this insight, few admitted that, in the future, the roles of the chairman and the CEO will need redesign.

Although, in admiration of the current generation of board chairmen, chairmen themselves, board members and the top managers of the firm drew attention to one concern, the over-dependence of the board and the overall company on the capabilities, health and resilience of the chairman. It was recognised that reliance on one person left the enterprise vulnerable, particularly as most chairmen are rarely replaced and step down for only reasons of ill health or age. However, the prospect of introducing limited tenure, with limited responsibilities for the role of the chairman in the future, was not welcomed by most of the study participants.

Conclusion

Certain parallels can be drawn between the reported governance and leadership practices on Turkish enterprises and those of Anglo-American firms.

For contrasting reasons, the role duality of the CEO/chairman of US com panies and the dominance of the executive and non-executive chairma role in Australia display similar characteristics to Turkish chairmen, pa ticularly in the determination and driving forward of the vision (Kakabads and Kakabadse, 2007). Similar to that of the USA, the Australian chairma is seen as providing long-term balance and stability to the board and to th firm, similar to the findings of this study of the role and contribution of th Turkish chairman.

Research also reveals that US board members feel themselves as restricte from forming ties with the management of the organisation (Kakabads et al., 2006). The reason is one of governance, in particular maintainin independence to protect objectivity of decision-making. Further, due t pressures of time and a "poverty" of informal ties, both UK and US boar members report limited use of board colleague's experience, thus reducin their ability as individuals to act together as a "board team" (Merton, 195 Suls and Green, 2003; Westphal and Bednar, 2005).

Members of Turkish boards are identified as suffering less from Angl American "inhibition" and more confident to raise issues sometimes fo mally, more often informally, due to exposure to long lasting "philos" tie This is an important point, for according to Forbes and Milliken (1999 bonding between group members affects a board's ability to work togethe and leads to higher levels of satisfaction, commitment to the group an greater levels of cohesiveness when under pressure. In turn, cohesive board tend to preserve their collective nature, positively influence future grou processes and enhance effort norms through their ability to influence mem bers' behaviour (Forbes and Milliken, 1999). Such delicate group processe are identified as particularly well handled by the chairmans of Turkis boards, who seem able to mitigate the potentially negative consequences o damaging relationships and nurture balanced power structures within th board. Most study participants indicated that Turkish board members' clos relationship with management provides them with direct access to informa tion concerning the enterprise's strengths and weaknesses, enabling ever further the problem solving capability of the board.

Thus, the effective Turkish chairman, usually the majority shareholder emerged as a skilful communicator able to pursue multiple conversation with most levels of the organisation. The chairman's primary concern emerged as the disciplined pursuit of business goals, and the maintaining o harmonious relationships with board members, management and externa stakeholders.

Further the spread of responsibilities of Turkish chairmen emerged a extensive. Despite that, the influence of the chairman on board member and the organisation is paramount. The chairman drives the organisation However, scant attention seems to be given by both chairman and boarc members to the protocols of governance. Yet our findings support othe research results, which conclude that no clear relationship exists between governance structure and corporate performance (Jensen and Meckling, 1976; Dalton et al., 1998; Weir and Laing, 2000). The nature and structure of any social grouping, including that of a board, is elusive and complex. As Heenan and Bennis (1999, p. 1) remind us, "the social world isn't nearly as orderly as the physical world, nor is it as susceptible to rule" as "people are untidy but informed and anything but predictable."

This study reveals that Turkish boards fare well on at least one criterion set by Forbes and Milliken (1999) for determining board effectiveness, service task performance (STP). STP is considered as composed of two elements, involvement in and providing expert and detailed advice on major strategic initiatives such as acquisition and restructuring and (second) that of board cohesiveness (Forbes and Milliken, 1999). Turkish boards emerge as effective in the determination and pursuit of company strategy. Equally, STP effectiveness is enabled by a distinct capacity for approval of major capital projects and other initiatives, and in nurturing "cohesive interactions" at board level due to family and/or philos ties and the chairman's capability to facilitate sensitive dialogue with all pertinent parties (Krackhardt and Stern, 1988; Kakabadse, 1991).

However, of critical concern is governance, particularly the opaque hiring and remuneration of management, low transparency of decision making as a result of informal meetings, unclear board selection processes and by implication, the configuration of Turkish boards. The "secretive," non-transparent nature of Turkish boards does little to endear foreign investment or the forming of partnerships with Turkish enterprises. The myriad of interwoven board, managerial and stakeholder relationships can be viewed as an overwhelming hurdle for foreign companies desiring business opportunities in Turkey.

> So, many of our boards and companies are just not ready for full western exposure. We have talented people but we have to change our ways. (Chairman, first-generation owner, Board 2)

Further, the desire for change in the area of governance did not emerge as a driving passion. Without the will to change but with the wish to be more international, an additional concern is identified, that of being unprepared to adapt business-wise and socially to the reality of an international competitive climate.

> Step-by-step, we all realised that within our company, in our production and also in our market share, both in Turkey and internationally, it's not possible to survive for long. The EU one way, one day, will come and collect all of us. Turkey cannot continue as a low cost economy. The day when we cannot pay for our company, or country debt, will come

because in Turkey, the private sector is based on the family business and 95% or even 98% are smaller and medium scale companies. When that day comes, we will face business and social problems. We talk a lot but we are not ready and do little about reforms, governance and new structures. (Chairman, first-generation owner, Board 2)

Thus, the study concludes that Turkish chairmans and Turkish board members are relationally skilled, strategically astute but policy vulnerable. To be skilled in influence and to be strategically "smart" mean being able to "do good business" and procure advantageous business deals. To be policy disadvantaged, however, leaves the enterprise and by implication the nation, open to damage, for policy determines corporate and national infrastructure and, as such, is the overarching framework to continued strategy excellence. The challenge of a disciplined governance application, at both the level of the enterprise as well as the state, remains unaddressed. This study supports Bugra's (1994) premise that neither institutional frameworks nor behavioural market regularities follow principles of universally rational behaviour. The policy design necessary for good governance in Turkish business enterprises is unlikely to change, at least in the short term, according to the results of this study.

Nevertheless, the study contributes to a better understanding of the chairman's role and an effect on board performance within Turkish family controlled, publicly listed companies. Further qualitative and quantitative based research is required examining the boardroom dynamics of family controlled enterprises and their impact on regulatory and policy-making bodies. If nothing else, the study reported in this paper confirms that examination of the idiosyncratic governance features of family-owned firms deserves greater attention from corporate governance academicians and professionals.

References

Ahmad, F. (1977) *The Turkish Experiment in Democracy: 1950–1975,* Westview Press, Boulder, CO.

Anderson, R.C. and Reeb, D.M. (2003) Founding-Family Ownership and Firm Performance: Evidence from the S&P 500. *Journal of Finance,* 58, 1301–28.

Andert, D.M. (2005) Independent Directors, Knowledge Symmetry and All Powers. *Corporate Governance: International Journal for Enhancing Board Performance,* 5(2), 20–2.

Ararat, M. and Ugur, M. (2003) Corporate Governance in Turkey: An Overview and Some Policy Recommendations. *Corporate Governance,* 3(1), 58–75.

Arnold, D. J. and Quelch, J. A. (1998) New Strategies in Emerging Markets. *Sloan Management Review,* 40(1), 7–20.

Attig, N., Gadhoum, Y. and Lang L. (2003) Bid-Ask Spread, Asymmetric Information and Ultimate Ownership. Working Paper, University of Quebec, Montreal.

Baysan, T., Blitzer, C. (1991) Turkey. In Papageorgiou, D., Michaely, M., Choksi, A.M. (eds), *Liberalising Foreign Trade: The New Zealand, Spain and Turkey:* Vol. 6, A Research Project of the World Bank, Basil Blackwell, Cambridge, MA.

Baysinger, B. and Hoskisson, R.E. (1990) The Composition of Boards of Directors and Strategic Control: Effects of Corporate Strategy. *The Academy of Management Review,* 15(1), 72–87.

Boje, D. (1991) The Storytelling Organization: A Study of Story Performance in an Office-Supply Firm. *Administrative Science Quarterly,* 36(1), 106–26.

Bruner, J.S. (1990) *Acts of Meaning,* Harvard University Press, London.

Bugra, A. (1994) *State and Business in Modern Turkey: A Comparative Study* (SUNY Series in the Social and Economic History of the Middle East), State University of New York Press, New York.

Buğra, A. (1998) Class, Culture, and State: An Analysis of Interest Representation by Two Turkish Business Associations *International Journal of Middle East Studies,* 30, 521–39.

Burkat, M., Panunzi, F. and Shleifer, A. (2003) Family Firm. *Journal of Finance,* 58, 2167–210.

Cadbury, A. (1992) *Report of the Committee on the Financial Aspects of Corporate Governance,* Gee Publishing, London.

Cascio, W.F. (2004) Board Governance: A Social Systems Perspective. *The Academy of Management Executive,* 18(1), 97–100.

CCPG (Corporate Governance Principles Guide) (2005) *Capital Markets Board (CMB),* Istanbul.

Charkham, J.P. (1995) *Keeping Good Company: A Study of Corporate Governance in Five Countries,* Oxford Paperbacks, Oxford.

Chatterjee, S. and Harrison, J.S. (2001) Corporate Governance. In Hitt, M.A., Freeman, R.E. and Harrison, J.S. (eds), *The Blackwell Handbook of Strategic Management,* Blackwell, Oxford, pp, 543–63.

Claessens, S., Djankov, S. and Lang, L. (2000) The Separation of Ownership and Control in East Asian Corporation. *Journal of Financial Economics,* 58, 81–112.

Cohan, J.A. (2002) "I Didn't Know" and "I Was Only Doing My Job": Has Corporate Governance Careened Out of Control? A Case Study of Enron's Information Myopia. *Journal of Business Ethics,* 40(3), 275–99.

Collins, J. and Porras, J. (1998) *Built to Last: Successful Habits of Visionary Companies,* Random House Business Books, London.

Coombes, P. and Wong, C.-Y. (2004) Chairman and CEO: One Job or Two? *The McKinsey Quarterly: A new era in Governance,* 2, 43–7.

Daily, C.M. and Thompson, S.S. (1994) Ownership Structure, Strategic Posture, and Firm Growth: An Empirical Examination. *Family Business Review,* 7, 237–49.

Dalton, D.R., Daily, C.M., Ellstrand, A.E. and Johnson, J.L. (1998) Meta-analytic Reviews of Board Composition, Leadership Structure, and Financial Performance. *Strategic Management Journal,* 19(3), 269–90.

De Geus, A. (2002) *The Living Company: Habits for Survival in a Turbulent Business Environment,* Harvard Business School Press, Boston, MA.

Demb, A. and Neubauer, F.F. (1992) The Corporate Board: Confronting the Paradoxes. *Long Range Planning,* 25(3), 9–20.

ECGI (European corporate governance institute) (2003) Corporate Governance Codes and Principles in Turkey. http://www.ecgi.org/codes/code.php?code_id=117 (accessed: 20.10.05).

Eisenhardt, K.M. (1989) Agency Theory: An Assessment and Review. *The Academy of Management Review,* 14(1), 57–74.

Elloumi, F. and Gueyie, J.P. (2001) Financial Distress and Corporate Governance: An Empirical Analysis, *Corporate Governance: International Journal of Business in Society,* 1(1), 15–23.

Ertürk, İ. (2003), Governance or Financialization: The Turkish Case, *Competition & Change*, 7(4), 185–204.

Faccio, M. and Lang, L.H.P. (2002) The Ultimate Ownership of Western European Corporations. *Journal of Financial Economics*, 65(4), 365–96.

Fama, E.F. and Jensen, M.C. (1983) Separation of Ownership and Control. *Journal of Law and Economics*, 26(2), 301–25.

Feldman, M.S. (2004) Resources in Emerging Structures and Processes of Change. *Organization Science*, 15(3), 295–309.

Forbes, D.P. and Milliken, F.J. (1999) Cognition and Corporate Governance: Understanding Boards of Directors as Strategic Decision-Making Groups. *The Academy of Management Review*, 24(3), 489–505.

Franks, J., Mayer, C. and Rossi, I. (2003) The Organisation and Evolution of Ownership and Control. Financial Working Paper, 12/2003, ECGI.

Franks, J.R. and Mayer, C. (1994) Corporate Control: A Synthesis of the International Evidence. IFA Working Paper, 165–92.

Gergen, M.M. and Gergen, K.J. (2003) Qualitative Inquiry: Tensions and Transformations. In Denzin, N.K. and Lincoln, Y.S. (eds), *The Landscape of Qualitative Research: Theories and Issues* (2nd Edition). Sage, London, pp. 575–610.

Glaser, B.G. and Strauss, A.L. (1965) *Awareness of Dying*, Aldine Transaction, USA.

Gunduz, L. and Tatoglu, E. (2003) A Comparison of the Financial Characteristics of Group Affiliated and Independent Firms in Turkey. *European Business Review*, 15(1), 48–54.

Harvey, J.B., Kanter, R.M. and Carlisle, A.E. (1998) The Abilene Paradox: The Management of Agreement. *Organizational Dynamics*, 17(1), 16–43.

Heenan, D. and Bennis, W. (1999) *Co-Leaders: Who Wields the Real Power in Organizations Today?* Wiley, New York.

Heracleous, L. (1999) Boards of Directors as Leaders of the Organization. *Corporate Governance: An International Review*, 7(3), 256–65.

Higgs, D. (2003) *Review of the Role and Effectiveness of Non-executive Directors*, The Department of Trade and Industry, London.

IIF Equity Advisory Group (2005) Corporate Governance in Turkey: An Investor Perspective – Task Force Report. http://www.iif.com/data/public/ IIFCorpGovTurkey_0405.pdf (accessed: 23.03.06).

Inselbag, I. and Gultekin, B. (1988), Financial Markets in Turkey. In Nas, T. and M. Odekon (eds), *Liberalization and the Turkish Economy*, Greenwood Press, Westport, CT, pp. 63–84.

Janis, I.L. (1971) Groupthink. *Psychology Today*, 5(6), 43–6, 74–6.

Jensen, M.C. and Meckling, W.H. (1976) Theory of the Firm: Managerial Behavior, Agency Costs, and Ownership Structure. *Journal of Financial Economics*, 3, 305–60.

Kabasakal, H. and Bodur, M. (2002) Arabic Cluster: A Bridge between East and West. *Journal of World Business*, 37(1), 40.

Kahl, J. (1957) *The American Class Structure*, Rinehart, New York.

Kakabadse, A. (1991) *The Wealth Creators: Top People, Top Teams and Executive Best Practice*, Kogan Page, London.

Kakabadse, A. and Kakabadse, N. (2001) *The Geopolitics of Governance: The Impact of Contrasting Philosophies*, Palgrave, Hampshire.

Kakabadse, A., Kakabadse, N.K. and Barratt, R. (2006) Chairman and Chief Executive Officer (CEO): That Sacred and Secret Relationship. *Journal of Management Development*, 25(2), 134–50.

Kakabadse, A., Ward, K., Korac-Kakabadse, N. and Bowman, C. (2001) Role and Contribution of Non-executive Directors. *Corporate Governance: International Journal of Business in Society*, 1(1), 4–8.

Kakabadse, N. and Kakabadse, A. (2007) Chairman of the Board: Demographics Effects on Role Pursuit, *The Journal of Management Development*, 26(2), 169–92.

Karademir, B., Ozgen, H., Osborn, R., Yaprak, A. (2005), *The Co-evolution of Institutional Environments, Markets, Organizational Capabilities, and Organizational Strategies: A Comparative Case Study of Turkish Family Holdings*, 21st Colloquium of European Group for Organizational Studies, Berlin.

Karpoff, J.M. (2001) The Impact of Shareholder Activism on Target Companies: A Survey of Empirical Findings. Presentation at the Norwegian School of Management.

Katz, D. (1959) Consistent Reactive Participation of Group Members and Reduction of Intergroup Conflict. *Journal of Conflict Resolution*, 3, 28–40.

Katz, D. and Kahn, R.L. (1966) *The Social Psychology of Organizations*, Wiley, New York.

Keyder, C. (1987), The Political Economy of Turkish Democracy. In R. Benatar, I. C. Schick and R. Margulies (eds), *Turkey in transition: New Perspectives*, Oxford University Press, Oxford, pp. 27–65.

Khanna, T., and Palepu, K. (2000), The Future of Business in Emerging Markets: Long-Run Evidence from Chile. *Academy of Management Journal* 43: 268–85.

Khurana, R. (2002) *Searching for a Corporate Savior: The Irrational Quest for Charismatic CEOs*, Princeton University Press, Princeton, NJ.

Krackhardt, D. and Stern, R. (1988) Informal Networks and Organizational Crises: An Experimental Simulation. *Social Psychology Quarterly*, 51, 123–40.

Kula, V. (2005) The Impact of the Roles, Structure and Process of Boards on Firm Performance: evidence from Turkey. *Corporate Governance*, 13(2), 265.

La Porta, R., Lopez-de-Silanes, F. and Shleifer, A. (1999) Corporate ownership around the world, *Journal of Finance*, 54, 471–517.

Lieblich, A., Tuval-Mashiach, R. and Zilber, T. (1998) *Narrative Research: Reading, Analysis and Interpretation*, Applied Social Research Methods Series, Volume 47, Sage, USA.

Lorsch, J.W. and MacIver, E. (1989). *Pawns or Potentates: The Reality of America's Corporate Boards*, Harvard Business School Press, Boston, MA.

Merton, R.K. (1957) *Social Theory and Social Structure* (Revised Edition), Free Press, USA.

Miller, D.T., Monin, B. and Prentice, D.A. (2000) Pluralistic Ignorance and Inconsistency between Private Attitudes and Public Behaviors. In Terry, D.J. and Hogg, M.A. (eds), *Attitudes, Behavior and Social Context: The Role of Norms and Group Membership*, Lawrence Erlbaum Associates, NJ, pp. 95–114.

Monks, R.A.G. and Minow, N. (2003) *Corporate Governance* (3rd Edition), Blackwell, Oxford.

Morris, M.H., Williams, R.W. and Nel, D. (1996) Factors Influencing Family Business Succession. *International Journal of Entrepreneurial Behaviour & Research*, 2(3), 68.

Nadler, D.A., Behan, B.A. and Nadler, M.B. (2006) *Building Better Boards: A Blueprint for Effective Governance*, Jossey-Bass, San Francisco, CA.

Nas, T.F. and Odekon, M. (eds) (1996) *Liberalization and the Turkish Economy*, Greenwood Press, New York.

Ng, W. and de Cock, C. (2002) Battle in the Boardroom: A Discursive Perspective. *The Journal of Management Studies*, 39(1), 23.

Ochberg, R.L. (1994) Life Stories and Storied Lives. In Lieblich, A. and Josselson, R. (eds), *Exploring Identity and Gender: The Narrative Study of Lives*, Sage, USA, pp. 113–44.

OECD (Organisation for Economic Co-operation and Development) (2002) *OECD Reviews of Regulatory Reform Turkey: Crucial Support for Economic Recovery – Performance and appraisal*, OECD, France.

Önder, Z. (2003) Ownership Concentration and Firm Performance: Evidence from Turkish Firms, *METU Studies in Development*, 30, 181–203.

Ongoren Law Office (2005) The Measures Protecting the Rights of Minority of Shareholders in Joint Stock Companies. http://www.ongoren.av.tr/news/en/05-11. php (accessed: 20.12.05).

Pass, C. (2004) Corporate Governance and the Role of Non-executive Directors in Large UK Companies: an Empirical Study. *Corporate Governance*, 4(2), 52–63.

Pentland, B.T. (1999) Building Process Theory with Narrative: From Description to Explanation. *The Academy of Management Review*, 24(4), 711–24.

Perman, S. (2006) Taking the Pulse of Family Business, *Business Week*, 12 February 2007, http://www.businessweek.com/print/smallbiz/content/feb2006/sb20060 (accessed: 10.07.2007).

Pettigrew, A. and McNulty, T. (1998) Sources and Uses of Power in the Boardroom. *European Journal of Work and Organizational Psychology*, 7(2), 197–214.

Proctor, G. and Miles, L. (2002) *Corporate Governance*, Cavendish Publishing, London.

Pye, A. (2002) The Changing Power of 'Explanations': Directors, Academics and Their Sensemaking from 1989 to 2000. *Journal of Management Studies*, 39, 907–25.

Riessman, C.K. (1993) *Narrative Analysis*, Sage, USA.

Roberts, J. (2002) Building the Complementary Board: The Work of the PLC Chairman. *Long Range Planning*, 35(5), 493.

Robinson, R.D. (1963), *The First Turkish Republic: A Case Study in National Development*, Harvard University Press, MA, USA.

Schaffer, B.S. (2002) Board Assessments of Managerial Performance: An Analysis of Attribution Processes. *Journal of Managerial Psychology*, 17(1/2), 95–115.

Shleifer, A. and Vishny, R. (1997) A Survey of Corporate Governance. *Journal of Finance,* 52, 737–83.

Stapledon, G. (1996) *Institutional Shareholders and Corporate Governance*, Clarendon Press, Oxford.

Suls, J. and Green, P. (2003) Pluralistic Ignorance and College Student Perceptions of Gender-Specific Alcohol Norms. *Health Psychology*, 22(5), 479–86.

The Wilshire Index (2004) Wilshire 5000 Index. http://www.fool.com/school/indices/wilshire5000.htm (accessed: 20.02.2004).

TOBB (The Union of Chambers and Commodity Exchanges of Turkey) (2004) Industrial Database. http://www.tobb.org.tr (accessed: 20.10.2004).

Van der Elst, C. (1999) De remuneratie van de raad van bestuur van de Bel-20 vennootschappen. Working Paper No 1999-11, Ghent University, Ghent.

Van der Elst, C. (2000) The Equity Markets, Ownership Structures and Control: towards an International Harmonisation? Working Paper No 2000-04, Financial Law Institute, Ghent University, Ghent.

van Hamel, J.A., van Wijk, H.E., de Rooij, A.J.H. and Bruel, M. (1998) Boardroom Dynamics – Lessons in Governance (Part 2). *Corporate Governance: An International Review*, 6(4), 284–88.

Van Hulle, C. (1998) Is het systeem van Corporate Governance belangrijk? Op zoek naar de impact van verschillen in modellen. *Referaat voor het Drieëntwintigste Vlaams Wetenschappelijk Economisch Congres*, Leuven.

Vincke, F. (1997) The Corporate Governance Debate in Belgium. In Hopt, K.J. and Wymeersch, E. (eds), *Comparative Corporate Governance: Essays and Materials*, Walter de Gruyter, Berlin, pp. 119–49.

Weir, C. and Laing, D. (2000) The Performance–Governance Relationship: The Effects of Cadbury Compliance on UK Quoted Companies. *Journal of Management & Governance*, 4(4), 265–81.

Weir, C. and Laing, D. (2001) Governance Structures, Director Independence and Corporate Performance in the UK. *European Business Review*, 13(2), 86–94.

Westphal, J.D. and Bednar, M.K. (2005) Pluralistic Ignorance in Corporate Boards and Firms' Strategic Persistence in Response to Low Firm Performance. *Administrative Science Quarterly*, 50(2), 262.

Westphal, J.D. and Khanna, P. (2003) Keeping Directors in Line: Social Distancing as a Control Mechanism in the Corporate Elite. *Administrative Science Quarterly*, 48, 361–98.

Wong, S. (2004) US Sets Global Trends behind Governance Shake-Up. *McKinsey & Company, a special IFLR supplement.* http://www.mckinsey.com/clientservice/organizationleadership/service/corpgovernance/pdf/Wong-US_sets_global_trends_behind_governance_shake-up_(IFLR)(Sept_2004).pdf (accessed: 20.01.2006).

World Federation of Exchanges (2004) Annual Report and Statistics 2004. http://www.fibv.com/publications/WFE%202004%20Annual%20Report%20and%20Statistics.pdf (accessed: 20.03.06).

Yeh, Y.H. and J.Y. Shu (2001) The Year-End Anomaly of Taiwan Family Control Groupings. *Review of Pacific Basin Financial Markets and Policies*, 4(1), 127–63.

Yurtoglu, B.B. (2000) Ownership, Control and Performance of Turkish Listed Firms. *Empirica*, 27(2), 193.

7
Boards of Steel: The Role and Contribution of the Non-executive Director (NED)

Nada Kakabadse, Oleg Tsvetkov, Vlad Uldatsov and Andrew Kakabadse

Introduction

Corporate governance is considered to be a pivotal subject in terms of organizational effectiveness and sustainability. In fact, the debate over the nature of the improvement of governance systems continues. The traditional focus on the separation of control from ownership is seen as key to determining the company's strategic development – in effect to steward how power is exercised (Berle and Means, 1932). From there on in, it took nearly 40 years of scholarly study (Mace, 1971) to ascertain 'what Directors really do?' With certain basics in place, the focus now is on relationships and interactions amongst the different actors of the firm, board of directors, senior managers, shareholders and other corporate stakeholders (Tricker, 1996; Cochran and Wartrick, 1988; Mace, 1971).

As well as identifying director tasks and activities, investigative scrutiny has also attracted negative comment concerning the role and contribution of boards and their directors. Van den Berghe and Levrau (2004) point to the passive and decorative nature of the board of directors. Drucker (1974) was equally scathing, drawing on terms such as 'ceremonial' and 'fiction' to describe the ineffective nature of boards. Lorsch and MacIver (1989) investigation of American boards found that too many boards of directors are too centred on their CEO, thus inhibiting independent, challenging comment from being made.

On the positive side, corporate boards are increasingly being viewed as essential and critical for the defence of shareholder funds (Romano, 1996). Cadbury (1999) considered boards of directors to be the bridge between shareholders and the management. Daily et al. (2003b) viewed the board as being central to the effective governance of the enterprise. Along this line, Adams and Ferreira (2007) confirmed the board as, "the legal authority overseeing the decision-making process in the firm." Brennan (2006) went further and placed boards as a line of defence against management, whilst Murphy (2006) of PricewaterhouseCoopers asserted that it is "fundamental" for companies to be led by an effective board of directors which is "collectively responsible for the success of the company."

However, these assertions are based on experience of and inquiry into enterprises which exist in the mature markets of the Anglo American economies. The role of corporate boards and non-executives (i.e., external directors) is more ambiguous in emerging markets where more idiosyncratic models of corporate governance are practiced. Garratt (1999) encapsulated the diversities of capitalism as spanning from the "liberal" or "casino capitalism" of the USA, through to the "crony" capitalism pursued in some parts of Asia and Japan, to the "gangster capitalism" found in the former Russian states. Additionally "state" capitalism is dominating the growth of China. There is also a great diversity and variety of corporate governance, ranging from the Anglo-American "market-oriented" or "shareholder" model of corporate governance (Corbetta and Salvato, 2004), to the "network-oriented" model found in Japan and Latin countries such as Italy and France (Weimer and Pape, 1999), to the "social partnership" or "stakeholder" model practiced in Germany (Corporate Governance, 2000).

To counter balance board experience within mature economies, this chapter explores the role and contribution of the non-executive directors (NEDs) of the boards of major Russian steel companies. A literature review of Russian corporate governance, focusing particularly on steel companies, is presented. This is followed by a study of the activities, roles and effect of Russian board directors. From there on, a discussion regarding the implications of the studies findings for Russian steel enterprises concludes this chapter.

Russian corporate governance: increasing usage of NEDs

The institutional upheaval of Russia after the collapse of the central planning system in 1991 punctuated a new era of a market-oriented economy imposed through "shock therapy" policies, on an unsuspecting population. What resulted was a serious financial crisis as per capita income fell by about 75 per cent. Vast sectors of the economy disappeared. Income inequality and unemployment grew dramatically. Hyperinflation wiped out many families' savings, thus leaving millions of Russians impoverished. What followed was a drop in the nation's population by more than 2 million, due largely to the steep decline in public health provision (Liveleak, 2007; Biography Online, 2007). Many state-owned enterprises were privatized, having to quickly adapt to market economy forces. Despite such disadvantages, large numbers of new viable operations emerged displaying varying degrees of success in terms of profitability and survival.

Only towards the end of the 1990s, after the Russian financial crises, did Russian and international financial organizations and intermediaries realize that suspect business behaviour on its own could not account for the economic collapse that had occurred. In fact, many of the problems had been caused by weak regulatory institutions. It became clear that inadequate corporate governance was considerably responsible for the financial loss, a realization that hit those international banks involved in lending to the Russian oil and gas sectors, which later spilled over into other sectors (Troschke, 1999, pp. 147–8, 155). In 2000, the State regained order and control, and set the economy on the road to recovery. Macroeconomic stability, rising oil prices and the revival of private initiative allowed the country, which almost went bankrupt at the end of last century, to now boast a $1.3 trillion economy, foreign-currency reserves of nearly $480 billion and a $144 billion stabilization fund for surplus oil and gas revenues, making Russia the sixth biggest market in Europe (*The Economist*, 2008). Russian annual growth of real income has been in double digits, whilst its GDP per head has risen from less then $2000 in 1998 to $9000 in 2008, at current rates of exchange (*The Economist*, 2008).

Russia's two "durable" key advantages, an educated work force and mineral resources, have provided the means with which to realize significant longer-term growth, so much so that by 2007, Russia experienced a boom in capital investment leading to record achievement (*Kommersant*, 2007). Although the state through law, regulation and formal policy has played a significant role in improving how corporations are governed in Russia, enterprises themselves are also paying increased attention to corporate governance issues and particularly to how a board of directors should exercise the authority to supervise the management of the business and the affairs of the corporation.

Of concern is how each director and executive officer is exercising their powers and discharging their duties. Do they act honestly, in good faith and in the best interests of the company? Is the director's "fiduciary duty" exercised with the due care, diligence and skill that any reasonably prudent person would similarly exercise in comparable circumstances?

Whether as a result of regulation, or shareholder guideline, a broad variety of areas are now scrutinized by the board, such as board structure and composition, director qualification and remuneration, and risk and compensation. These checks ensure that boards of directors adequately oversee the management of the organization and act in the best interests of the company and all of its shareholders. Further, the use of independent directors in Russia has been growing at a rate of 25–30 per cent per annum since 2003, reflecting the urge to make firms more transparent and to improve their performance and quality of strategic vision (Dagayeva, 2006). According to Standard & Poor (2008), Russian corporate governance has made substantial improvement in transparency concerning ownership mostly in connection with IPOs, with 80 per cent of the Russian twenty majors being listed in London and New York, and with most having foreign independent directors on their boards. Foreign independent directors hold 18 per cent of Russia Board positions and constitute a majority of 57 per cent of independent directors (Standard and Poor, 2008).

However, Russian steel industry corporate governance differs from Western practice in terms of board structure and composition exemplified by their NED ratio, their "independence" and their selection process which are mostly determined by the will and interest of a single shareholder. A single shareholder, in contrast to counterparts in Western companies, has fewer conflicts of interests and does not need the board to protect him (or her) from opportunistic top managers (Harrison, 2002). Neither does the single shareholder need to be further empowered by the board as the individual already has the greatest authority with which to determine the direction the business should take. If a major concern of corporate structure is rooted in the "separation of diffuse capital providers (shareholders) and capital users (management)" and if the boards' role is to help reduce associated costs (Brennan, 2006), then it follows that in closely held structures (i.e. single shareholder) such a disadvantage is *a priori* eliminated, and therefore, there are neither "associated costs" nor the need for "cost-reducers."

The search consultants, Heidrick and Struggles (2007), referring to Standard and Poor's (2006) study of independent directors on boards of Russian companies with an international listing, note that most NEDs fall into one of the following categories (in descending order of frequency):

- active executive of a major company, unrelated to the issuer;
- former executive of the issuer's industry;
- financer or auditor;
- academic or scientist;
- former civil servant.

Analysis of the personal data (Dagayeva, 2006), of 166 independent directors from 90 public and private companies in Russia, describes an "average" NED as having an annual salary of $125 thousand, 95 per cent of whom are male, 40 per cent of cases are foreign, and who officially do not

1. represent either shareholders or top management;
2. own any shareholding in the company;
3. have any joint (or shared) business with the company and
4. serve as a consultant.

The Russian National Association of Non-Executive Directors (2006) found that over 40 per cent of the "average" NEDs in Russia are experienced in finance and/or economy; that 33 per cent are professional managers; 20 per cent are industrialists and 6 per cent academics and politicians. The other characteristics of an "average" NED on Russian Boards include:

(1)   he (she) is often recruited through personal ties, but if a firm plans to "go global" or to list it shares abroad, a head-hunting agency is hired;

(2)   59 per cent of NEDs are 50–60 years old; 24 per cent are in their 40–50s; 16 per cent are aged 30–40 and only 1 per cent is younger than 30 years old.

Those major Russian companies with the "go global" urge are singling out NEDs with experience in industry consolidation, vertical integration and geographic expansion (Heidrick and Struggles, 2007). Thus the prevailing view is that strategy in Russian companies is directly related to participating in consolidation processes in keeping with those sweeping over the global steel industry. However, some corporate governance scholars (Kakabadse and Kakabadse, 2007, 2008; Kakabadse et al., 2006) argue that at the heart of good corporate governance is not board structure, which receives considerable attention in terms of regulation, but instead board process and especially consideration of how board members competencies enable working together as a group. This latter area of board and director dynamics is deemed to have received inadequate attention.

Corporate governance of Russian steel companies

The Russian steel industry, currently ranked fourth in world's steel league tables and which contributes approximately 7 per cent to the global steel output, is highly consolidated. It consists of only four major groups that form over 70 per cent of national steel output (*Metal Bulletin Weekly*, 2006). One of the most distinguishing features of the Russian steel sector is its totally private ownership where the "control of the [Russian steel industry] lies with a handful of independently minded entrepreneurs" (*Metal Bulletin Weekly*, 2006, p. 3). Moreover, major Russian steel entrepreneurs usually assume strategic and even operational management responsibilities over their steel businesses, happily combining the functions of controlling ownership and top management ("owner-managers") in their companies (Harrison, 2002).

Since the last market downturn cycle in 2001, Russian steel companies and their competitors worldwide have been enjoying 7 years of market boom and favourable pricing due the skyrocketing demand for steel. During this period of prosperity, Russian steel owner-managers have embarked on a drive for the recruitment of experienced and capable NEDs on to their boards. Whilst the dominant theoretical assumption holds that NEDs are normally called upon to join corporate Boards when the organization is struggling for survival or are trying to overcome a "performance crisis" (Pettigrew, 2002), Russian steel companies are countering this experience. Almost all major Russian steel companies entered Western stock exchanges by listing small percentages (8–12 per cent) of their shares, recruiting NEDs to their boards and adopting Western standards of corporate governance, whilst at the same time retaining their "oligarch" run business nature. One man is in charge of everything!

The phenomena of all major Russian steel-making companies becoming owned and controlled by individual "owner-managers" (holding 80 per cent of shares in some companies) emerged as a result of mass privatization in Russia in the early 1990s (Jenkins, 2002). These owner-managers usually took the position of chief executive officer (CEO), president or chairman of their group. Such corporate governance is often referred to as "autocracy," or "authoritarianism," because decisions are made by the undivided authority of the owning top manager (Bradford and Bernstain, 2006). In the Russian post-socialist period, there have been only two known cases where owner-managers of steel businesses have voluntarily acceded their ownership and control:

- In February 2006, Vladimir Iorich, CEO and equal partner-owner of the Mechel Steel Group, passed over his shareholding to the Board's Chairman Igor Zyuzin, who then consolidated the positions of CEO and board Chairman (Vinkov and Sivakov, 2006).
- In mid-2006 Alexander Abramov, the president of the Evraz Steel Group suddenly retired from his position, sold his shares and resigned from the position of Chairman.

However, the closed control model of corporate governance in the Russian steel business has its reverse side which affects strategic vision and decision making. Oleynik (2007) points to the "conditional" and non-absolute nature of "ownership" in Russia, especially in the raw materials sector. Oleynik (2007) views this conditionality as being political in character, one that depends upon the level of political relationship between the businessman and government institutions (local or federal level), and as such leads to contextual instability. Oleynik (2007, p. 4) hypothesizes that owners of big businesses in Russia can "hardly be too confident of the future" and that this uncertainty has multiple negative effects on long-term investment and strategy.

Oleynik's (2007, p. 4) argument that the "conditional nature of ownership usually calls forth risky choices concerning short-term business moves – just to make maximum profits in the shortest possible time" may prejudice the mere possibility of developing a long-term strategy in the Russian steel industry. If Oleynik (2007, p. 4) is correct, then how will boards, composed of independent foreign directors, be able to play one of their "taken-for-granted" roles, that of being strategists?

Moreover the study of "family-owned" and closely held corporate governance models, where "single, competent and all-powerful entrepreneurs" rule, suggests that there is a need for the "increasingly large and active external boards of directors" (Corbetta and Salvato, 2004, p. 120). According to Corbetta and Salvato (2004), there are several reasons for the growing importance of the board's role in closely held firms, namely the need to be more transparent through exposure to public listing, internationalization and changes in the relationship between banks and companies. Drawing on contingency theory, where the firm's performance is the result of the proper alignment of its "endogenous variables" with its "exogenous context," Corbetta and Salvato (2004) powerfully emphasize the importance of the functions of the Board.

Bartholomeusz and Tanewski (2006) studied 100 listed, family controlled and non-family controlled companies and found their corporate governance structures to be substantially different. In particular, family-controlled firms may have a lower proportion of "disinterested or independent" directors on their boards, than do the non-family firms, thus maintaining a tighter control "with little opportunity for external discipline." The study carried out by Credit Suisse of 172 family-owned companies where a family or individual owns not less than 10 per cent, found that families are more effective in running the company than (truly) publicly owned corporations with atomized shareholding (Overchenko and Grozovsky, 2007). The in-built advantage of family companies includes a longer strategic perspective, a focus on core business and a powerful entrepreneurial drive peculiar to the business owners (Overchenko and Grozovsky, 2007). It is an interesting observation that the most successful and long-term strategically oriented steel groups are family owned, having their origins in the BRIC (Brazil, Russia, India and China) countries (Wilson and Roopa, 2003). Research into corporate ownership in 49 countries suggests that

> in the world as a whole, the average ownership of the three largest shareholders is 46 percent and the median 45 percent. Dispersed ownership in large public companies is simply a myth. Even in the United States, the average for the 10 most valuable companies is 20 percent (which is partly explained by the fact that Microsoft, Walmart, Coca-Cola and Intel are on the list, and all have significant ownership concentration), and the median is 12 percent. Presumably, if we looked at smaller companies, the numbers we would get for ownership concentration would be even larger. The finance textbook model of management faced by multitudes of dispersed shareholders is an exception and not the rule. (La Porta et al., 1998, p. 1146)

Certain researchers have come to conclude that an organization is considered to be a "family firm" if more than 50 per cent of ordinary voting shares are owned by members of the largest single family group related by blood or marriage (Cromie et al., 1995; Westhead et al., 2001); or the company is perceived as family by its Chief Executive/Managing Director or Chairman (Westhead et al., 2001); or managers are members of a single dominant family group (Daily et al., 2003a). The board of non-executive directors' role in such a firm is to link the firm with its external groups such as customers, suppliers, bankers, and to secure "critical resource, including prestige and legitimacy" (Westhead et al., 2001, p. 372).

The study

On the basis of increasing understanding of the role and contribution of the NEDs in closely held Russian steel companies, the aim of this study is to explore how NEDs as independent outsiders can contribute to the improvement of enterprise performance especially in the domain of strategic decision making in owner-manager corporations. The study was conducted during July–August 2007. The study drew on documentary evidence (Finnegan, 1998) and semi-structured interviews (Barnes, 2001). Documentary evidence included annual company reports, industry reports, and press and media reports. Four steel companies were selected for scrutiny based on their media exposure and reputation within the Russian steel industry. The interview sample consisted of twelve non-executive and executive board directors from the four selected steel companies. Through open-ended questions and semi-structured interviews, the role of independent directors was explored. The available documentary evidence was qualitatively analysed in order to provide background to each selected case drawing on analytical induction (Blaikie, 2000) in order to make sense of primary data.

Background of the four Russian steel companies: Evraz, NLMK, MMK and Severstal

By 2006, the Russian steel industry had become highly consolidated with four major groups, Evraz, Novolipetsk (NLMK), Magnitogorsk (MMK) and Severstal, jointly producing 70 per cent of the national steel output of over 70 million tones (Table 7.1).

Russian steel companies also gained recognition through international league tables. Table 7.2, compiled by Saghdiev and Kudashkina (2007), lists the world's Top-200 most respected companies as reported by the American Reputation Institute (*RepTrak Pulse 200*). Saghdiev and Kudashkina (2007) analysed and ranked some of the 600 largest companies in terms of revenue by assessing each company's evaluation along several indices. Depending upon their scoring, the companies were then ranked as having an "excellent" (>80), "strong" (70–79), "medium" (60–69), "weak" (40–59) or "bad"

Table 7.1   Russian steel

Indicators	Evraz	NLMK	MMK	Severstal
Raw steel output, per million, 2006	15.2	9.13	12.5	11.1
Output 2005–2006 y-o-y change, %	(+) 10	(+) 8	(+) 9	(+) 5
Net profit, $ billion	1.39	2,07	1.43	1.18
Net profit 2005–2006 y-o-y change, %	(+) 51	(+) 50	(+) 51	(−) 30
Revenue $ billion	8.29	6.04	6.42	12.42
Revenue 2005–2006 y-o-y change, %	(+) 27	(+) 38	(+) 19	(+) 7
Ebitda profit, $ billion	2.65	2.63	2.01	2.99
Ebitda 2005–2006 y-o-y change, %	(+) 43	(+) 26	(+) 33	(−) 2

Source: Compiled by the authors from companies' 2005–06 reports.

Table 7.2   Reputation ranking of Russian major steelmakers by American Reputation Institute

Indicators	Evraz	NLMK	MMK	Severstal
Rank in 2006	Not included	279	87	192
Rank in 2007		174	14	63
RepTrak Pulse (scores)		69.82	81.17	75.81
Reputation		Medium	Excellent	Strong

Source: Compiled by Saghdiev and Kudashkina (2007).

(<40) score in terms of reputation. The 2007 reputation champion was Danish Lego with a score of 85.01.

Three out of four Russian companies were included in the Top-200 most respected companies as reported by the American Reputation Institute. However, the Evraz group, although one of Russia's most active and dynamic steel groups, was not included in the American Reputation Institute ranking list.

Further, all four enterprises have been listed on the London Stock Exchange (LSE) (Table 7.3). Among the major steel players in Russia, only the Mechel Steel Group, not covered by this research, has made its IPO in New York.

Table 7.3 Listing of Russian steelmakers at LSE

Indicators	Evraz	NLMK	MMK	Severstal
Year of listing	2005–2006	2005–2006	2007	2006
Flotation, % of shares	13.3	7	10	9
IPO price, $ billion	0.762	0.609	~ 1.0	1.1
Firm capitalization, $ billion	5.7	8.7	11.2	12.2

Source: Compiled by the authors from companies' 2005–06 reports.

According to primary and secondary data, Russian steel companies hold a preference for being listed on the London Stock Exchange (LSE) rather than in New York (NYSE), due to the LSE's regulatory flexibility. All study participants point to the LSE being more adaptable and less cumbersome, and as such more close to the Russian model of practice. For example, although both institutions require a listed company (or an issuer) to have independent directors at the LSE, NEDs must constitute not less than half of the total number of Board members excluding the Chairman (LSE's Combine Code on Corporate Governance, 2003). In contrast, the NYSE regulation is for the "majority" of the Board to be composed of NEDs (The NYSE Listed Company Manual). The LSE practices a "comply or explain" principle and provides exception for the NED/Executive ratio for closely controlled enterprises (i.e. those where one shareholder owns more than 50 per cent) as in the case of all four Russian steel companies in this study.

In the major Russian steel companies, the functions of ownership and top management are usually combined, with the owner realizing the roles of either CEO or Chairman. The structure of the ownership and Board configuration of the four enterprises are presented in Table 7.4.

All four companies have a different board composition in terms of the proportion of NEDs and separation or duality of the chairman/CEO roles. However, the obvious similarities are the enterprises' highly consolidated ownership and owner's position as a top-manager in whatever formal post. The exception is Evraz.

Recruitment of NEDs according to their professional background and experience varies amongst the companies in this study (Table 7.5). Two companies, Evraz and NLMK, each have two NEDs with expertise and knowledge of the steel industry on their boards. Both Evraz and NLMK also have the lowest ratio of interlocking directorships among their independent Board members, which theoretically may provide them with more time for attending to strategy issues. Whether or not part-time directors with limited expertise in steel industry-related issues and oversaturated time-schedules

Table 7.4 Ownership and board structure of major Russian steelmakers

Indicators	Evraz*	NLMK	MMK	Severstal
% Owner of shares	R. Abramovich 41%	V. Lisin 82%	V. Rashnikov 80%	A. Mordashov 83%
CEO or President	A. Frolov (salaried CEO)	A. Lapshin (salaried president)	V. Rashnikov (owner president)	A. Mordashov (owner CEO)
Board size	9	8	10	10
NEDs	3	3	4	5
Foreign NEDs	3	2	2	5
Board Chairman	Salaried CEO	Company owner	Company owner	NED

Note: *In early January 2006, Alexander Abramov (until then Evraz's majority owner, CEO and president) suddenly retired from his presidency (leaving it to Valery Khoroshkovsky), and on May 1 left Evraz chair to Alexander Frolov. In August 2006 Abramov and Frolov sold their 41 per cent stake in Evraz for $3 billion to Millhouse Capital, an investment company owned by London-based billionaire and the Chelsea FC owner Roman Abramovich.

Source: Compiled by the authors from companies' 2005–06 reports.

Table 7.5 NEDs' professional background

Board membership features	Evraz	NLMK	MMK	Severstal
Professional background				
• current related (steel or mining) executive	1	–	–	–
• formerly related (steel or mining) executive	1	2	–	–
• currently unrelated (non-steel) executive	1	–	1	3
• financer/auditor/lawyer	–	1	2	1
• academic/scientist/consultant	–	–	–	1
• former civil servant	–	–	1	–
Interlocking directorship*	2	4	8	30

Note: *Indices of interlocking Directorship are simple sums of all positions/involvements which the NEDs have beside their steel boards.

Source: Compiled by the authors using Heidrick and Struggles' (2007) recruitment criteria.

from interlocking directorships can be effectively involved in determining strategy is debatable. The academic literature provides mixed evidence, while certain consultancies (Heidrick and Struggles, 2007) emphasize the boards' strategic role and hence the necessity for the NEDs to devote the necessary time to attending to board affairs.

Although the literature emphasizes the special role of the NED in making a "valuable contribution to determining corporate strategy," through providing "guidance to achieving strategic goals" and the allocating of "corporate resources to support strategic plans" (Murphy, 2006), NED contribution to strategy is structurally emphasized through their participation on Board committees. In our sample, the structural role of the "watchers and keepers" is mostly emphasized on the Evraz, MMK and Severstal Boards, where the NEDs chair both the remuneration and audit committees (Table 7.6). Structurally, Evraz's Board provides the forum for NEDs to formally have maximum involvement in determining strategy on the Board's strategic committee.

Severstal formed a strategy sub-committee in 2008, and has co-opted two of its senior executives (Gregory Mason and Vadim Makhov) on to that forum. That does not mean that the NEDs are not involved in the strategy determination process. It is just that the dominant strategic role is played by its owner and top executives with the free and active involvement of the NEDs, although their roles are not so structurally emphasized.

A particular challenge for steel companies is that of increasing profitability and also cost effectiveness through consolidation. The companies in our study seemingly draw on the experience of their NEDs to varying degrees in terms of contribution to the steel consolidation process (Table 7.7).

In the case of Evraz and NLMK, it is postulated that a relationship exists between the NED's "strategic" impact and the enterprises activity in global consolidation. However, that relationship does not hold with MMK, which has no NED strategists on its board, but which still demonstrates active strategic behaviour in terms of its global expansion. Severstal, on the other hand, has a history of consolidation investment and acquired capacity and draws extensively on the experience of its NEDs.

Table 7.6   Formal roles of NEDs on boards of Russian steelmakers

Committees	Evraz	NLMK	MMK	Severstal
Strategy	Chair (NED)	NED	Company owner	two executives
Remuneration	Chair (NED)	NED	Chair (NED) + 1 NED	Chair (NED) + 1 NED
Audit	Chair (NED)	NED	Chair (NED) + 1 NED	Chair (NED) + 2 NEDs
Investments	Not available	Not available	Executive VP	Not available
No of NEDs involvement	3	3	4	5

Source: Compiled by the authors from companies' 2005–06 reports.

Table 7.7 Strategic consolidation of Russian steel majors and their boards strategic membership

Strategic activity	Evraz (2007)	NLMK (2006–07)	MMK (2007)	Severstal[a] (2007)
Number of NED steel strategists on the Board	2	2	–	–
Major steel acquisitions of 2003–07, and planned further expansion activity	1. Vitcovice Steel (2005, Czechia) 2. Palinie Bertoli (2005, Italy) 3. Oregon Steel (2006, USA) 4. Highveld (2007, RSA)	1. DanSteel (2006, Denmark) 2. VIZ-Stal (2006, Russia) 3. JV with Duferco (2006, Switzerland) 4. Winner Steel (2007, USA)	Plans: 1. A 2.6 mtpy flats plant in Turkey. 2. A 1.5 mtpy flats plant in USA. 3. A 0.3 mtpy steel service centre in Russia	1. Rough Steel (2003, USA) 2. Lucchini (2005, Italy) 3. SeverCorr – a 1,6 mtpy greenfield flat minimill in the US
Total related investments, $b	~ 3.0	~ 1.9	(planned) 2.2	> 3.0
Steel capacity acquired, million t	> 3.2	~ 3.8	(planned) 4.2	~7

Note: [a]In 2008 Severstal made series of major acquisitions in the US, buying three additional steelworks with about 8 million tons capacity in total. The purchases have included: Sparrows Point in Maryland, WCI Steel of Ohio and Esmark which owns Wheeling-Pittsburgh Steel in West Virginia. Thus, Severstal North America becomes the fourth-largest producer in the US with about 12,7 mtpy annual capacity.

Sources: Compiled by the authors from industry monitoring journals.

Evraz Group

The Evraz Group was formed in the early 1990s through the privatization of the three then state-owned steel-making plants in the Urals and Siberia. Through consecutive buy-outs of shares from atomized shareholders, Alexander Abramov (one of Evraz's traders) gradually consolidated his ownership and by the early 2000s became a majority owner of the group. In early January 2006, Alexander Abramov (Evraz's owner, CEO and President) retired from the presidency, and on May 1st retired as the Chairman of Evraz. As already mentioned in August 2006, Abramov and Frolov sold their 41 per cent stake in Evraz for $3 billion to Millhouse Capital, the investment company owned by the Russian, London-based billionaire and Chelsea FC owner Roman Abramovich.

In accordance with its Corporate Articles, Evraz's Board is in charge of "all acts of administration and disposition in compliance with the corporate objectives of the company" (Evraz Corporate Articles, 2007). The members of the board of directors are elected for a 1-year term by a majority vote of shareholders at the annual general meeting (AGM). The board is composed of nine members, of which three are "deemed to be independent" in line with company criteria. All three of Evraz's independent directors are foreign citizens who act as chairmen of the boards' committees, such as remuneration, strategy and audit. Three other members of the Board represent the group's major shareholder – Millhouse Capital UK Ltd. Evraz's CEO also serves as the chairman of the board of directors, thus occupying duel roles. In his CEO position, the majority shareholder is in charge of the day-to-day management of the Evraz group and reports directly to the board, which also means the chairperson (in effect himself). The CEO is assisted by his top-team of eleven senior managers including vice-presidents (VP), who are selected and appointed by the board. The group corporate structure is illustrated in Figure 7.1.

In the Russian steel business, it is more common that the CEO is the company's owner, and as such accepts both capital and management responsibilities. In other words, the CEO/owner determines strategy. Abramov (2005, p. A5), the founder of Russia's biggest steel group Evraz, explains

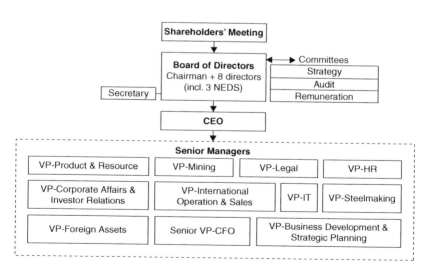

Figure 7.1 Apparent structure of corporate governance at Evraz
Source: Compiled by the authors.

these corporate dynamics, "Evraz is like my child. European managers hired by me just do their job. They stop taking care of the company if and when they retire."

MMK

MMK was formed in the early 1990s through the privatization of the single largest Soviet integrated iron and steel works of Magnitogorsk in the Urals. It took Victor Rashnikov about 10 years to consolidate his ownership of MMK to over 80 per cent.

   MMK appears to have the most complicated system of corporate governance amongst the major Russian steelmakers. The board consists of nine directors of which four appear to be independent, including two foreign citizens. The board is chaired by the MMK owner and president, who also serves as chairman of the board's strategic planning and corporate governance committees. The MMK board has four committees, namely, the committees of investment, policy, strategy (which includes responsibility for interaction with government bodies), audit and remuneration. In contrast with Evraz, MMK's two foreign members of the board, one of which is an ex-diplomat and the other being the regional director of British Petroleum, are neither chairpersons or appear on the board's sub-committees. MMK's four executives and board members are titled vice-presidents (VPs), with responsibilities for corporate issues, property management, operations and strategic development. The latter two VPs are also members of the management board, a body consisting of 21 members. This body is managed by two additional VPs and a trade-union head (Figure 7.2).

NLMK

NLMK was formed in the early 1990s through the privatization of the Soviet Union's then most modern integrated iron and steel works of Novolipetsk in central Russia. It took Vladimir Lisin about 10 years to consolidate his ownership of NLMK to over 80 per cent.

   NLMK has the smallest Board amongst the major Russian steelmakers consisting of seven members, which includes three NEDs, two of which are foreign citizens. The board is chaired by the NLMK owner. Both foreign directors are professional metallurgists, one, a professor, and are members of both the strategy and remuneration committees. NLMK's charter directly allots strategic decision making to the board, leaving day-to-day operations as a prerogative of the management board composed of a nine-member collegial executive body, consisting of vice-presidents, headed by the president who also acts as chairman of the management board and reports to the board of directors (Figure 7.3).

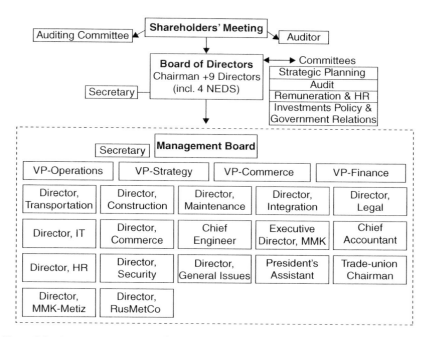

Figure 7.2 Apparent structure of corporate governance at MMK
Source: Compiled by the authors.

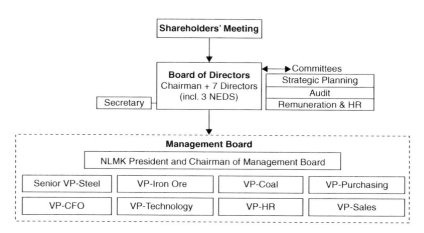

Figure 7.3 Corporate governance structure at NLMK
Source: Compiled by the authors.

Severstal

Severstal was formed in the early 1990s through the privatization of the Soviet Union's integrated iron and steel works of Cherepovets in North-West Russia. It took Alexei Mordashov less than 5 years to become the owner of more than 80 per cent of the company.

The WSD's (2007) report entitled, "World-Class Steelmakers: Best in Class," portrays 24 steel companies, who in their opinion are "growth oriented, have a culture of excellence, are led by age hardened management and are positioned to win in the future." The WSDs best in class are quantitatively ranked against an average score of 23 factors. As of April 2007, Russian Severstal has been positioned as number 1 with a winning average score of 7.93 out of 10.

Members of Severstal's board of directors are elected for 1 year by the annual general meeting of its shareholders. Also elected is the chairman by a majority vote of all board members. CEO duality (i.e., combining the CEO and chairman roles) is not permitted according to the company's charter. Severstal's board consists of five executive and five independent directors, chaired by a non-executive chairman (Figure 7.4). The company's audit committee operates completely independently and is chaired by the non-executive chairman and comprises two other members. The remuneration committee is chaired by a non-executive director and also includes the chairman of the board and the owner/CEO of Severstal. The newly formed

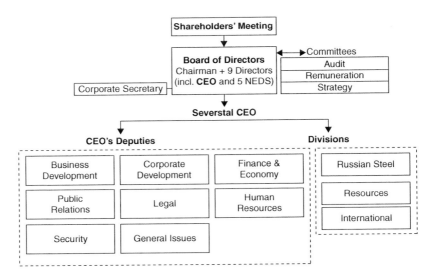

Figure 7.4 Corporate governance structure of Severstal

Source: Compiled by the authors.

strategy committee is staffed with two top executives as well as a proportion of the NEDs.

Interview study findings

Data analysis from twelve interviews identified four emergent themes (Pentland, 1999), namely, the contrasting nature of Russian steel enterprises, drivers for NED recruitment, independence of the board and NED contribution to strategy.

Nature of Russian steel enterprises

The majority of respondents consider the phenomenon of the highly concentrated ownership of the steel industry to be the distinguishing feature of the Russian corporate model contrasting it from its Western counterparts (Table 7.8).

Further, the respondents are unanimous in assuming that the combination of controlling shareholding and top management function (owner-manager) has a significant effect upon the structure and processes of corporate governance, including the board's role, composition and proportion of NEDs on the board (Table 7.9).

Drivers for recruiting NEDs

The increasing trend of recruiting NEDs onto the boards of Russian steel companies once they become public is driven by an expectation of enhancing reputation amongst investors, thus in turn improving the companies' market aspirations. However, when questioned on the reasons for going public, not a single participant mentioned the raising of additional cash for the owner(s) of the business, an unusual omission when considering why pursue IPO. It seems that for Russian steel owner-managers, going public is

Table 7.8 Russian steel company governance

Contrasting features of Russian corporate governance
High concentration (consolidation) of ownership
Less delegation, more concentration of power
Lack of transparency, low protection for minority shareholders
Management's immaturity in understanding of the role of NEDs
General immaturity in terms of governance and board role when compared to the history of western management

Source: Compiled from interviews.

Table 7.9 Owner-manager: determining corporate governance in closely held firms

Contrasting features of Russian corporate governance

Owner-managers are sole architects of corporate governance in their firms

Owner-managers are sole architects of corporate governance in their firms until they go public and have to conform to regulation, laws and rules

Owner-managers greatly determine corporate governance in their firms, but they have to take into account political and economic risks

Owner-managers greatly determine corporate governance in their firms, but their options are influenced by low-cost and high-margin conditions

Source: Compiled by the author on the basis of interviews.

Table 7.10 Drivers for hiring NEDs onto the boards of Russian steel companies

Drivers

Regulatory requirement of going public in Western markets
To increase credibility within Russia and abroad
To gain knowledge and experience
To improve the overall system of corporate governance
To enforce greater transparency and bring maximum value to all stakeholders
To build a system of process control

Source: Compiled from interviews.

seen as more of an image consideration than an economic move, at least at this current stage of their enterprise's evolution.

Table 7.10 presents the participants view of what drives Russian steel enterprises to hire NEDs onto their boards. The prime requirement for NED recruitment onto Russian Steel company boards is to draw on their experience of industry consolidation through merger, acquisition and international alliances. Additionally, the study participants highlight that stock market relations and reputation are major drivers, followed by knowledge and experience, greater transparency and creating systems of process control.

Although the raising of capital through stock exchange listing is perceived as a requirement for growth, in the Russian context only limited listing of up to 25 per cent is foreseen for the future (Table 7.11). In the words of one participant:

> The Russian steel industry is now very different from what it was a decade ago. It is now commercially focused and competitive. Enterprises are

Table 7.11   Russian steel companies "free-float" in the West

Options
"Small free-float means lack of liquidity. Free float must be increased if enterprise is to grow."
"Depends on how long Russian steelmakers can retain a profit margin advantage from lower energy, labour and transportation costs."
"No – as it would dilute owners' control."
"No – until Russian steel is further consolidated."
"No – as IPO purpose has been to assess companies valuation."
"Only slightly increase of free-float is foreseen. Russian law allows not more than 25% of corporate shares to be sold abroad."

Source: Compiled from interviews.

asset and cash rich. They are not pressed to raise capital on the stock exchange, but they need to prove to the market that they can be trusted and have an effective governance system in place in order pursue international acquisitions, alliances and partnerships.

The analysis of secondary and primary data indicates that beside regulatory requirement, company valuation, inviting publicity and attracting limited funds, the pursuit of IPOs and the appointment of NEDs on board, signal an important message to potential partners and/or "targets" of global expansion. The companies in this study are active consolidators focusing on mature markets, such as Western Europe and the USA. So for them, pursuing IPOs and recruiting prominent NEDs are as much strategic moves to prepare public opinion for further consolidations or partnership.

Independence of boards

The participants agreed on the importance of the "independence" of directors (Table 7.12). Equally there was a sharing of view that "independent" and "non-executive" are synonymous. Board independence is perceived as separation of the chairman and CEO roles. The majority of participants take the view that the board's independence requires that its members are "non-commissioned" within the hosting company's chain of command. The majority of the participants viewed "independence" as not an end in itself, but as a means to adequately perform the roles of "advisor," "keeper" and "watcher."

It is interesting that the majority of the participants consider that NED independence (Table 7.13) and chair/CEO role separation allows for board independence, despite the fact that the majority of the shares are controlled by one person.

Table 7.12   Meaning of independence for non-executive directors in Russian steel companies

Options
"Independence (of a Board member) means no economic or political interest. An 'independent' director is one who is independent of management and free from any business or other relationships which could significantly interfere with the director's ability to act in the best interests of the company."
"Independent" and "non-executive" are synonymous
"Non-executive are those who are not incorporated in any executive body of the company. There can be 'non-independent' non-executives."

Source: Compiled by the author on the basis of interviews.

Table 7.13   Board independence versus professionalism

Role separation	Interviewees
Is board independence and chair separation important, essential and attainable under highly consolidated ownership?	Yes, as independent members and Chair act as arbitrators to challenging the company's strategic course and rules (majority)
	No, as board's familiarity with the industry are more important factors for company effectiveness

Source: Compiled by the author on the basis of interviews.

The majority of the respondents consider that only when the board is truly independent can adequate challenge and guidance to management be provided (Table 7.14). Lack of industry background and interlocking directorships are not seen as serious obstacles to boards being able to be effective and efficient. Only three out of the ten participants put industry knowledge and familiarity ahead of NED common sense, reputation and experience. In the words of one participant,

> If you are steel expert you do not need another steel expert on your board.
>
> Rather you need NEDs that have skills that the rest of the board does not have.

The composition of the board is perceived as being important in the Russian context. The majority of participants suggested that the board requires a variety of different skills and not only industry specific skills.

Table 7.14   Role of boards: Russian steel industry

Roles of the board of directors
To provide opinion, consultancy, guidance and challenge to management
To steward the strategy, culture, top-team performance and governance of the company
To protect minority shareholders
Depends upon owner-manager's position towards the role of the board

Source: Compiled from interviews.

Industry specific skills were perceived to exist within the host company whilst other expertise such as the capability to respond quickly to changing competitive conditions, marketing, finance and an understanding of foreign stock exchanges, are seen as necessary competencies to have on boards.

In the words of one participant,

> The CEO is brilliant, he has done his homework and understand what skills he needs. Then he went to a professional search firm who found the skills he needed for his board.

NED contribution to strategy

Regarding board involvement in strategy determination, the participants were quite undivided in their opinion. Determining strategy is strictly management's prerogative with the board playing some form of auxiliary role (Table 7.15). In the words of one CEO,

> I am satisfied with my board. I trust that they will protect the interest of the shareholders and that means having input into the strategic process as well as questioning proposed strategies.

Though all the respondents in this study positioned the responsibility for strategy determination to management, certain consultancies (Heidrick and Struggles, 2007) and academics (Govorun, 2007) are specific about the role of the board and NED involvement in strategy emphasizing greater input particularly under circumstances of global expansion (Govorun 2007; Table 7.16)

Though the participants of this study consider strategy determination to be the responsibility of management and limit the boards' role to watchdog, advisory and consultancy functions, in the course of the study it was observed that certain independent foreign NEDs provide more than indirect

Table 7.15　Board contribution to corporate strategy?

Options
Management is responsible for deciding and implementing corporate strategy and tactics. Whilst • "Board and its Chairman should ensure consistency of strategy – as any deflection dilutes the share price and minimizes shareholder value;" • "Board should approve and agree the strategy;" • "Board should ensure the clarity of strategy;" • "the Board's role in corporate strategy is to advise, counsel and warn."

Source: Compiled from interviews.

Table 7.16　Six drivers to hire NEDs to a Russian public company: level of strategy involvement

Reason to hire NEDs	Relation to strategy issues
NEDs watch over interests of all shareholders	More friendly conditions for merger and acquisition
NEDs increase company transparency	Softening of "political" issues in certain developed regions
Investors are ready to pay more for companies with NEDs on boards	Increase company's market value – particularly in case of strategic alliances
NEDs uphold and build up company reputation among foreign third parties	Make company an attractive partner
Well-connected NEDs are company's spanners	Co-optation of strategic information and resources
NEDs are prominent advisors	Introduction of additional strategic knowledge

Source: Compiled by authors using Govorun's (2007) "six reasons to hire NED."

assistance on strategy matters, and often step up as active participants in the strategy-forming process for their host corporation.

Conclusions and implications

The literature reveals mixed evidence regarding the boards' strategic role. Some experts and academics see strategy as being among the board's major duties (Heidrick and Struggles, 2007; Ruigrok et al., 2006; Murphy, 2006;

McNulty and Pettigrew, 1999), whilst others seem to be quite reserved about part-time NED strategic capability (Brennan, 2006; Demb and Neubauer, 1992).

This research argues that the role of boards (including NEDs) of closely held Russian steel companies is greatly determined by the will, aspiration and intentions of their owner-managers. Because it is strictly the owner-manager who frame and determine company mission and vision, the same applies to the structure of corporate governance and the composition of board in particular. Although the candidates, in most cases, are found by search firms or through personal contacts, it is indeed the owner-manager who assigns the parameters and qualities (including professional background) of the candidates for positions on the board of directors.

The implication of the finding that the owner-manager structures and composes the board is that:

- Board composition, and the professional background and experience of the NEDs can be used to evaluate the company's strategic goals and plans, irrespective of whether they are aimed for more global expansion or for organic growth and development particularly in local/regional markets.
- Board characteristics reflect the owner-manager's self-appraisal and vision of the company at each stage of the development of the industry. This, in turn and subject to the owner manager's position in the steel world, is likely to influence the shape and configuration of the industry, bringing socially constructed features into that reality.
- Steel industry related professionals on boards of Russian steel companies are likely to play a greater part in the board's strategic role and company's predator positioning within global steel consolidation.

Let us return to the study of Evraz and NLMK. The boards of these two companies have two NEDs (Evraz Strategic Committee, also chaired by a foreigner) with steel professional backgrounds. Until recently, these two companies out of the four have demonstrated the most active strategic behaviour, more aggressively expanding globally than their counterparts. Both Evraz and NLMK also have the lowest ratio of interlocking directorships among their NEDs, which theoretically may provide them with more time for attending to the strategy issues of their hosting companies.

The above conclusions hold importance for steel companies, their strategic development and corporate governance processes in Russia. Analysing board of director composition and dynamics may turn out to be an additional instrument with which to measure how companies view their future strategic paradigms and even their life cycle.

The research findings suggest that recruiting NEDs to Russian steel company boards may reflect deeper concerns over longer team ownership and succession. Yakovlev and Danilov's (2007) report, "Russian Corporations on

20-Years Horizon," projected that in 5–7 years certain major Russian companies will have the Russian state as their controlling shareholder. From a longer perspective of a further 20 years ahead, when the first generation of entrepreneurs retires, the structure of corporate ownership in Russia will change dramatically as most of the shareholdings will be sold in the stock exchanges across the world.

This research has not been able to either confirm or to deny this forecast. Only one participant has mentioned preparation for retirement from the business as being among the obvious reasons of hiring NEDs to boards of closely held Russian steel companies. But the reality may be that none of the major Russian steel companies have and probably will not be able to have their direct family-related successors actively involved in the control and management of their steel business. Being in their 40–50s, the owner managers will sooner or later be facing the question of succession of their steel business, an unavoidable double-edged, economic and moral challenge. Perhaps the increasing use of NEDs on boards is also a reflection of a subconscious concern about the future.

References

Abramov, A. (2005), I have been never been considered as a successful entrepreneur by anybody, in Kornelyuk, N., Interview with Alexander Abramov, the head of Evrazholding. *The Profile Business Weekly*, 18 July.

Adams, R. B. and Ferreira, D. (2007), A Theory of Friendly Boards, *The Journal of Finance*, Vol. LXII, No. 1, February, pp. 217–50.

Barnes, D. (2001), Research Methods for the Empirical Investigation of Process of Formation of Operations Strategy, *International Journal of Operations & Production Management*, Vol. 21, No. 8, pp. 1076–95.

Bartholomeusz, S. and Tanewski, G. A. (2006), The Relationship between Family Firms and Corporate Governance, *Journal of Small Business Management*, Vol. 44, No. 2, pp. 245–67.

Berle, A. and Means, G. (1932), *The Modern Corporation and Private Property*, Macmillan, New York.

Biography Online (2007), Biography Boris Yeltsin, http://www.biographyonline.net/politicians/russian/boris-yeltsin.html (accessed: 20 February 2008).

Blaikie, N. (2000), *Designing Social Research: The Logic of Anticipation*, Polity Press, Cambridge.

Bradford, L. D. and Bernstain, V. (2006), Every Team Has Its Own Currency Exchange, *Expert Business Weekly*, No. 44, 27 November–3 December.

Brennan, N. (2006), Boards of Directors and Firm Performance: Is There an Expectations Gap? *Corporate Governance*, Vol. 14. No. 6, pp. 577–93.

Cadbury, A. (1999), What Are the Trends in Corporate Governance? How Will They Impact Your Company, *Long Range Planning*, Vol. 32, pp. 12–9.

Cochran, P. L. and Wartrick, S. L. (1988), Corporate Governance – A Review of the Literature, *Financial Executives Research Foundation*, Morristown, NJ.

Corbetta, G. and Salvato, C. A. (2004), The Board of Directors in Family Firms: One Size Fits All?, *Family Business Review*, Vol. XVII, No. 2, June.

Corporate Governance Editorial (2000), Whose Time Has Come?, Vol. 8, No. 4, October, Blackwell Publishing, Oxford.

Corporate Governance Editorial (2003). Non-executive Directors: Key Characteristics, Vol. 11, No. 4, October, Blackwell Publishing, Oxford.

Cromie, S., Stephenson, B. and Monteith, D. (1995), The Management of Family Firms: An Empirical Investigation, *International Small Business Journal*, Vol. 13, No. 4, pp. 11–34.

Dagayeva, A. (2006), Portrait of Independent Director. *Vedomosti Business Daily*, No. 233, p. 8, 13 December.

Daily, C., Dalton, D. R. and Cannella, A. A. (2003a), Corporate Governance: Decades of Dialogue and Data, *The Academy of Management Review*, Vol. 28, pp. 371–82.

Daily, C. M., Dalton, D. R. and Cannella, A. A. Jr (2003b) Introduction to Special Topic Forum-Corporate Governance: Decades of Dialogue and Data, *Academy of Management Review*, Vol. 28, pp. 371–82.

Demb, A. and Neubauer, F. (1992), *The Corporate Board: Confronting the Paradoxes*, Oxford University Press, New York and Oxford.

Drucker, P. F. (1974), *Management: Tasks, Responsibilities, Practices*, Harper and Row, New York.

Evraz Group Management Structure (2007), available at: http://evrazgroup.com/about/ management/ (accessed: 1 July 2007).

Finnegan, R. (1998), Using Documents, in Sapsford, R. and Jupp, V. (Eds), *Data Collection and Analysis*, Sage, London, Thousand Oaks, New Delhi.

Garratt, B. (1999), Developing Effective Directors and Building Dynamic Boards, *Long Range Planning*, Vol. 32, pp. 28–35.

Govorun, J. (2007), Independent from Their Job. Why Major Russian Public Companies Recruit Independent Director-Foreigners, *Smart Money Business Weekly*, No. 31, August.

Harrison, A. (2002), Case Study Research, in Partington, D. (Ed.), *Essential Skills for Management Research*, Sage, London, Thousand Oaks, New Delhi.

Heidrick and Struggles (2007), Independent Foreigners on the Boards of Directors of a Russian Company. Importance of a Successful Overseas IPO, *English Translation of Russian Report*.

Jenkins, M. (2002), Cognitive Mapping Management, in Partington, D. (Ed.), *Essential Skills for Management Research*, Sage, London, Thousand Oaks, New Delhi.

Kakabadse, N. and Kakabadse, A. (2007), Chairman of the Board: Demographics Effects on Role Pursuit, *Journal of Management Development*, Vol. 26, No. 2, pp. 169–92.

Kakabadse, A. and Kakabadse, N. (2008), *Leading the Board: The Six Disciplines of World-Class Chairman*, Palgrave, London.

Kakabadse, A., Kakabadse, N. and Barratt, R. (2006), Chairman and Chief Executive Officer (CEO): That Sacred and Secret Relationship, *Journal of Management Development*, Vol. 25, No. 2, pp. 134–50.

Kommersant (2007), The Russian Investment Boom Continues, *Russian Daily Online*, July 23, p. 1, http://www.kommersant.com/p788945/finance_macroeconomics/ (accessed: 20 February 2008).

La Porta, R., Lopez-de-Silanes, F. and Shleifer, A. V. R. (1998), Law and Finance!, *Journal of Political Economy*, Vol. 106, No. 6, pp. 1113–55.

Liveleak (2007), Former Russian leader Boris Yeltsin Dies, http://www.liveleak.com/ view?i=f67_1177341166 (accessed: 20 February 2008).

Lorsch, J. W. and MacIver, E. (1989), *Pawns or Potentates: The Reality of America's Corporate Boards*, Harvard Business School Press, Boston.

Mace, M. L. (1971), Directors – Myth and Reality, *Graduate School of Business Administration*, Harvard University, Boston, MA.

McNulty, T. and Pettigrew, A. (1999), Strategists on the Board, *Organization Studies*, Vol. 20, No. 1, p. 47.

Metal Bulletin Weekly (2006), Editorial: Russians Spread Wings Overseas. 25 December.

Murphy, R. (2006), Powers & Duties of the Non-executive Director, *Accountancy Ireland*, Vol. 38 No. 6, pp. 35–7.

Oleynik, A. (2007), The Economical Anatomy of the Tragedy. The State and the Business, *Vedomosty Daily Business Paper*, Vol. 30, No. 97, p. A4.

Overchenko, M. and Grozovsky, B. (2007), The Family Values. Why Private Companies Are More Dynamic Than Public Ones, *Vedomosti Business Daily Newspaper*, 5 February.

Pentland, B. T. (1999), Building Process Theory with Narrative: From Description to Explanation, *Academy of Management. The Academy of Management Review*, Vol. 24, No. 4, pp. 711–24.

Pettigrew, A. (2002), Executives and Strategy: An Interview by Kenneth Starkey, *European Management Journal*, Vol. 20, No 1, pp. 20–5.

Romano, R. (1996), Corporate Law and Corporate Governance, *Industrial and Corporate Change*, Vol. 5, pp. 277–339.

Ruigrok, W., Peck, S. I. and Keller, H. (2006), Board Characteristics and Involvement in Strategic Decision Making: Evidence from Swiss Companies, *Journal of Management Studies*, Vol. 43, No. 5, pp. 0022–2380.

Russian National Association of Non-Executive Directors (2006), A Collective Portrait of an Independent Director on a Russian Board, in Dagayeva, A. Portrait of Independent Director, *Vedomosti Daily*, No. 233, p. 8, 13 December.

Saghdiev, R. and Kudashkina, E. (2007), The Respected Business, *Vedomosti Business Daily*, 31 May, No. 98, p. B6.

Standard & Poor (2008), Special Report: Russia Post-2008: Road to Riches or Slippery Slope, *Standard & Poor's*, Division of the McGraw-Hill Companies.

Standard and Poor (2006), Portrait of a Board of Directors of a Public Russian Company. *Standard & Poor's*, Division of the McGraw-Hill Companies.

The Economist (2008), Smoke and Mirrors, 1 March, Vol. 386, No. 8569, pp. 27–9.

Tricker, B. (1996), *Pocket Director*, The Economist Books, London, UK.

Troschke, M. (1999), *Die Energiewirtschaft Rußlands im Transformationsprozeß: eine ökonomische und politische Analyse*, LDV, Munich.

van den Berghe, L. A. A. and Levrau, A. (2004), Evaluating Boards of Directors: What Constitutes a Good Corporate Board?, *Corporate Governance*, Vol. 12, No. 3, October.

Vinkov, A. and Sivakov, D. (2006), They Have Got Tired: One of Mechel's Founders Leaves the Business, *Expert Business Weekly*, February, pp. 20–6.

Weimer J. and Pape, J. C. (1999), A Taxonomy of Systems of Corporate Governance, *Corporate Governance*, Vol. 7, pp. 152–66.

Westhead, Paul, Cowling, M. and Howorth, Carole. (2001), The Development of Family Companies: Management and Ownership Imperatives, *Family Business Review*, Vol. XIV, No 4, December.

Wilson, D. and Roopa, P. (2003), Dreaming with BRICs: the Path to 2050, *Global Economics*, Paper No. 99, 1 October.

World Steel Dynamics, consultancy (eds.) (2007), World-Class Steelmakers. Best in Class. *Monitor Report*, March 2007.

Yakovlev, A. and Danilov, Y. (2007), Russian Corporations on Their 20-Year Horizon, in Petrachkova, A. The Future of Corporations, *Vedomosti Business Daily*, 19 January.

8

How do International Joint Venture (IJV) Directors Contribute to Board Effectiveness Evidence from Practice

Jelena Petrovic, Nada Kakabadse and Andrew Kakabadse

Introduction

Despite the acknowledged importance of international joint venture (IJV) board directors for IJV success (Child, 1998; Bamford and Ernst, 2005) and the impressive amount of research into different aspects of IJV operations, such as motives for IJV formation, performance/instability, control, human resource management, inter-partner relationships and trust (Parkhe, 1998; Schuler, 2001; Yan and Luo, 2001; Werner, 2002; Reus and Ritchie, 2004), a review of the literature shows that insufficient attention has been given to examining IJV board functioning and the roles played by individual IJV directors in contributing to board effectiveness. Apart from certain insights concerning what IJV board directors are expected to do, what qualities they should display in their role and the issues they are likely to encounter, little is known about the nature of their behaviour and their contribution to board effectiveness. Consequently, our understanding of how directors of IJV boards contribute to board effectiveness is incomplete.

This paper presents the findings and resulting conclusions from thirteen case studies conducted in three Serbian–foreign joint ventures based in Serbia as a part of an inquiry into IJV director contribution to board effectiveness. This chapter is in four sections. The first part presents a brief review of the corporate governance (CG) and IJV literature. The chapter continues by providing an outline of the methodology adopted in this research. This is followed by presentation of the empirical evidence of IJV board director contribution and discussion of the findings in relation to the previously reviewed literature. Finally, the paper offers a model that captures the contribution to board effectiveness from an individual IJV board director's perspective, highlighting implications for theory and practice.

Literature review: a need for practical evidence

The corporate governance (CG) literature emphasises the importance of board effectiveness for company success and the role that each board director plays in contributing to board effectiveness (Renton, 1999; Nicholson and Kiel, 2004; Kiel and Nicholson, 2005; Westphal and Bednar, 2005; Kemp, 2006). Concern over board effectiveness is reinforced in the context of IJVs due to their distinctive, "fragile" form of governance – shared sovereignty and incomplete contracting (Pearce, 1997). This implies two or more companies deciding the strategic direction and operational issues of the joint company (Ravasi and Zattoni, 2001; Boersma et al., 2003). IJVs are viewed as "hybrid organisations" because they combine elements of both hierarchies and contracts (Parkhe, 1993; Madhok, 1995; Child, 1998). Whereas "traditional" organisations rely primarily on agency governance in terms of fulfilling plans and meeting targets, in IJVs plans and targets are likely at best to be highly tentative (Child and Rodrigues, 2003). Consequently, despite a common reason for forming an IJV, there is invariably a divergence of interests between parent companies with regard to their IJV, which may exhibit a "mixed motive scenario" involving both co-operation and competition (Hamel, 1991; Yan and Gray, 2001; Buckley et al., 2002). This can easily lead to partners' conflicts over priorities and a temptation to behave opportunistically, that is, to achieve benefits from collaboration, beyond the level mutually agreed upon, in areas where the IJV contract is incomplete (Hamel, 1991; Yan and Luo, 2001; Zeng, 2003). This adversely influences IJV performance (Harrigan, 1985; Pothukuchi et al., 2002).

The simultaneous popularity of IJVs and the dissatisfaction with their performance have led to a literature which suggests that IJV board directors can play a crucial role in IJV success (Child, 1998; Li et al., 1999; Carver, 2000; Garrow et al., 2000; Hsieh and Lin, 2005; Bamford and Ernst, 2005). Given that in IJVs, the partners' representation on the IJV board is their only direct, legal connection to their IJV, reflecting the equity ownership of the IJV (Schaan, 1988; Kumar and Seth, 1998; Sharma, 1998; Carver, 2000), IJV board directors have been seen as one of the effective ways of controlling the risks associated with opportunistic partner behaviour and ensuring that partners' interests are protected (Yan and Gray, 1994; Luo et al., 2001).

The literature, however, also points to the need for greater attention to, and a more sophisticated understanding of, the process of governing IJVs (Madhok, 1995; Hsieh and Lin, 2005; Bamford and Ernst, 2005). It is noted in the literature that the behaviour of senior IJV directors is still poorly understood and that research opportunities exist for studying the governance of IJVs, the functioning of IJV boards in particular (Hambrick et al., 2001; Goodall and Warner, 2002; Adobor, 2004; Hsieh and Lin, 2005).

Moreover, numerous authors in the CG literature note that there has been a limited empirical study of the inner workings of boards, the actual behaviour of board directors, and their perceptions about their role and contribution (Forbes and Milliken, 1999; Leblanc, 2001; Pye and Pettigrew, 2005; Westphal and Bednar, 2005; Kemp, 2006). As noted by Leblanc (2001, p. 14), "board process or how a board of directors actually functions is a 'black hole,' both theoretically and empirically."

Methodology overview

The qualitative exploratory case study was the methodology adopted for this research. The case, that is, unit of analysis, is the individual IJV board director. The cases/participants included thirteen board directors (local and foreign partner representatives) from three Serbian–foreign joint ventures based in Serbia. The directors were members of a multi-tier board consisting of four different IJV governing bodies[1]: (1) The Assembly ("shareholding body" that "sets" the strategic direction through its ratification of the strategic decisions proposed by the Management Board), (2) Management Board ("strategic management body" that made strategic decisions and directed the CEO in implementing the strategy), (3) CEO ("executive body") and (4) Supervisory Board ("monitoring body" that controlled the legality of the company's documents and the Management Board's and CEO's activities).

Data were collected during the period between March 2003 and November 2004. A semi-structured interview was used as the main data collection method. Since a case study is known as a triangulated research methodology (Yin, 1989; Voss et al., 2002; Patton and Appelbaum, 2003), apart from interviews, an additional method/source of evidence used in the study was informal observation taken to include all information gathered on-site about a particular case, as well as secondary research of literature and relevant IJV documentation (e.g., Serbian Company Law documents, press releases about cases/participants and their IJVs, company documents provided by the informants).

The researchers conducted a conceptual/thematic analysis of data. Given that the intention of the research was not to assess IJV director contribution to board effectiveness beyond individual statements, but to track the concurrence of the study participants' perceptions about their contribution, at the start of the data analysis each case (IJV board director) was treated as a unique, stand-alone entity. From analysis of each individual case, a number of themes and sub-themes emerged that relate to those aspects that are central to the research. Following the data analysis strategy suggested by Eisenhardt (1989) and Miles and Huberman (1994), emerging themes and sub-themes from each individual case were then compared across cases and the themes concurrent between cases discussed in order to draw conclusions and propositions about IJV director contribution to board effectiveness.

Research findings

In the literature, the terms "role" and "contribution" are used interchangeably to refer to behaviours associated with a particular position in an organisation (Katz and Kahn, 1978; Roberts et al., 2005). The findings, however, show that role and contribution are differentiated in the eyes of the participants: role refers to the pre-determined tasks and goal, whilst contribution is about how these tasks and goal are being performed and/or fulfilled.

The directors see their tasks and goals as board tasks and IJV goals (the partners' shared vision about their IJV) that are determined by the law/IJV contract and the IJV partners respectively. This indicates the strong impact of context on IJV board director behaviour. The structured legal framework and statutory regulation of CG in Serbia and the IJV partners' shared vision about the IJV provide the framework in which IJV board directors operate. A detailed discussion of these and other influences on IJV board director contribution is, however, outside the scope of this paper.

This study revealed that individual IJV board directors meet their role requirements, that is, contribute to board effectiveness, through:

- Displaying and developing certain qualities (e.g., *knowledge of business, being* informed and prepared),
- Developing interpersonal relationships (e.g., competence-based trust),
- Developing and maintaining trust and chemistry on the IJV board,
- Maintaining the partners' shared vision about the IJV,
- Balancing different partners' agendas,
- Increasing board decision-making efficiency, and
- Increasing transparency about IJV operations.

The study identified the processes that explain how participants "produce" the above behaviours, that is, achieve individual-level "outcomes" (director qualities and interpersonal relationships) and board-level "outcomes" (IJV board trust/chemistry, the partners' shared vision, a compromise on the partners' agendas, board decision-making efficiency and transparency about IJV operation) that are considered important for board effectiveness. This is following criticisms of the literature that many studies lack direct evidence of the boardroom processes (Pettigrew, 1992) and also tend to describe behaviours that make up a role, rather than explain how and why this behaviour occurred (Rodham, 2000).

The processes that the IJV director engages in when fulfilling his/her role (contributing to board effectiveness) are presented and discussed below in detail and include informal, frequent and open communication, questioning and challenging others, showing initiative and actively participating in boardroom discussions, consultation, devoting sufficient time to their role (learning and reading advance materials), carefully considering options, demonstrating success, "keeping on track," monitoring and controlling the other partner's representatives, and relying on the contract.

Informal communication

Informal communication was viewed by the participants as important for developing their knowledge of business, for the balancing of different partners' agendas, for developing and maintaining board (inter-partner) trust, and increasing board decision-making efficiency. In effect, the findings show that formal board meetings were considered as almost irrelevant as board decisions were largely made on an informal basis and then formally confirmed at the board meeting:

> Our views are shared and known through our everyday, informal communication. Because everybody receives the agenda in advance, before the board meeting, all of us have discussed it and made a decision before the meeting. At the official board meeting, we just confirm the decision. (CASE 7 [CEO, IJV2])

> The board itself is not really important – it is simply a place where you can meet and confirm the decision that has already been taken through informal communication. (CASE 9 [Chairman, Management board, IJV2])

> We need to manage priorities without waiting for the Management Board to officially meet. (CASE 3 [CEO, IJV1])

> My input regarding how the results should be achieved is, in fact, prior to the board meeting. When we have a board meeting all the issues have been already pre-discussed informally in depth, we really know the situation and are so well prepared that we can take any decision with confidence. Therefore, the board is only a place where our decisions are formally confirmed. (CASE 13 [NED, Management board, IJV3])

These findings support those of Ravasi and Zattoni (2001) and Goodall and Warner (2002) in that informal communication is important and the purpose of the IJV board meeting is to formalise agreements already reached. However, other authors in the IJV field (Schaan, 1988; Carver, 2000; Buchel, 2002) take a different view and argue that formal board meetings represent a key strategic decision forum where significant matters are appropriately monitored and reviewed. Still, in terms of the importance of informal communication for enhancing board inter-partner trust, the findings of this study are in line with the IJV literature where informal communication is posited as an effective mechanism for trust-building (Parkhe, 1998; Buchel, 2000; Currall and Inkpen, 2002).

In relation to the CG literature, the findings correspond to previous authors and researchers' recommendations that informal meetings between board directors provide the opportunity to exchange and test ideas in greater depth than may be permitted at formal board meetings (Ingley and Van der Walt, 2003; Roberts et al., 2005). The results also support the findings of Roberts et al. (2005) that informal contact with the executives builds non-executive directors' (NEDs') knowledge in a way that is likely to increase the perceived credibility of their boardroom contribution.

Frequent communication

Regarding frequency of formal board meetings, the study findings show that the Assembly met at least once per year, whilst the official Management and Supervisory board meetings in all three IJVs averaged four times per year. This, generally, falls within the range of frequency of IJV board meetings found by previous IJV studies (Daniels and Magill, 1993; Yan and Gray, 1994; Groot and Merchant, 2000; Ravasi and Zattoni, 2001). The length of IJV board meetings – 3 to 4 hours on average in all three IJVs – also corresponds to that reported in the IJV literature (Groot and Merchant, 2000; Ravasi and Zattoni, 2001). Irrespective of the number of formal meetings, the study respondents reported the importance of informal communication for making decisions against the frequency of formal communication.

Frequent communication emerged as a critical way in which the IJV board director was informed and prepared, balanced different partners' agendas and contributed to board (inter-partner) trust and decision-making efficiency:

> Obviously, there are some formal meetings of the Management Board that we have to attend…. Still, when we meet we already know what the situation is because we have already discussed all the things through our frequent informal communication, over the phone, through email or at our informal meetings. (CASE 8 [NED, Management Board, IJV2])

> You can't develop a true partnership and contribute to trust between the board members if you meet only a few times per year. (CASE 9 [Chairman, Management Board, IJV2])

> Having very frequent communication and discussion with others – formally or informally – is not only important for building trust between us but also for developing our shared view about how to achieve the IJV vision. (CASE 13 [NED, Management Board, IJV3])

The significance of frequent communication for balancing different partners' agendas and developing trust on the board is a finding in line with the previous literature on IJVs, where frequent communication between the partners is considered important for facilitating finding of the partners' common interests and shared vision about their IJV (Kanter, 1994; Madhok, 1995; Buchel, 2000; Boersma et al., 2003), as well as for developing trust between the partners (Parkhe, 1998; Buchel, 2000; Arino et al., 2001; Buckley et al., 2002; Li and Hambrick, 2005). Frequent communication is also seen in the CG literature as a means of building shared understanding among Board Directors (Sundaramurthy and Lewis, 2003; Westphal and Bednar, 2005) as well as contributing to trust of each other's expertise and judgement (Coulson-Thomas, 1991; Forbes and Milliken, 1999; Conger and Lawlor, 2002; Ingley and Van der Walt, 2003).

Open communication

Open communication emerged as an important contribution to balancing different partners' agendas, and developing and maintaining board (inter-partner) trust, as well as for increasing transparency about IJV operations:

> Since it is the IJV, you have to take into account that your partner company has its own interests, which means that you have to try to understand their point of view. Here, it is important that in every conversation you have with other directors, you always openly express your opinion.... I am such a person that I openly communicate my opinion and give everybody a chance to try to convince me otherwise. I maybe even risk saying some things openly, given that I am employed by the IJV, but I think that being open and having good intentions is very important. I would never hide a problem. (CASE 1 [Assembly member, IJV1])

> If I feel there are some issues, I openly tell others about them. I never do things behind someone's back – I always have a direct and open approach. (CASE 5 [Deputy CEO, IJV1])

> I don't hesitate to openly communicate to others.... I equally openly communicate with all of the Management Board members and there is no Serbian versus Italian side.... This is because our mutual relationship is extremely fair, open and completely honest.... It is important to find people who are ready to have such openness because then the IJV Board Director's contribution is much easier. (CASE 7 [CEO, IJV2])

> So far, it has not occurred yet that we didn't come to a consensus of what to do, because we all communicate openly with each other. And that really depends on chemistry between the people on the IJV board. (CASE 13 [NED, Management Board, IJV3])

Again, in keeping with the literature on IJVs, open communication between the partners when searching for solutions that satisfy both partners' needs is viewed as essential for contributing to the high levels of trust required between the partners to enable transparency in the reporting of corporate data (Madhok, 1995; Lin and Germain, 1998; Parkhe, 1998; Buchel, 2000; Pearce, 2000; Arino et al., 2001; Buckley et al., 2002; Currall and Inkpen, 2002; Child and Rodrigues, 2003; Bamford and Ernst, 2005; Li and Hambrick, 2005).

The results also support the CG literature, where the willingness of all board members to communicate openly with their colleagues and to say what they think, even if their views differ from others at a board meeting, is considered to require the adoption of multi-perspectives by the board members (Charan, 1998; Kakabadse et al., 2001; Cadbury, 2002; Sherwin, 2003; Huse, 2005) which also helps to build the directors' mutual trust and confidence (Coulson-Thomas, 1991; Cadbury, 2002; Roberts, 2002; Conger and Lawlor, 2002; Sherwin, 2003; Kiel and Nicholson, 2005). It is however necessary to note that the level of openness of communication between IJV board directors appears to be much higher at informal meetings than at formal ones where, as noted by one of the directors, "the responsibility for each word counts."

Questioning/challenging others

Questioning and challenging others and playing the "devil's advocate" to proposed courses of action emerged as an important process through which the participants balance different partners' agendas and increase transparency about IJV operations. For some of the directors, penetrating questioning of management was reported as a crucial part of their contribution to board effectiveness:

Although I don't have experience of sitting on the board of a 'real' Western company, I am aware of the need to question what the executives do. For the board to be effective, it is important that none of our questions be left unanswered by the executives... I think that so far, we have been effective in questioning the executives' decisions and operation even though we could see that not always did they feel comfortable in this respect. (CASE 2 [Employee Representative, Supervisory Board, IJV1])

Everybody is playing both the role of an advisor or one that proposes decisions and also the role of 'devil's advocate'. If, for example, CASE 10 [CEO] suggests something, before I agree with that, I first think very carefully about his proposal and openly tell him about all the negative aspects of his suggestion I might come up with. (CASE 11 [Chairman, Supervisory Board, IJV3])

Roberts et al. (2005, p. 14) concur highlighting "the effectiveness of board accountability; of asking questions and the actions that can follow directly from this," where questioning is seen not only to enable the addressing of specific concerns about executive performance but also to set norms for executive behaviour. Numerous authors in the CG field (Coulson-Thomas, 1991; Forbes and Milliken, 1999; Sonnenfeld, 2002; Roberts, 2002; Nadler, 2004; Huse, 2005; Westphal and Bednar, 2005) consider the fact that *board directors* ask questions, challenge one another's assumptions and beliefs and offer a counter view to be an important contribution to board effectiveness.

Showing initiative and actively participating in boardroom discussion

The findings showed that the participants actively contributed to the dialogue of the board, offered constructive suggestion to help determine pertinent IJV strategy and increase transparency about IJV operations:

> You should not play your role in terms of just 'procedural box ticking' or to satisfy your petty, personal interests. You have to be active, engaged and show interest. For example, the Management Board members always invite me to their meetings. Although I don't have a right to vote there, I still have a right to discuss things. This is important, because my role is mostly 'exposed' – I am the Assembly representative in the IJV and one who has to convince the shareholders. So, if I have doubts and dilemmas regarding the Management Board's decision, that is, if the decision is not prepared well, then there is a huge risk that the Assembly won't accept it. (CASE 1 [Assembly member, IJV1])

> How an IJV board member contributes really depends on how active, engaged and interested he or she is.... For example, our board members like discussion and always find something to question.... So we [the executives] really have to be well prepared and completely open about what is going on. (CASE 3 [CEO, IJV1])

> I believe that my contribution has been very successful – I am very active and give a lot of input! (CASE 13 [NED, Management Board, IJV3])

Proactive director initiative and active participation in board discussion are considered important for board effectiveness (Charan, 1998; Forbes and Milliken, 1999; Conger and Lawlor, 2002; Ingley and Van der Walt, 2003; Nadler, 2004; Kiel and Nicholson, 2005; Huse, 2005). The study results also indicate that decisions reached on IJVs boards are often initiated by NEDs and that the IJV board is directly involved in the development of strategic alternatives, thus supporting the previous literature (Ravasi and Zattoni, 2001). It is therefore argued that the IJV boards in this study are characterised by a "maximalist" board culture (Pettigrew and McNulty, 1995).

Yet, a minority of the participants took an opposite view and considered that the board should not act like a "police officer" and dictate what the executives do. This could be seen as related to what Roberts et al. (2005) call "being involved but NED," namely the dichotomy between a weak board with poor "independence" and one with powerful NEDs who slow down board decision-making and flexibility by exercising too much control.

Consultation

Most of the study participants mentioned that they consult others and actively seek out information on boardroom issues, before and after formal meetings, much in keeping with the findings and "recommendations" in the CG literature (Forbes and Milliken, 1999; Conger and Lawlor, 2002; Sonnenfeld, 2002; Nadler, 2004). Consequently, although the executives were placed as formally responsible for preparing the boardroom agenda, the agenda appears to be the result of a collective input based on frequent, informal consultation between executives and NEDs:

> I consult with other IJV board members many times before the formal board meeting.... In essence, we [the executives] try to make sure that the Management Board members will be happy with a decision we propose...Consulting other directors on an informal basis is particularly useful when it comes to reconciling our different interests. (CASE 3 [CEO, IJV1])

> In preparing the agenda for the board meetings, I frequently consult with other board members because they are all very well informed about the IJV operations and have a good knowledge of business. (CASE 10 [CEO, IJV3])

Although in contrast with studies of the Anglo/Saxon board model whereby executive-driven agendas are concluded to be useful tools for CEO control over the board (Carver, 2000; Sundaramurthy and Lewis, 2003; Nadler, 2004), this study's findings support Hermalin and Weisbach's (1988) view that CEOs utilise directors as sources of information in the formulation of strategy. Although the study results partly support Roberts' (2002) notion about boards acting as "rubber stamps," what also emerges is that executives anticipate NEDs' concerns before bringing issues to board meetings.

Devoting sufficient time to their role
(learning and reading advance materials)

Apart from frequent and informal communication and consultation, the directors affirmed the importance of devoting sufficient time to their role, particularly in terms of learning and reading professional materials, in order to be informed and prepared:

> You have to have as much information as possible in order to establish how you are going to contribute....That's why I read a lot, I am constantly learning and updating my knowledge. (CASE 1 [Assembly member, IJV1])

I need to be well prepared…This means spending lots of time learning about and analysing how each of the IJV parts functions and what improvements are needed, how to cut the costs and similar…. There are situations that require in depth knowledge of a problem. So I need to keep up to date with new developments in the field. I read many professional materials.(CASE 2 [Employee representative, Supervisory Board, IJV1])

One of the vital elements of my contribution is that I take a lot of time to prepare. It is important that you don't go from one board meeting to another where you only discuss and prepare. (CASE 13 [NED, Management Board, IJV3])

Again these findings are in line with the results of other studies concerning director contribution (Forbes and Milliken, 1999; Renton, 1999; Conger and Lawlor, 2002; Nadler, 2004; Roberts et al., 2005; Shen, 2005). Investing time in learning and the sharing information about IJV issues not only improve director performance but also act as a basis for IJV success (Schuler, 2001).

Carefully considering options

Careful consideration of current circumstances and decision-related alternatives emerged as important issue for board effectiveness:

Depending on the way I prepare the set of alternatives, I can influence the Board's strategic choice…. For that, you have to know as much as you can, having all the possible alternatives very clearly defined, including the weaknesses and strengths of everyone, balancing the pros and cons. Otherwise, you can leave some parts unclear and unexplored and a problem can arise exactly from those parts. (CASE 8 [NED, Management Board, IJV2])

Denis et al. (2000) termed such behaviour as "immersion" – a necessary precursor to promoting effectiveness.

Demonstrating success

The participants view is that demonstrating success enhances directors' trust in their leadership and management skills. This, in turn, increases the participants' ability to influence decision-making on the IJV board:

Since the company's strategic vision is profitable growth, if we [the executives] offer this profitable growth, then nobody has a reason to challenge us. At our meeting held this December, we [the executives] announced to the IJV Management and Supervisory Board and the Assembly that we had a huge growth and opportunities for growth, as well as an extremely high profit…. When you have operating results like this, there is no person who would challenge decisions you propose…So there is no question really posed on the Management Board – our decision-making is very simple. (CASE 10 [CEO, IJV3])

IJV partners' "competence-based" trust (an ability to perform the required task) is seen as being developed mainly through the successful performance of their IJV (Inkpen and Currall, 1998; Boersma et al., 2003; Hsieh and Lin, 2005).

"Keeping on track"

"Keeping on track" in terms of ensuring that IJV board decisions are directed towards the achievement of the partners' shared vision is no easy matter. As Parkhe's (1998, p. 428) has recommended, IJV managers should be observant of the divergence of partners' strategic orientation because "even the strategic fit of a once-perfect match may diminish as the partners' evolving internal capabilities, strategic choices and market developments pull them in separate directions."

> Sometimes it seems that at the beginning, the partners have found each other, but later their ways of thinking start to diverge. Consequently, their goals or agendas start to diverge, although they perhaps had the same goal at the beginning. That situation cannot lead to IJV success. Hence, the IJV needs to be constantly 'kept on track', that is, managed towards the fulfilment of the initially agreed vision regarding the IJV. If someone tries to 'leave the track', I would say, 'Wait, we have agreed this and not that'. The most important thing is to keep focused on the ultimate result we have to achieve – the partners' common goal for the IJV. (CASE 7 [CEO, IJV2])

> As we all agreed on the vision at the beginning of the IJV operation, when we are deciding about how to reach it, we should always have in mind that vision. That's why I am keeping everybody on the right track. So, when we are discussing an issue, I ask everyone whether it is in our strategic vision. If it isn't, we shouldn't discuss it. (CASE 12 [Chairman, Management Board, IJV3])

Monitoring and controlling the other partner representatives

Certain of the study participants admitted to monitoring and attempting to control the thinking and behaviour of the other partner representatives, despite their acknowledgement that such a behaviour negatively affects board (inter-partner) trust:

> For IJV success to be achieved, you not only need to have a common interest regarding the IJV but a high level of mutual trust between

the partners from the very start. Unfortunately, this was not the case with our IJV.... Hence we've lost a year monitoring and learning about each other's ways of thinking and agendas. (CASE 1 [Assembly member, IJV1])

Although we trust each other, we are still different partners' representatives.... For this reason and also so as not to incur some unnecessary costs that would decrease each partner's part of the profit, we need to control each other. (CASE 2 [Employee representative, Supervisory Board, IJV1])

Other studies confirm the practice of monitoring other partner delegates, although this is considered to undermine the desire to collaborate (Kanter, 1994; Madhok, 1995; Garrow et al., 2000; Arino et al., 2001); such acts are viewed as "justified" by the fact that IJVs spawn mistrust between the partners (Pearce, 1997; Parkhe, 1998). Hence

giving the other side the benefit of the doubt (reflecting too much trust) sets oneself up for exploitation, while treating all poor outcomes as opportunistic behaviour (reflecting too little trust) creates a spiral of joint retaliation. (Parkhe, 1998, p. 432)

Relying on the contract

Confronted with determining partner relations, certain study respondents reported turning solely to contractual obligation as a way of negotiating through different partners' agendas:

I am trying to be constructive but not at the expense of the German partner's interests, since they gave us a helping hand when we were in a crisis. Of course, this is going to be the case as long as they do what we have agreed and as long as it is in accordance with the Law. For example, there was a problem regarding a newspaper, which I managed to resolve. That newspaper was, at some point, an item on the boardroom agenda. The German partner wanted to get rid of it but I said something like, '...if we still decide to cease the newspaper today, please note that, in that case, we will need to follow the legal procedure which means, changing the contract'. (CASE 4 [Vice Chairman, Management Board, IJV1])

Reminding partners of their contractual obligations is referred to as "legalistic strategy" in terms of IJV partner conflict resolution (Lin and Germain, 1998; Wang et al., 2005) and usually is considered as a last resort to sustain the IJV (Boersma et al., 2003).

Conclusion: a model of IJV director contribution

The empirical evidence of IJV directors' contribution to board effectiveness presented in this paper shows that IJV directors contribute to board effectiveness through a number of processes that result in and are affected by individual-level and board-level "outcomes," as illustrated in Figure 8.1.[2]

Given that identifying both the behaviour of individual directors and factors that affect and are affected by their behaviour is seen as paramount for understanding of board dynamics (McNulty and Pettigrew, 1999; Long et al., 2005), the empirical evidence discussed in this paper and illustrated in Figure 8.1 thus opens the "black box" of previous CG research. In addition, in contrast with many studies of board dynamics which fail to distinguish between individual and collective inputs and outputs (Pye and Pettigrew, 2005), this research makes a clear distinction between levels of analysis (i.e., individual director and board).

Overall, the findings show that the behaviours, processes and qualities displayed by IJV board directors correspond in many ways to those recommended by the CG literature (e.g., open and frequent communication, questioning and challenging others, showing initiative and actively participating

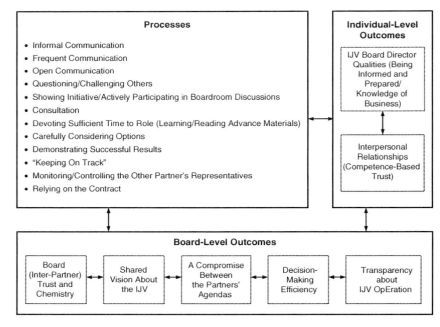

Figure 8.1   IJV director contribution to board effectiveness
Source: Petrovic, 2006.

in boardroom discussions, devoting sufficient time to their role, carefully considering options and being informed and prepared). In addition, viewed from a board-level perspective, the four factors that emerged as important for board effectiveness – directors' shared vision, trust, transparency and decision-making efficiency – are recognised in the CG literature as determinants of board effectiveness (Kakabadse and Myers, 1996; Forbes and Milliken, 1999; Renton, 1999; Sonnenfeld, 2002; Cascio, 2004; Pye and Pettigrew, 2005).

On the other hand, there are also processes that emerged as unique to IJVs (e.g., monitoring and controlling the other partner's representatives). Additionally, the fifth board-level "outcome" that emerged from the findings – a compromise on the partners' agendas – is unique to IJV boards: for an IJV board to be effective, its decisions need to represent a compromise between different partners' agendas. This further means that, in comparison to "normal" boards which are characterised by a "CG paradox" in terms of control versus collaboration approaches (Sundaramurthy and Lewis, 2003), IJV boards face a "double CG paradox," because the issue is not only about the relationship between the NEDs and executives but also about that between different partner representatives. Therefore, the study confirms the speculations in the literature (Carver, 2000; Child and Rodrigues, 2003; Hsieh and Lin, 2005) that the IJV shared form of governance alters "traditional" CG practice. Such a situation might also explain why informal communication emerged as by far the most important process of the IJV board director's contribution.

The general contribution of this chapter thus includes the enhancing of our understanding of the IJV board director role, an extending of the study of the board director role in the CG literature to IJVs, and a contribution to the studies of board dynamics and IJV boards which have been largely under-researched. Moreover, little is known about the CG systems of transitional economies in general (Dockery and Herbert, 2000) and, in effect, no single study has been pursued regarding IJVs based in Serbia. Hence, this research provides a unique perspective as it is the first attempt to explore IJV board director contribution in this context. The research is of interest to practitioners as it offers a better understanding of the issues and nuances associated with governing of IJVs, as well as knowledge of IJV board director behaviour within a particular CG system.

Notes

1. Since November 2006, this form of board structure in Serbia has ceased to exist. This is due to new Company Law in Serbia (Serbian Official Gazette, 2004), which has "merged" the governance bodies of Management Board and CEO into one. It is also important to note that, although there are no specific provisions in the Law that refer to IJVs, specific provisions for these forms of companies apply and are incorporated in IJV contracts. The three IJVs in this research are all limited liability companies.

2. It is important to note here that there are other "individual-level" outcomes that also emerged as having an impact on the processes and outcomes. However, detailed discussion about each of these outcomes and their impact is outside the scope of this paper.

References

Adobor, H. (2004), High performance management of shared-managed joint venture teams: Contextual and socio-dynamic factors, *Team Performance Management,* Vol. 10, No. 3/4, pp. 65–76.

Arino, A., de la Torre, J. and Ring, P. S. (2001), Relational quality: Management trust in corporate alliances, *California Management Review,* Vol. 44, No. 1, pp. 9–131.

Bamford, J. and Ernst, D. (2005), Governing joint ventures, *McKinsey Quarterly,* Vol. 15, pp. 12–6.

Boersma, M. F., Buckley, P. J. and Ghauri, P. N. (2003), Trust in international joint venture relationships, *Journal of Business Research,* Vol. 56, No. 12, pp. 1031–42.

Buchel, B. (2000), Framework of joint venture development: Theory building through qualitative research, *Journal of Management Studies,* Vol. 37, No. 5, pp. 637–61.

Buchel, B. (2002). Joint venture development: Driving forces towards equilibrium. *Journal of World Business,* Vol. 37, No. 3, pp. 199–207.

Buckley, P. J., Glaister, K. W. and Husan, R. (2002), International joint ventures: Partnering skills and cross-cultural issues, *Long Range Planning,* Vol. 35, No. 2, pp. 113–34.

Cadbury, A. (2002), *Corporate Governance and Chairmanship,* Oxford University Press, Oxford.

Carver, J. (2000), The opportunity for re-inventing corporate governance in joint venture companies, *Corporate Governance,* Vol. 8, No. 1, pp. 75–80.

Cascio, W. F. (2004), Board governance: A social systems perspective, *Academy of Management Executive,* Vol. 18, No. 1, pp. 97–100.

Charan, R. (1998), *Boards at Work: How Corporate Boards Create Competitive Advantage,* Jossey-Bass, San Francisco.

Child, J. (1998), Resource provision, key appointments and control in international joint ventures – the case of China, *Chinese Management Centre Working Study* CMC, 1998-005-01, University of Hong Kong, Hong Kong.

Child, J. and Rodrigues, S. B. (2003), Corporate governance and new organizational forms: Issues of double and multiple agency, *Journal of Management and Governance,* Vol. 7, No. 4, pp. 337–60.

Conger, J.A. and Lawlor, E. (2002), Individual director evaluations: The next step in boardroom effectiveness, *Ivey Business Journal,* Vol. 66, No. 5, pp. 28–31.

Coulson-Thomas, C. (1991), What the personnel director can bring to the boardroom table, *Personnel Management,* Vol. 23, No. 10, pp. 36–9.

Currall S. C. and Inkpen, A. C. (2002), A multilevel approach to trust in joint ventures, *Journal of International Business Studies,* Vol. 33, No. 3, pp. 479–95.

Daniels, J. D. and Magill, S. L. (1993), "Protection of competitive advantage in U.S./Asia-Pacific joint ventures from high-technology industries", in: Culpan, R. (Ed.), *Multinational Strategic Alliances,* International Business Press, New York, pp. 167–82.

Denis, J. L., Langley, A. and Pineault, M. (2000), Becoming a leader in a complex organization, *Journal of Management Studies,* Vol. 37, No. 8, pp. 1063–99.

Dockery, E. and Herbert, W. E. (2000), Corporate governance and enterprise restructuring in transition economies: Evidence from privatised Polish companies, *Managerial Finance*, Vol. 26, No. 9, pp. 80–92.

Eisenhardt, K. M. (1989), Building theories from case study research, *Academy of Management Review*, Vol. 14, No. 4, pp. 532–50.

Forbes, D. P. and Milliken, F. J. (1999), Cognition and corporate governance: Understanding boards of directors as strategic decision making groups, *Academy of Management Review*, Vol. 24, No. 3, pp. 489–505.

Garrow, V., Devine, M., Hirsh, W. and Holbeche, L. (2000), *Strategic Alliances: Getting the People Bit Right*, Roffey Park Institute, Horsham.

Goodall, K. and Warner, M. (2002), Corporate governance in Sino-Foreign joint ventures in the PRC: The view of Chinese directors, *Journal of General Management*, Vol. 27, No. 3, pp. 77–92.

Groot, T. L. C. M. and Merchant, K. A. (2000), Control of international joint ventures, *Accounting, Organizations and Society*, Vol. 25, No. 6, pp. 579–607.

Hambrick, D. C., Li, J., Xin, K. and Tsui, A. (2001), Compositional gaps and downward spirals in international joint venture management groups, *Strategic Management Journal*, Vol. 22, No. 11, pp. 1033–53.

Hamel, G. (1991), Competition for competence and inter-partner learning within international strategic alliances, *Strategic Management Journal*, Vol. 12, Special issue, pp. 83–103.

Harrigan, K. R. (1985), *Strategies for Joint Ventures*, Lexington Books, Lexington.

Hermalin, B. E., and Weisbach, M. S. (1988), The determinants of board composition. *Journal of Economics*, Vol. 19, No. 4, pp. 589–606.

Hsieh, H-Y. and Lin, A. (2005), Conceptual model of post-formation governance in cross-border partnership, *Journal of American Academy of Business*, Vol. 7, No. 2, pp. 302–7.

Huse, M. (2005), Accountability and creating accountability: A framework for exploring behavioural perspectives of corporate governance, *British Journal of Management*, Vol. 16, Special issue, pp. 65–79.

Ingley, C. B. and Van der Walt, N. T. (2003), Board configuration: Building better boards, *Corporate Governance*, Vol. 3, No. 4, pp. 5–17.

Inkpen, A. C. and Currall, S. C. (1998), The nature, antecedents, and consequences of joint venture trust, *Journal of International Management*, Vol. 4, No. 1, pp. 1–20.

Kakabadse, A. and Myers, A. (1996), Boardroom skills for Europe, *European Management Journal*, Vol. 14, No. 2, pp. 189–200.

Kakabadse, A., Ward, K. and Korac-Kakabadse, N. (2001), Role and contribution of non-executive directors, *Corporate Governance*, Vol. 1, No. 1, pp. 4–7.

Kanter, R. M. (1994), Collaborative advantage: The art of alliances, *Harvard Business Review*, Vol. 72, No. 4, pp. 96–108.

Katz, D. and Kahn, R (1978), *The Social Psychology of Organisations* (2nd Edn), Wiley, New York.

Kemp, S. (2006), In the driver's seat or rubber stamp? The role of the board in providing strategic guidance in Australian boardrooms, *Management Decision*, Vol. 44, No. 1, pp. 56–73.

Kiel, G. C. and Nicholson, G. J. (2005), Evaluating boards and directors, *Corporate Governance*, Vol. 13, No. 5, pp. 613–31.

Kumar, S. and Seth, A. (1998), The design of coordination and control mechanisms for Management joint venture – parent relationships, *Strategic Management Journal*, Vol. 19, No. 6, pp. 579–99.

Leblanc, R. (2001), Getting inside the black box: Problems in corporate governance research, *Joint Committee on Corporate Governance*, Available from: http://www.cica.ca/multimedia/Download_Library/Research_Guidance/Risk_Management_Governance/GettingInside_Leblanc.pdf (accessed 3 August 2005).

Li, J., and Hambrick, D. C. (2005), Factional groups: A new vantage on demographic faultiness, conflict, and disintegration in work teams, *Academy of Management Journal*, Vol. 48, No. 5, pp. 794–813.

Li, J., Xin, K., Tsui, A. and Hambrick, D. C. (1999), Building effective international joint venture leadership teams in China, *Journal of World Business*, Vol. 34, No. 1, pp. 55–68.

Lin, X. and Germain, R. (1998), Sustaining satisfactory joint venture relationships: The role of conflict resolution strategy, *Journal of International Business Studies*, Vol. 29, No. 1, pp. 179–96.

Long, T., Dulewicz, V. and Gay, K. (2005), The role of the non-executive director: Findings of an empirical investigation into the differences between listed and unlisted UK boards, *Corporate Governance*, Vol. 13, No. 5, pp. 667–79.

Luo, Y., Shenkar, O. and Nyaw, M-K. (2001), A dual-parent perspective on control and performance in international joint ventures: Lessons from a developing economy, *Journal of International Business Studies*, Vol. 32, No.1, pp. 41–58.

Madhok, A. (1995), Opportunism and trust in joint venture relationships: An exploratory study and a model, *Scandinavian Journal of Management*, Vol. 11, No. 1, pp. 57–74.

McNulty, T. and Pettigrew, A. (1999), Strategists on the board, *Organization Studies*, Vol. 20, No. 1, pp. 47–74.

Miles, M. B. and Huberman, A. M. (1994), *Qualitative Data Analysis* (2nd Edn), Sage, Thousand Oaks, CA.

Nadler, D. A. (2004), Building better boards, *Harvard Business Review*, Vol. 82, No. 5, pp. 102–11.

Nicholson, G. J. and Kiel, G. C. (2004), A framework for diagnosing board effectiveness, *Corporate Governance*, Vol. 12, No. 4, pp. 442–60.

Parkhe, A. (1993), "Messy" research, methodological predispositions, and theory development in international joint ventures, *Academy of Management Review*, Vol. 18, No. 2, pp. 227–68.

Parkhe, A. (1998), Understanding trust in international alliances, *Journal of World Business*, Vol. 34, No. 3, pp. 219–40.

Patton, E. and Appelbaum, S. H. (2003), The case for case studies in management research, *Management Research News*, Vol. 26, No. 5, pp. 60–71.

Pearce, R. J. (1997), Toward understanding joint venture performance and survival: A bargaining and influence approach to transaction cost theory. *Academy of Management Review*, Vol. 22, No. 1, pp. 203–25.

Pearce, R. J. (2000), The general manager's perspective on how factionalism can impact the behaviors and effectiveness of top managers inside a shared management joint venture, *Journal of Management and Governance*, Vol. 4, No. 3, pp. 189–206.

Petrovic, J. (2006), International joint venture (IJV) directors' contribution to board effectiveness: Learning from practice. *The 4th Workshop of the European Institute for Advanced Studies in Management (EIASM) on International Strategy and Cross-Cultural Management*, 29–30 September. Toulouse, France.

Pettigrew, A. M. (1992), On studying managerial elites, *Strategic Management Journal*, Vol. 13, Special issue, pp. 163–82.

Pettigrew, A. M. and McNulty, T. (1995), Power and influence in and around the boardroom, *Human Relations*, Vol. 48, No. 8, pp. 845–73.

Pothukuchi, V., Damanpour, F., Choi, J., Chen, C. and Park, S. H. (2002), National and organisational culture differences and international joint venture performance, *Journal of International Business Studies*, Vol. 33, No. 2, pp. 243–65.

Pye, A. and Pettigrew, A. (2005), Studying board context, process and dynamics: Some challenges for the future, *British Journal of Management*, Vol. 16, Special issue, pp. 27–38.

Ravasi, D. and Zattoni, A. (2001), Ownership structure and the strategic decision process: A comparative case study, *SDA Bocconi Research Division Working Paper*, No. 1-46, Available from the Social Science Research Network (SSRN) Electronic Paper Collection: http://ssrn.com/abstract=278238 (accessed: 24 October 2005).

Renton, T. (1999), *Standards for the Board* (2nd Edn), Institute of Directors, London.

Reus, T. H. and Ritchie, W. J. (2004), Interpartner, parent, and environmental factors influencing the operation of international joint ventures: 15 years of research, *Management International Review*, Vol. 44, No. 4, pp. 369–95.

Roberts, J. (2002), Building the complementary board: The work of the plc Chairman, *Long Range Planning*, Vol. 35, No. 5, pp. 493–520.

Roberts, J., McNulty, T. and Stiles, P. (2005), Beyond agency conceptions of the work of the non-executive director: Creating accountability in the boardroom, *British Journal of Management*, Vol. 16, Special issue, pp. 5–26.

Rodham, K. (2000), Role theory and the analysis of managerial work: The case of occupational health professionals, *Journal of Applied Management Studies*, Vol. 9, No. 1, pp. 71–81.

Schaan, J. L. (1988), How to control a joint venture even as a minority partner, *Journal of General Management*, Vol. 14, No. 1, pp. 4–16.

Schuler, R. S. (2001), Human resource issues and activities in international joint ventures, *International Journal of Human Resource Management*, Vol. 12, No. 1, pp. 1–52.

Sharma, D. D. (1998), A model for governance in international strategic alliances, *Journal of Business and Industrial Marketing*, Vol. 13, No. 6, pp. 511–28.

Shen, W. (2005), Improve board effectiveness: The need for incentives, *British Journal of Management*, Vol. 16, Special issue, pp. 81–9.

Sherwin, L. (2003), Building an effective board, *Bank Accounting and Finance*, Vol. 16, No. 5, pp. 22–8.

Serbian Official Gazette (2004), *Company Law*, Serbian Official Gazette, No. 125/04.

Sonnenfeld, J. A. (2002), What makes great boards great, *Harvard Business Review*, Vol. 80, No. 9, pp. 106–13.

Sundaramurthy, C. and Lewis, M. (2003), Control and collaboration: Paradoxes of governance, *Academy of Management Review*, Vol. 28, No. 3, pp. 397–415.

Voss, C., Tsikriktsis, N. and Frohlich, M. (2002), Case research in operations management, *International Journal of Operations and Production Management*, Vol. 22, No. 2, pp. 195–219.

Wang, C. L., Lin, X., Chan, A. K. K. and Shi, Y. (2005), Conflict handling styles in international joint ventures: A cross-cultural and cross-national comparison, *Management International Review*, Vol. 45, No. 1, pp. 3–21.

Werner, S. (2002), Recent developments in international management research: A review of 20 top management journals, *Journal of Management*, Vol. 28, No. 3, pp. 277–305.

Westphal, J. D. and Bednar, M. K. (2005), Pluralistic ignorance in corporate boards and firms' strategic persistence in response to low firm performance, *Administrative Science Quarterly*, Vol. 50, No. 2, pp. 262–98.

Yan, A. and Gray, B. (1994), Bargaining power, management control and performance in international joint ventures: A comparative case study, *Academy of Management Journal*, Vol. 37, No. 6, pp. 1478–517.

Yan, A. and Gray, B. (2001), Antecedents and effects of parent control in international joint ventures, *Journal of Management Studies,* Vol. 38, No. 3, pp. 393–416.

Yan, A. and Luo, Y. (2001), *International Joint Ventures: Theory and Practice*, M. -E. Sharpe, New York.

Yin, R. K. (1989), *Case Study Research: Design and Methods* (2nd Edn), Sage, London,

Zeng, M. (2003), Management the cooperative dilemma of joint ventures: The role of structural factors, *Journal of International Management,* Vol. 9, No. 2, pp. 95–113.

9
The Chairman of the Board of Directors: Role and Contribution

Eleanor O'Higgins

Introduction

From the early 1990s, there has been a growing awareness of the relevance of positive leadership in corporate governance for the sustainability of companies and the business system. This awareness stems from manifest failures in corporate governance, which gave rise to scandals worldwide, and arguably, to the global banking crisis of 2008. An early scandal, which was a factor initiating corporate governance reform in the UK, was the 1991 Maxwell downfall, when it was revealed that Robert Maxwell, Chairman and CEO of Maxwell Communications Corporation, had caused a GBP 441 million-sized hole in the company pension fund to cover hidden personal debts of GBP 4 billion. Subsequent analysis highlighted a number of corporate governance deficiencies and lack of accountability and controls because of the concentration of power that had facilitated Maxwell's fraudulent activities.

Subsequent corporate governance reform was designed to curb power at the top of organizations. One plank of this objective has been calls by academics and shareholder activists alike to separate the roles of chairman and CEO (Chung and Burgess, 2008; MacAvoy and Millstein, 2003). The intention is that the chairman, who heads the board, which represents the interests of investors, can constrain the CEO and his/her senior management team from behaving in a self-serving way that runs counter to shareholders' interests. This conforms to agency theory, a view that emphasizes the controlling aspects of corporate governance and the chairman's role in particular (Benz and Frey, 2007). Notwithstanding these arguments, companies in the USA remain attached to unitary power, with only 129 of the S&P 500 separating the role. Moreover, many of these separate chairmen are insiders or otherwise not independent, and the Corporate Library, a corporate governance research firm reckons that only 63 or 12.6 per cent of the S&P 500 have genuinely independent chairman (Chung and Burgess, 2008).

However, in the 2000s, the possibilities of the role of chairman beyond its controlling function have come to the fore (Cadbury, 2002; Directorbank,

2008; Dulewicz et al., 2007; Harper, 2005; Kakabadse and Kakabadse, 2008; Lechem, 2002; Praesta, 2005; SpencerStuart, 2008). The UK Combined Code regards the chairman as pivotal in creating the conditions for overall board and individual director effectiveness, both inside and outside the board-room (Financial Reporting Council, 2003). The influence of an effective chairman can extend far beyond the boardroom, as the potential of the chairman to make a positive contribution to the long-term success and sus-tainability of the organization is recognized. In line with this development of the chairman's role, this chapter examines the augmented role of the chairman (What?), the ways in which the role is best conducted (How?), the personal attributes of successful chairmen (Who?), and the pitfalls and issues in realizing the potential of the expanded role of the chairman (Why and why not?).

While this chapter recognizes the different board structures around the world, it assumes a growing sentiment in favor of and convergence toward the appointment of a separate independent chairman, working with a CEO. Thus, what are presented are parameters of effectiveness that are universal in thinking about outstanding chairmen.

The expanded role of the chairman

The UK Combined Code (Financial Reporting Council, 2003) is a good starting point in delineating the role of the chairman. The Code incorpo-rated the recommendations of Derek Higgs' review on corporate govern-ance, commissioned by the Government (Higgs, 2003).

Specifically, the Combined Code spells out the responsibility of the chair-man to

- Run the board and set its agenda. Agendas should be forward looking and concentrate on strategic matters.
- Ensure that the members of the board receive accurate, timely, and clear information, to enable the board to take sound decisions, monitor effect-ively, and provide advice to promote the success of the company;
- Ensure effective communication with shareholders and that the members of the board develop an understanding of the views of the major invest-ors. Although not included in the Higgs Report or the Combined Code, ensuring effective communication with a broad array of legitimate stake-holders is now recognized as partly the chairman's role.
- Manage the board's time to ensure sufficient scope for discussion of com-plex or contentious issues, including arranging appropriate informal pre-paratory meetings in advance of board meetings.
- Building an effective and complementary board, initiating change, and planning succession in board appointments and managing the develop-ment of the board and individual directors. This involves taking the lead

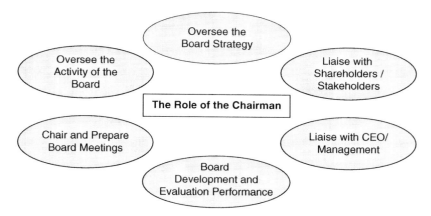

Figure 9.1 The role of the chairman
Source: Compiled by the author.

in providing a properly constructed induction programme for new direct-ors, facilitated by the company secretary. It also involves identifying and meeting the development needs of individual directors. It is the responsi-bility of the chairman to address the development needs of the board as a whole with a view to enhancing its overall effectiveness as a team.

• Another aspect of board development is an annual evaluation of the per-formance of individuals and of the board and its committees.

The role of the chairman breaks down under a number of headings (Lechem, 2002):

• Managing the board, which includes organization of meetings and agen-das, as well as communicating between meetings
• Developing a more effective board, which means enhancing board contri-bution and development in terms of membership and training
• Working with management, especially the CEO. This role includes liais-ing between management and shareholders and the board
• Managing shareholder relations
• Liaising with other parties, usually in conjunction with the CEO.

The chairman's role is summarized in Figure 9.1.

How should the chairman carry out his/her role?

The success of the expanded role of the chairman really depends on the manner in which it is enacted. Cadbury (2002) makes the point that the role of the chairman is variable, in the sense that how it is carried out depends on the personal history and characteristics of the chairman him/herself, on those with whom s/he interacts, especially the CEO and board colleagues, and on the nature and history of the company. The role may also vary over time, and circumstances, that may call for stability or change at different periods. However, there are some principles of excellence in chairmanship that are constant, transcending individual differences.

Board meetings and agendas

The Combined Code states that the chairman sets the agenda, style, and tone of board discussions to promote effective decision making and constructive debate. Chairing board meetings, having devised the agenda, is at the core of the chairman's role, because the board is the formal locus of power, and it should be within the meeting forum that key decisions on the future of the company are made. Although chairing meetings is an activity that defines the chairman's role, it is one that is furthest from the public eye (Cadbury, 2002). Also, since no amount of preparation can control how a meeting will develop, Cadbury likens the chairman's job to that of an orchestra conductor, but more difficult, since company "chairmen have to be their own composers and they cannot be sure in advance what tunes their soloists will play, or whether they will perform at all" (Cadbury, 2002, p. 79). However, both chairmen and conductors are ultimately responsible for the performance.

The success of a meeting is measured by the extent to which it has reached the best conclusions. The best conclusion is not merely a satisficing one that is politically acceptable, but it must be optimum for the company's achievement and sustainability. Success is more likely if the chairman can get board members to contribute to the best of their abilities. The development, balance, flow, and scope of board discussion must be balanced against the scarce resource of time by the chairman.

The conduct of board meetings was studied in a survey of chairmen/directors in Ireland (Praesta, 2005). The survey was conducted with 70 randomly selected directors from the *Irish Times* Top 1000 companies. Cumulatively, these participants held 373 directorships, of which 36 participants held 119 chair roles. These covered publicly quoted companies, private companies, state companies, and non-profit organizations. The survey concluded that the following chairman behaviors are required at board meetings:

- Good listener
- Establishes trust, openness, and good relations
- Facilitates inclusiveness
- Allows the discussion to flow
- Encourages challenge and open debate

How is the chairman likely to get the best out of each board member at a meeting? Harper (2005) offers some sensible advice. The chairman should adopt attitudes of respect, patience, humor, and goodwill. Listening is an essential habit for chairmen, to truly appreciate and understand the inter-action, not to impose one's views, lest it inhibits input from others. Another essential behavioral trait is respectfulness to each board member. This means being accepting of others, not favoring some directors over others, giving credit where it is due, and not embarrassing others in public. Respect not only sets an example to others but also allows the scope to be direct and tough when required, as others are more likely to accept it if it is not seen in personally insulting terms.

Yet, the chairman must also maintain discipline and control. Harper (2005) suggests that an ostensible commitment to the board as a group and to its objectives, alongside an even-handed approach, gives the chairman the authority to impose discipline, and to deal with individuals who may be disruptive of group goals. Discipline is also enhanced by timely, decisive, positive starts to board meetings. This should include a brief statement of what needs to be achieved at the meeting as per the agenda.

Orchestrating meetings to arrive at optimum conclusions requires open discussion, without losing focus. This means allowing points to be aired that may not be useful to them, but nonetheless stimulate ideas that others build upon, as a way of bringing out valuable knowledge and insights. The chairman should also be alert to miscommunication in the form of over-generalizations and ambiguities. These require clarification, in case differ-ent interpretations are applied to decisions taken. The chairman's task also consists of avoiding too early closure on an issue before all aspects of it have been fully considered. An effective chairman will know when to adjourn an item on which agreement cannot be reached. Generally, well-run boards usually reach decisions by consensus, rarely requiring actual vote counts. It is better for the chairman to defer a decision, pending more information, or consultation than to insist on a majority vote when the board is split. Forcing a vote may not yield the most informed decision, but even worse, could be divisive far into the future.

Agendas

Setting the meeting agenda is the responsibility of the chairman, in col-laboration with the CEO and board secretary. The agenda has to reflect priorities in board duties. The inclusion and order of items will influence outcomes. Cadbury (2002) categorizes agenda items under three types. Items of report, such as financial updates, from management keep the board informed about company progress, and are relevant to the board's monitoring function. Compliance reviews would also be presented, such as government-stipulated returns, or reports to do with matters like health and safety (Lechem, 2002). A second type of agenda item is a general one of matters where management is looking to the board for advice, for example, an issue coming up the line, such as pressure from environmental pressure groups. These are managerial issues, and not for board execution.

The danger with the first two types of items is that boards can get bogged down in these, to the detriment of the most critical function of board meetings. This involves considering matters for decision. It is up to the chairman to apportion board time to concentrate on such important matters. These decisions have to do with strategic choices and important corporate policies, vital to the future of the company. They may involve significant expenditure of resources. The chairman, in conjunction with the board secretary, has to ensure that board members are furnished with all the necessary documentation to enable them to inform themselves and give some thought to the issues at hand. In addition, the agenda should reflect the duties of the board, as contrasted with the duties of management, and it is up to the chairman then to keep the discussion on track to avoid micromanagement.

Preparation for board meetings by the chairman should also consist of meeting the CEO and senior executive team in advance, according to the survey of Irish directors (Praesta, 2005). The survey also found a consensus advocating timely circulation of board papers and minutes, the latter to ensure that clear follow-up actions are identified and processed.

Establishing and maintaining relationships

As board leader, the chairman is at a nexus of relationships, within the board itself, within the company, and with parties external to the company. The chairman has to promote effective relationships and open communication, both inside and outside the boardroom. Despite the chairman's central role in the network of actors, s/he has little or no official power over many of them, and even when s/he does, must use the power with a light touch. Nonetheless, the chairman must still influence these myriad of actors. Thus, the chairman must lead by example by acting with goodwill and commitment to the aspirations of the company, ready application of skills for its benefit, as befits the duty of a director. Outside the boardroom, the chairman should also behave in an exemplary way that inspires trust and respect from other members of the company and from outside stakeholders.

The importance of relationships in the chairman's role is illustrated in the UK Non-Executive Director Awards 2006. Judges deemed that outstanding chairmen spend significant time mentoring, developing, and advising their colleagues, are team builders, encourage contributions from fellow directors, and achieve consensus. Yet, they challenge and probe colleagues (Dulewicz et al., 2007).

The key relationships for the chairman are summarized in Figure 9.2.

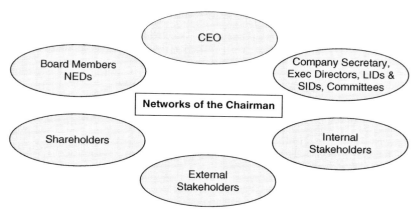

Figure 9.2   Networks of the chairman
Source: Compiled by the author.

The CEO relationship

There is no doubt that the key relationship for the chairman is that with the chief executive. This relationship is critical for the contribution of the board and the success of the company. It involves both a clear division of labor between the two figures at the top of the organization, but at the same time, a great deal of collaboration between them. The chairman has to establish a close relationship of trust with the chief executive, providing support and advice while respecting executive responsibility, according to Higgs (2003). One of the advantages of division of labor at the top of the organization is the colossal amount of work to be done, so that two individuals, each suited to different aspects of the job, can share the leadership more effectively and efficiently than one person alone could do. Typically, it is accepted that the CEO bears the primary responsibility for strategy implementation, while the chairman is responsible for the composition and conduct of the board and its committees in the board's directorial role. However, the delineation is not clear, and there is actually unavoidable overlap, especially as regards strategy, but also responsibility for the external face of the company (Roberts and Stiles, 1999). The strategy overlap makes sense since strategy formulation and implementation are not easily separated.

The ambiguity in separating the roles of chairman and CEO is both an opportunity and a problem. It presents an opportunity for flexibility, with one person or the other taking on the lion's share of a task as contingencies dictate. On the other hand, unless there is a relationship of confidence and trust between the two individuals, ambiguity may create tension and conflict, because one individual suspects the other of usurping their position – usually the CEO believing that the chairman is interfering with management by micromanaging.

The actual division of labor and balance of influence between chairmen and CEOs varies between companies, and may vary within companies at different times. An important aspect of the relationship is emotional, and the emotional tone is set through the process of building the relationship from the beginning. This will depend on how the relationship is initiated, and factors determining this include whether either or both of the two individuals is an insider or outsider, whether the one individual had any influence in choosing the other for his/her role, and how the individuals evaluate each other's competence and personality. These findings were based on in-depth interviews with 30 chairman/CEO dyads in the UK (Roberts and Stiles, 1999).

A clear and shared vision for the company between chairman and CEO is necessary. Since the purpose of a vision is to inspire both internal and external stakeholders critical to the company, it has to be led by those most responsible for determining it and driving it forward (Kakabadse and Kakabadse, 2008). Once the Chairman and CEO are addidum about the vision, the board and top management have to throw their weight behind it too. How is this unity of vision best created? A trusting relationship is a precondition, and the early months are the time for initiating and developing the relationship, for better or worse. Critical incidents at an early phase can set the stage for confidence building. Confidence is required to deal with points of tension, and so it is a delicate matter to have established some trust before encountering any conflicts. It must be borne in mind that everyone is aware of the chairman's board leadership role in ensuring effective implementation of board decisions, at the same time that the chairman is developing a trusting relationship with the CEO. Part of this involves choosing, monitoring, and dismissing the CEO.

Based on their interview findings, Roberts and Stiles (1999) offer some guidelines on building the critical relationship between chairman and CEO. Initially, it is recommended that the Chairman and CEO hold a formal discussion on their respective roles and relationship. A regular routine of meetings between the two individuals is another basis of relationship building. Both parties should learn a lot from these meetings, to be applied for the benefit of the company. It will also prevent unpleasant surprises on both sides (Roberts, 2002). In a thriving relationship, the power of the chairman will derive from a complementarity of roles with the CEO, rather than at the expense of CEO power. Interestingly, Roberts (2002) found that CEOs appreciated chairmen who were experienced and strong. From the chairman's point of view, complementarity means taking pleasure in the successes of the CEO, rather than seeing it as a diminution of his/her own contribution. On the other hand, if the chairman has acted in support of the CEO, as acknowledged by both individuals, the relationship is truly complementary, even if the chairman enjoys the fruits of the joint work accomplished in a less high profile, public way than the CEO.

Complementary rests on a number of dimensions – skills, experiences, knowledge, temperament, business focus, and values (Roberts, 2002). For example, the chairman might have long experience of working with institutional investors, while the new CEO might be a novice, and could use the chairman's support in developing his/her networks. The notion of complementarity also explains how the chairman can, at the same time, support and monitor the CEO. This is seen by both individuals' commitment to accountability, which becomes a joint commitment in the context of ongoing dialogue that facilitates problem solving and learning. This desire for accountability installs a set of standards in the minds of executives, as led by the CEO, and influences everyday behavior accordingly.

Relationships with Non-Executive Directors (NEDs)

As the leader of the board, the chairman has to deal with the succession planning of NEDs (Cadbury, 2002). Thus, s/he has to find and attract the most suitable NEDs and maximize their contribution. This means choosing people with the right competences, experience, and personal attributes, who will exercise independent judgment. It entails taking a good look at the existing NEDs and assessing which of them should be retained when the time comes for re-election, but it should be appreciated that director contributions may improve over time (Kakabadse and Kakabadse, 2008). Then, the chairman has to find suitable replacements for board vacancies, usually in consultation with the CEO (Roberts, 2002). A chairman with vibrant networks and a good reputation can help to attract able candidates – but, of course, the chairman must be careful not to be over-reliant on "old-boys" networks.

Having attracted suitable NEDs, the chairman must ensure proper induction, as well as involvement. This means cultivating board relationships based on common purpose, mutual support, respect, and credibility. In addition to involvement at board meetings, the effective chairman will also confer with NEDs between meetings, as necessary, especially in the context of upcoming thorny issues that need deliberation in advance. NEDs can be an excellent source of counsel and trusted objective criticism (Harper, 2005). However, it is important not to meet individual NEDs in a divisive, or faction creating way. This requires transparency, in the sense that everyone knows that the chairman is having these discussions and what they are about. It is also recommended that chairmen convene meetings of all the NEDs, without the presence of executives, to allow free discussion, and enhance accountability. Executives should be aware that such meetings take place as a matter of course, so that they are not seen to be clandestine, or conspiring against management. The chairman has to call upon NEDs in a way that does not separate them unduly from the management team, so that the complementarity of skills between NEDs and executives is allowed to flourish in a collegiate manner, and the NEDs do not get bogged down in management details (Kakabadse and Kakabadse, 2008). The input of NEDs may be augmented if they hold positions as executive directors in other organizations, since it makes them appreciate the differences between direction and management (Cadbury, 2002).

Executive directors

The chairman has to relate to executive directors, just as to any other directors. Since executive directors hold dual roles, that is, executives and directors, like the CEO, they are on both sides of the direction/management divide. This may place them in an invidious position, since, in their executive jobs, they are normally answerable to the CEO. Yet, as a fellow board member, they are not answerable to the CEO. It may be difficult for executive directors to question or criticize the CEO, when they are identified with his/her policies and approaches. However, an effective chairman will appreciate these sensitivities and work around them to get the benefit of the views, knowledge, and skills of the executive directors, who offer insider perspectives beyond those of the CEO alone. In this sense, the chairman has to make executive directors feel equal to any other directors, including the CEO, so that they have the confidence to contribute as full members of the board.

Senior Independent Directors (SIDs)

The notion of SIDs and Lead Independent Directors (LIDs) came about from the US system of combining the chairman/CEO roles. As a compromise, it has been suggested that boards appoint a lead director from among the independent outside directors to consult with the chairman/CEO on matters to do with the selection of board committees, meeting agendas, processes, and information (Cadbury, 2002). A LID may intervene significantly in a crisis or a period of transition, and gets involved with evaluation of the chairman/CEO and the board as a whole (Kakabadse and Kakabadse, 2008). It appears that the LID derives influence, not so much from official power structures, but from personal authority. However, this role is more dependent on the consent of the chairman/CEO than is the case with an independent chairman where the chairman and CEO roles are each formally recognized. Thus, a LID is unlike an independent chairman with a prescribed positive role and scope to develop the board and its contribution, offering advanced input to the company.

Even in the presence of an independent separate chairman, the UK Combined Code recommends the appointment of a SID. The role may appear to be redundant, except in crises when the chairman is dysfunctional and the shareholders and others look to the SID for a solution (Kakabadse and Kakabadse, 2008). However, there is scope for a SID to make a significant contribution, according to Cadbury (2002). The chairman can harness the expertise of the SID by seeking counsel and support from him/her on an informal basis. Also, the SID is involved in board development and assessment and in evaluating the chairman's performance and arranging for chairman succession (unless s/he is a candidate). The SID is likely to chair the remuneration committee, and should be available for consultation with shareholders, if required. The partial monitoring role of the SID with respect to the chairman may create sensitivities and tensions, which have to be handled in a constructive manner for the sake of board effectiveness.

Internal stakeholders

The chairman interacts with various other internal stakeholders, as necessary. This includes the finance director whose professional independence is relied upon, especially when the chairman reports the company's results publicly. The chairman and NEDs may also find it helpful to liaise with managers and other company employees who are not board members, as part of valuable learning about the company, for example, visiting facilities away from company headquarters to try to understand the business. These relationships are usually mediated by the CEO, and indeed, such outside board encounters are most beneficial when done with the blessing and facilitation of the CEO and other executive directors.

The company secretary works closely with the chairman in ensuring smooth board administration, preparing for board meetings and looking after minutes, helping to prepare the annual report, and ensuring corporate regulatory compliance. The secretary may provide support with arrangements for director induction and development. Sometimes, the company secretary has legal training. Cadbury (2002) makes the point of how invaluable a good company secretary can be to enable the chairman to carry out his/her job to best effect.

Board committees

It is up to the chairman to ensure clear structure for and the effective running of board committees. The chairman takes the lead in decisions to establish particular committees to make the board work more effectively and efficiently, and in choosing committee members. Some committees, such as the Audit Committee, are compulsory under various Codes. The purpose of the Audit Committee is to monitor financial reporting and risk, including the internal audit function. In the UK Combined Code, the Audit Committee is expected to be comprised entirely of independent directors and to include at least one member who is financially literate. Another universally found committee is the remuneration committee to monitor the performance and agree on the remuneration of top operational management, including the CEO. Nomination committees are now also universal, formed to ensure board renewal and succession, to choose new NEDs in a transparent way that seeks the best people, not just comfortable cronies from existing networks of the chairman and other directors, including executives. Corporate governance committees are an increasing phenomenon to oversee how the board is performing its functions, and to disclose on it in the annual report (Lechem, 2002). Many committees are formed for special purposes and include both executive and NEDs working together. Non-directors may also be co-opted on to such committees. Examples are health and safety committees, or international business committees.

In all instances of the establishment and appointment of board committees, the chairman has to bear in mind that committees perform delegated work, and ultimately, the board is responsible for the activities and outcomes of the committees, and takes the final decisions on any recommendations arising out of committees. Orchestrating and coordinating committees is a complex and difficult task. First, the committee must be necessary, either for regulatory or for effectiveness/efficiency purposes. The decision to set up a discretionary committee necessitates a deep and broad knowledge of the company, and it has to be based on a first-class sense of judgment, probably after consultation. Then, the members chosen for the committees must have the competences to make a real contribution. It is important to choose proficient chairmen for the committees. Yet, the work has to be distributed, since the same people cannot be expected to sit on too many committees. There may be personal sensitivities and jealousies about who is appointed to which committees. Since most committees, with the exception of audit, remuneration, and corporate governance committees, include both executives and NEDs, this provides an opportunity for both groups to learn from each other and form productive relationships. On the other hand, unreasonable behavior on the part of either group may cause lasting damage in the running of the company. It is up to the chairman to ensure that those serving as chairmen of the committees have the skills to bring people together to optimize group and personal outcomes.

Shareholders

The most obvious contact between chairmen and shareholders occurs at the annual general meeting, when the annual report is presented and shareholders get a chance to pose questions face-to-face. However, the chairman, CEO, and finance director meet with institutional investors regularly, since these shareholders hold such large stakes. A study found that promoting investors' confidence and high returns was the most highly cited desirable behavior of chairmen (Dulewicz et al., 2007). Activities typical of this behavior were persuading shareholders, especially through difficult strategic periods for the company, and identifying inherent value in the company and ensuring communication of this to shareholders. Effective chairmen do not forget new and private investors, even if they concentrate on relations with existing institutional investors. Today, chairmen and boards have to be aware of investors who insist on certain standards of conduct in the way that business is done, that is, investors who confine themselves to socially responsible investment, as an increasing number of funds of this kind are being established. Generally, a good chairman will be to the forefront of engaging with activist investors, defusing situations before they become a cause célèbre, which may have negative reputational repercussions.

External stakeholders

Interacting with external stakeholders such as suppliers, customers, and the public is usually the purview of the CEO, but the chairman has a role in reviewing and approving critical statements, reports, and other documents for the media and other key stakeholders (Kakabadse and Kakabadse, 2008). However, the chairman can make a valuable contribution beyond this, especially if s/he has access to networks with key stakeholders. For example, the chairman might facilitate contacts with governments, regulators, and government agencies, or even with competitors to work on common industry problems such as environmental issues. Other important stakeholders are lobby groups, charities, and other not-for-profit bodies. Chairmen may assist CEOs to liaise with important stakeholders, or may communicate directly themselves, with the consent and cooperation of the CEO. Dulewicz et al. (2007) describe instances of effective communication with stakeholders as having a direct effect, like facing up to a belligerent press, and an indirect effect, as demonstrating support to the workforce and boosting their confidence.

Setting the ethical tone at the top

It is widely agreed that a chairman cannot do his/her job unless s/he sets clear standards of integrity and leads the board in upholding the standards (Cadbury, 2002; Dulewicz et al., 2007; Kakabadse and Kakabadse, 2008; Lechem, 2005; Praesta, 2005). Cadbury states that chairmen and boards have to establish their companies' standards of behavior, ensure that they are communicated throughout the organization, and that the company's reward system reinforces them. Dulewicz et al. (2007) found that integrity and high ethical standards are enacted by chairmen who insist on upholding standards, especially when there may be a temptation to take the expedient way out. The chairman is also an important role model, ethically speaking.

The Irish survey conducted by Praesta found a consensus that the ethical tone of a company pervades its every action internally, as well as the messages it sends to external stakeholders. The chairman, with the CEO, plays an important leadership part in ensuring that ethical behavior becomes second nature in the organization and that all actions are carried out legally and ethically. Part of this is compliance with corporate governance standards, although mere compliance is not enough. It is up to the chairman to ensure that upholding ethical standards should be the subject of formal reviews.

An important aspect of integrity revolves around fiduciary duties of duty and care of all directors. This means that they are required to serve in good faith, implying independence that does not place the director in a conflict of interest situation. According to Higgs (2003), a NED is considered independent when the board determines that the director is independent in character and judgment, and there are no relationships or circumstances that affect the director's judgment. Thus, independence is not only an absence of concrete compromising relationships but also a matter of character.

Directors are expected to act truthfully and honestly in the exercise of their duties (Harper, 2005; Lechem, 2002). As leader of the board, the chairman has to create a sense of obligation among all directors to fulfill their fiduciary duties and to act as stewards of the company. A study on the role of shareholders, directors, and others defines stewardship as the process by which these actors seek to "influence companies in the direction of long-term sustainable performance that derives from contributing to human progress and the well-being of the environment and society" (Tomorrow's Company, 2008, p. 3).

Kakabadse and Kakabadse (2008) state that "as the ultimate steward of the organization, the chairman lives trust and integrity on behalf of the organization" (p. 113). They emphasize the need for consistency between espoused ethical values and behavior. This is not always easy, given the pressures and complexities of business life. Self-understanding alongside an intimate knowledge of the organization may be helpful in diagnosing obstacles that prevent the individual chairman from sticking to principles when facing uncomfortable challenges, essential in ensuring consistency and ethical integrity.

Attributes of the effective chairman

What kind of a person makes an effective chairman? Various surveys and inquiries have studied this question, and there are some common findings on desirable attributes (Cadbury, 2002; Directorbank, 2008; Dulewicz et al., 2007; Harper, 2005; Kakabadse and Kakbadse, 2008; Praesta, 2005; SpencerStuart, 2008). The common attributes reported in these studies break down under a number of headings:

- Integrity and high ethical standards
- Communication skills

- Personal authority and presence
- Cognitive abilities
- A sense of purpose

Integrity and high ethical standards

As the leader who sets the ethical tone, the chairman must be credible in his/her own personal moral conduct and character. This entails proved trustworthiness, and no compromises or evidence of double standards, in not only his/her own behavior but also in the high expectations set for others. Effective chairmen take the directorial duties of loyalty and due care very seriously, acting to safeguard the company from reputational risk. Their integrity would be recognized by critical stakeholders such as investors, and this would be a boon to the company.

Communication skills

It stands to reason that as someone whose discharge of duties depends on many other people, singly and in groups, the chairman needs to be an effective communicator, since the chairman wields influence largely by personal qualities, rather than by imposing control or dominance, and communication via persuasion becomes central. Good communicators must make their points with clarity, but they should also be good listeners and inquirers. Articulateness in marshalling arguments and sensitivity to the practical and emotional needs of others is important. Of course, persuasion and influence should not be based on cynicism or manipulation and must be authentic, grounded in respect for the other. This does not mean shying away from difficult conversations, or tackling awkward situations.

Personal authority and presence

Credibility and communication, both internal and external, are enhanced by personal presence and authority. Individuals with personal presence command respect for their expertise, track record, integrity, and wisdom. When this person speaks, people sit up and listen. Sometimes, they are charismatic. Part of personal presence is political skills that are essential in engaging all stakeholders, bringing people together, and managing relationships. Yet, it is desirable that the chairman not be an egotistical individual who craves the limelight and wants public credit for corporate achievements, since his/her job as head of the board is primarily to support the CEO and senior management in running the company successfully.

Cognitive abilities

This quality refers to the ability to size up a situation quickly, to grasp the core issues, and exercise excellent judgment. To some extent, it is based on knowledge of a sector, and/or on life and professional experience, but it is more, because it requires a constructive application of knowledge and experience to current situations and problems. Part of it is critical thinking, the capacity to examine an issue analytically, not to accept ideas at face value without understanding them and their further implications. Further, effective chairmen should be able to envisage alternative scenarios and recombine old elements, as contributors to strategic thinking.

A sense of purpose

The chairman has a clear direction in leading the organizational mission and is passionate about making it a reality, inspiring others. S/he is focused on the board's key tasks and issues, making sure they are addressed. Thus, s/he insists on getting things done and on following through, not content to let things drift, whether it is a board discussion or implementation of agreed actions. The chairman does not waiver from long-term greater aspirations for the company, and will not be defeated by obstacles and crises along the way.

Other attributes

Various other desirable attributes have been mentioned in studies on what makes a great chairman. These include broad experience, having a network of contacts, good team builders, empathetic, adopting a flexible approach, and having a keen appreciation of the difference between directing and managing. These characteristics may contribute to the others, for example, broad experience offers material for exercising cognitive abilities.

Issues in the role of the chairman

Chairman selection and remuneration

Much of what has been written and observed about chairmen assumes an in situ person in the post. But, how does the chairman get there? Very little is known about how chairmen are actually selected, and the process goes on behind closed doors. Given that it is such a tall order to find a person with all the vital characteristics, experience, knowledge, and so on, shouldn't there be guidelines on how to go about the search and selection process? Moreover, who is it that does the search and selection? Even this is shrouded in mystery.

Thus, there are many questions to be answered:

- Who should best lead the process? Is it the incumbent chairman? Is it a board subcommittee? Is it the SID, if one exists?
- What stakeholders are consulted? CEO and other senior managers? Institutional shareholders? Other key stakeholders as circumstances demand?
- What is the source of new chairmen? Existing board members? Outgoing or former CEO (although generally frowned upon)? Outsider from within the same industry? Outsider from a different industry?

- Any special attributes required? For example, political influence – former politician.

The answers to the questions may well be contingent on circumstances, and what is required at the time. For example, a company in decline may require a "company doctor" type who has successfully chaired companies requiring a turnaround. Generally, there are various considerations to take into account in finding a new chairman, according to Cadbury (2002). This chapter has delineated the fundamental qualities to do the job, under all circumstances. Of course, the candidate must be willing to accept the chairman's role, and that s/he is not the chief executive.

Another relatively nontransparent aspect is how the chairman's levels of remuneration are decided, and by whom.

Chairman removal

The issue of chairman selection also brings up that of deselection, that is, under what circumstances should an incumbent chairman be dismissed? Cadbury (2002) states that when a chairman has lost the confidence of the board, and/or of shareholders, it is an occasion for his/her removal from office. The reasons for loss of confidence are variable, ranging from incompetence or bad faith, resulting in a breakdown of key relationships. When there is a SID or Deputy Chairman, it is up to this person to deal with the matter. Otherwise, it may take a faction of the board to take the lead. Things can get very unpleasant, depending on how the situation is handled, for example, discretion versus publicity, and terms of dismissal.

Cadbury suggests that formal procedures for selection and removal of the chairman are very helpful. In this respect, a board committee for the purpose, led by the SID is the usual mechanism for evaluating the chairman's performance. A survey of nearly 400 directors sitting on more than 900 boards confirmed that 40 per cent of UK boardrooms have no structures in place to remove an ineffective chairman (Directorbank, 2008). Almost 8 out of 10 revealed that they had worked with an ineffective chairman and most companies do not know how to fire them. This is a problem, since only 18 per cent of respondents thought it is worth trying to improve an underperforming chairman through coaching and mentoring, clarifying the role, and helping to identify issues and weaknesses and work on eliminating them. However, it is unclear who would work with the chairman on the attempted improvements, but the circumstances may be too uncomfortable for everyone involved, and may end up undermining the chairman's position and dignity.

The ineffective chairman

There is a degree of consensus about what makes an ineffective chairman. The ineffective chairman is lacking in the traits and behaviors that comprise the make-up of the effective chairman. The Directorbank (2008) survey lists the characteristics of ineffective chairmen. These include the ditherer who is unable to make decisions, who cannot communicate or listen, and who fails to keep the board on course. Other undesirable traits are poor leadership and control of the board, and a lack of independence of mind – being too partisan and partial. The unsuccessful chairman may be too aloof and not involved, or may suffer from arrogance, being over-opinionated and domineering. Other failings are cognitive ones, that is, a failure to understand the business or sector. Kakabdse and Kakabdse (2008) also delineate some of the defects of poor chairmen. One of these is overintrusiveness, in effect, micromanagement. Another is being egotistical, competing with the CEO. On the other hand, chairmen may also fail by being oversubservient to the chief executive.

Conclusion

This chapter has outlined the potential expanded role of a chairman whose position is separate, but complementary to that of the CEO. It envisages that the chairman, leading the board of directors, has a vital part to play beyond monitoring and controlling the CEO and management. The expanded role makes a positive contribution to helping the CEO to enhance performance for the benefit of the organization. However, to realize the potential of the expanded role, the individual filling the chairman job must satisfy demanding requirements in character, personality, and behavioral style, to fulfill the criteria for a world-class chairman (Kakabadse and Kakabadse, 2008). The notion of being world class accommodates the fact that there is variety in corporate governance forms and institutional arrangements around the world. However, irrespective of the arrangements, what this chapter has attempted to demonstrate is that there are fundamental general requirements of a first-class chairman. It assumes a separation of roles between chairman and CEO, a form increasingly recognized as enabling an enhancement of accountable leadership when it works well.

It is not clear how it is possible to find and select people of sufficient caliber to take on the chairman position. The difficulty of the task of finding high-quality chairmen is underlined by the fact that an overwhelming majority of directors have worked with chairmen that they consider to be hopelessly ineffective. It is also evident that underperforming chairmen are difficult to remove, but increased success in effective chairman recruitment should minimize the need for removal anyway. This issue deserves more scrutiny, by learning from past successes as to how it was done, or from failures as to what not to do.

References

Benz, M. and Frey, B.S. (2007), "Corporate governance: What can we learn from public governance?," *Academy of Management Review*, 32:1, 92–104.

Cadbury. A. (2002), *Corporate Governance and Chairmanship: A Personal View*, Oxford University Press, Oxford.

Chung, J. and Burgess, K. (2008), "Calls in US for split of top jobs gain momentum," *Financial Times*, May 28, 24.

Directorbank (2008), *What Makes an Outstanding Chairman?* London, October 2008.

Dulewicz, V., Gay, K. and Taylor, B. (2007), "What makes an outstanding chairman? Findings from the UK non-executive director of the year awards," *Corporate Governance: An International Review*, 15:6, 1056–69.

Financial Reporting Council (2003), *The Combined Code on Corporate Governance*, The Financial Reporting Council, UK.

Harper, J. (2005), *Chairing the Board – A Practical Guide to Activities and Responsibilities*, Kogan Page, London & Sterling, VA.

Higgs, D. (2003), *Review of the Role and Effectiveness of Non-executive Directors*, UK Department of Trade and Industry, London.

Kakabadse, A. and Kakabadse, N. (2008), *Leading the Board: The Six Disciplines of World-Class Chairmen*, Palgrave Macmillan, Basingstoke and New York.

Lechem, B. (2002), *Chairman of the Board: A Practical Guide*, John Wiley & Sons, Hoboken, N.J.

MacAvoy, P.W. and Millstein, I.M. (2003), *The Recurrent Crisis in Corporate Governance*, Palgrave Macmillan, Basingstoke & New York.

Praesta (2005), *The Art of Chairing a Board*, Praesta Ireland, Dublin, May 2005.

Roberts, J. (2002), "Building the complementary board: The work of the chairman," *Long Range Planning*, 35:5, 493–520.

Roberts, J. and Stiles, P. (1999), "The relationship between chairmen and chief executives: Competitive or complementary roles?," *Long Range Planning*, 32:1, 36–48.

SpencerStuart (2008), *Cornerstone of the Board the Non-executive Chairman: Offering New Solutions*, London, January 2008.

Tomorrow's Company (2008), *Tomorrow's Owners: Stewardship of Tomorrow's Company*. London, October 2008.

10
The Recruitment and Evaluation of Boards of Directors in China

Nada Kakabadse, Hong Yang and Richard Sanders

Introduction

The cultural and market differences existing in Asia–Pacific markets create challenges in developing and implementing appropriate corporate governance systems. In China, it is particularly challenging, given the ill-developed nature of markets and supporting infrastructure in its transitional economy (e.g., Hovey, 2005; Zhang, 2006; Chen, 2005; Voß and Xia, 2006; OECD, 2007; Barton and Huang, 2007). With the emergence of capital markets in China, the current boom in institutional investment and the increasing establishment of legal frameworks (Qu and Leung, 2006), the implementation of systems of corporate governance is having a significant impact on China's own economic development and integration into global markets (Ewing, 2005). Although China's economy has shown continuous growth over the last 30 years of transition, future growth should not be taken for granted; indeed, it has been known for countries and companies with weak corporate governance systems to suffer larger collapses when hit by adverse shocks (Johnson and Shleifer, 2004). Weaknesses associated with the supervisory board, the board of directors and external audit are the main reasons for the prevalence of fraud committed by top management (Yuan and Yuan, 2007). Many issues such as the selection and evaluation mechanisms of board of directors employed by corporations and the training and qualifications of board of directors have become even more important. Scholars have suggested that China needs a continuous evolution of the existing systems, thereby improving the overall policy and institutional environment, strengthening the enforcement of existing laws and encouraging a continuous evolution of internal systems of control, with particular attention paid to improving shareholder rights and the accountability of boards of directors (Hu, 2005; Lin, 2001).

This chapter explores the recruitment and evaluation mechanisms employed by Chinese SOEs and their implications for corporate governance. It draws on a number of sources including semi-structured interviews and secondary data. The paper is divided into four main sections in addition to the introduction. The first section reviews the literature on Chinese corporate governance. The second presents the methodology applied to this particular empirical study. This is followed by the third section that outlines the data collected from the semi-structured interviews based on the boards of directors' perceptions on corporate governance practices in their companies. The final section discusses the implications of current elements of the Chinese corporate governance system, including major aspects of corporate governance practices such as the procedures followed in selection and evaluation, training and development and the independence of boards of directors. The conclusion highlights the theoretical and practical implications of the paper and argues that the recruitment and evaluation processes create a unique governance issue that requires further research in order to establish an efficient corporate governance system promoting independence, accountability and expertise.

Institutional background

Historical perspective

Starting in 1978, China's economic reform launched a new era in China's new political and economic life. The reform intended to liberate companies from bureaucratic control hindering their management and to improve the productivity of SOEs (e.g., Naughton, 1995; Koppell, 2007). Li and Wu (2002), however, state that this reform strategy has not had a persistent and economically significant effect on enterprise performance for several reasons. Ultimately, the reforms proved to be inadequate because managers were not penalised for poor performance and were insufficiently accountable to their government owners (Ewing, 2005). The poor performance of SOEs motivated the Chinese government to shift the focus of SOE reform to ownership and corporate governance restructuring (e.g., Ewing, 2005).

In 1992, the Chinese Communist Party (CCP) formally recognised the market economy as the ultimate destination of economic reform and formally endorsed private property rights (Zhang, 2002). The Company Law (1993) specified that governance structures are "to meet the needs of establishing a modern enterprise system, to standardise the organisation and activities of companies, to protect the legitimate rights and interests of companies, shareholders and creditors, to maintain the socio-economic order and to promote the development of the socialist market economy" (Chinese Company law, 1993, cited in Hua et al., 2006:404). A very important aspect of the reforms was the move towards a "socialist market economy" and the official opening of China's two Stock Exchanges encouraged more than 80 per cent of the SOEs to be transformed into corporate entities under the Company Law (Yao, 2004). The objective of such action was to raise finance from domestic and foreign investors to provide listed SOEs with new funds

(Mallin, 2004; Braendle et al., 2005). SOEs are required to form boards of directors, hold shareholder meetings and establish boards of supervisors to independently oversee and evaluate the behaviour of directors and managers (McNally, 2002:4). A well-functioning governance system is required to help align managerial incentives with economic value creation (Ewing, 2005).

From 1990 to 2000, the number of Chinese listed companies increased from 10 to 1121, with an annual increase rate of 53.2 per cent (Chen, 2005). There are two conflicting goals and a trade-off has been made between immediate economic growth and long-term sustainability of economic growth (Cooper, 2002). Problems exist at both the microeconomic and macroeconomic levels because of the lack of a corporate culture and institutions, the presence of political influence and agency costs (Wu, 1999). This strategy is now widely perceived to have not been successful at least in terms of the profitability of SOEs (Tian and Lau, 2001; Zhang, 2006). The performance of the majority of listed companies has declined after their restructuring and listing, mostly due to the flawed governance structures and inadequate performance incentives caused by continued state ownership (Green, 2004). Additionally, a thin capital market with few investment opportunities has made it easy for listed firms to raise equity even without sound corporate governance (Lin, 2000; Leung et al., 2002). According to Cheng (2007), 70 per cent of the companies listed on China's domestic markets do not meet international standards in terms of profit, returns and other indicators (Takeshi, 2007: 36). Apart from ownership transformation, the corporate governance of SOEs has come to be regarded as the crucial obstacle to China's further economic reform (Huchet and Richet, 2002).

Investors in China have protested that they have been greatly disadvantaged by the prevalence of non-tradable shares, typically held by central and local governments, which make up around two-thirds of outstanding common shares of China's 1350 listed companies (Tucker, 2006). In 2002, the Chinese government realised that without the reduction of state ownership, fundamental and sustainable improvements could not be achieved despite the significant progress to date in developing various instruments of corporate governance (Tenev and Zhang, 2002). The Chinese government mentioned officially non-tradable shares as a major hurdle for domestic financial development and stated its commitment to face the problem in the near future (Beltratti and Bortolotti, 2006). In 2005, the Chinese Securities Regulatory Commission (CSRC) announced an initiative to convert non-tradable shares into tradable shares. The new initiative, called "Administrative Measures on the Split Share Structure Reform of Listed Companies," provides the ground rules to allow for the conversion of the shares[1] (CSRC, 2005). As of December 2006, 96 per cent of the listed SOEs had completed the conversion process (People's Daily, 2006). The corporate governance system was expected to be changed fundamentally by this reform. SOEs had to define clear board responsibilities, increase representatives of tradable shareholders on boards and strengthen the function of collective decision making (Wan and Yuce, 2007). Investors would gain more power and exert more pressure on the proper information disclosure and transparency, the proper functioning of the board of directors and supervisory boards, the independence of auditors and so on (Voß and Xia, 2006; Table 10.1).

Chinese boards

Young et al. (2008) state that emerging economies have normally attempted to adopt the legal frameworks of developed economies such as the Anglo-American system, either as a result of internally driven reforms (e.g., China, Russia) or as a response to international demands (e.g., South Korea, Thailand). The Chinese model has elements of the Anglo-US model of corporate governance by way of a board of directors and shareholders meetings (Hovey, 2005) (Figure 10.1). The board of directors is the main decision-making authority with members working closely with management on the day-to-day operations of the company (Lin, 2004; CFA Institute, 2007). The boards, however, are dominated by executive directors, who make up two-thirds of the board on average, with less than 5 per cent of all directors showing any degree of independence (Liu, 2005, p. 447). According to Chen (2005), boards of directors in China have the power to formulate business and investment plans and these plans are approved at the shareholder's meeting whilst recognising inefficient supervising capacity. According to Xu (2004), on average, the largest shareholder (i.e., the state) owns 43 per cent of the issued shares and the second largest owns less than 5 per cent. The state, as the largest shareholder in SOEs, maintains effective control and intervenes in the day-to-day operations of the companies. The Company Law (2005) states that the executive directors have the duty of upholding the interests of the company but not of addressing the director's fiduciary duties (Chen, 2005). These directors, therefore, have no incentive to motivate the activities of the directors and managers and consequently contribute little to the improvement of corporate governance (Yuan and Yuan, 2007).

There has been a long debate as to whether independent directors in listed companies in China have a particular responsibility to minority shareholders where the evidence shows high ownership concentration and frequent misappropriation of funds by majority shareholders (OECD, 2007). Although Chinese listed companies have independent directors, they lack a basic understanding of their role (Leung et al., 2002). The appointment of independent directors on boards was not the result of market development, but was promoted by compulsory government enforcement (Lu, 2006). Independent directors in China account for less than one-third of the board in Chinese publicly trade corporations, in comparison with 75 per cent in large US listed companies and 50 per cent in UK firms (Ewing, 2005). By the

Table 10.1 Reform of SOEs in China

Stage	Time Period	Corporate Governance of SOEs
Original	Before 1978	All SOEs were totally owned by government of China. SOEs were not market-based enterprises in terms of production, marketing and distribution
		Governance: government was the sole investor who intervened in every aspect of SOEs without any supervision. SOEs'reform was provoked by the problem of low efficiency in the early 1980s and was designed to reduce the control by government
Primary	1978–92	The government retained the right to select agents or contractees
		Party Committee Employees Representative Committee Trade Unions in firms played important role in terms of governance
Transitional	1992–2002	SOE's reform transformed from management-oriented reform into enterprise system innovation. Most of the state-owned companies carried out "corporatisation" according to Company Law after 1993
		The checks and balances were weak in Chinese companies
		There was weak outside monitoring by stakeholders in firms, capital markets and credit institutions
		There was a concentration of control that very often was closely connected to the state

		Concentrated ownership structure with state as the controlling shareholder
		Lack of markets for corporate control
		Lack of independence of the boards of directors: most of the directors on boards were executive directors and representatives of big shareholders
		Codes and standards of corporate governance of Chinese listed companies have been formulated
Converging	2002–Present	CSRC: Independent directors system: Has required all Chinese listed companies to have 3 independent directors before June 2002 and 1/3 independent directors on the board by June 2003
		Diversification of ownership by diluting state shares
		Measures taken to standardise the relationship between listed companies and controlling shareholders
		Beginning of emphasis on board functions
		Performance-based incentive system set up: share option plans

Source: Adapted from Tian and Lau (2001) and Tenev and Zhang (2002).

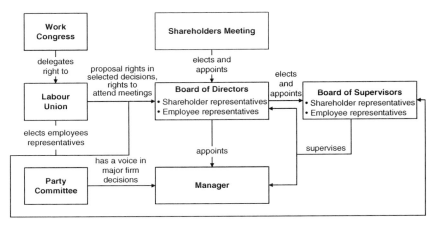

Figure 10.1   Corporate governance of China's listed firms
Source: Nee et al., 2007.

end of 2004, 4681 independent directors were employed by 1377 Chinese listed companies in total, equivalent to three independent directors for each listed company on an average (OECD, 2005). China needs to fill over 3000 independent director positions in its listed companies (Tai and Wong, 2003, cited in Rajagopalan and Zhang, 2008). However, currently many of them are not truly independent in that a "key man" often dominates the decisions of the board (Economist, 2000, 2001, cited in Hovey and Naughton, 2007). According to a survey done by Tenev and Zhang (2002), only 3.1 per cent of all directors had some degree of independence, compared to 62 per cent in the US and 34 per cent in the UK. Leung et al. (2002) noted that there was still a short supply of qualified directors that fit the CSRC criteria, making it difficult to meet the demands for a composite board and providing a continued challenge to SOEs to improve their corporate governance standards.

Clarke (2003, 2006) argues that under China's current institutional environment, particularly the legal environment that affects the viability of any proposed solution, the duty of independent directors who owe a duty of good faith and diligence cannot be made. The establishment of the system of independent directors in China has been promoted by compulsory government enforcement rather than being the natural result of market development (Lu, 2005). This is a particular issue in China where there is concentrated ownership and frequent irregular misconduct by the major shareholders. Clarke (2006) believes that independent directors are a potential solution to China's corporate governance problems. From Lawler and Finegold's (2005) research, although there were no significant relationships between board effectiveness and the practice of having independent chairs or board of directors, the formal corporate governance guidelines can provide a vital structure for boards and can help them to be more effective in their deliberations and decision-making processes. Firth et al. (2007a, b) conclude that independent directors help to align the interests of shareholders with the interests of the CEO. The rationale behind independent boards is to ensure they behave in the shareholders' interest rather than managerial interests and to motivate them to be more accountable by going beyond box-ticking practices, engaging deeply in their monitoring and strategic advice roles (Finkelstein and Mooney, 2003).

Recruitment and evaluation of board of directors

Chen (2005) argues that a key condition for success would be the appointment and remuneration of the board of directors based on competence and performance. The OECD (2005) principles of corporate governance require that the board should fulfil certain key functions, including ensuring a formal and transparent board nomination and election process. The boards of directors at SOEs are expected to go more deeply into a number of technical issues, thus helping to share out directorial responsibilities and reduce conflicts of interest (Chen, 2004). The main role of the nomination committee is to carry out a systematic procedure to evaluate the existing balance of skills, knowledge and experience on the board and utilise this when preparing a candidate profile for new appointments (Mallin, 2004). Lu (2006) states that Chinese corporations still lack nominating committees for directors and corporate governance committees. Regarding director selection, although the Company Law (2005) stipulates that the shareholders' general meeting is responsible for selecting and removing directors, it does not stipulate who is responsible for nominating directors (Lu, 2006). The process of nomination and compensation review is primarily handled by the management team or directed by the state (CFA Institute, 2007). Garnaut et al. (2005) note that the influence of Party committees on personnel appointments leads to skewed management incentives where managers tend to spend considerable effort presenting the right political image and nurturing good relations with superiors in the Party hierarchy. Managers can be transferred (promoted or demoted) to other SOEs suddenly and based on political criteria, without taking into account the interests of the company and its shareholders, curtailing the effective monitoring of managerial behaviour, distorting management incentives and creating a tendency toward insider control (Garnaut et al., 2005). As a result, SOE managers behave more like professional bureaucrats than professional managers (Zhang, 2007). Cheng (1998) argued that the lack of an effective performance-based compensation system resulted from several factors including multiple agency layers in the agency chain, the indistinguishable input of management under socialism, the bureaucratic executive appointment system, as well as serious information asymmetry problems. Evaluation systems that reward best practice and align management with a performance orientation, therefore, must be established (Hovey and Naughton, 2007). Ewing (2005) argue that the regulators could advocate bonus performance standards including indices for stock price, returns to shareholders and other proxies for shareholder value and promote stock-based performance incentives by introducing equity ownership of managers and directors.

Methodology and data

The approach adopted in this research was qualitative in nature. Twenty-one in-depth, semi-structured interviews were undertaken with participants who currently held a role in the board, including board of directors, enterprise management and supervisory agencies, allowing respondents to reveal their views and perceptions. The process of finding interviewees and setting up interviews is central to the outcomes of the research (Rapley, 2004). A purpose sampling approach (Glaser and Strauss, 1967) allowed us to draw samples from relevant organisations. There is also an effect of snowball sampling (Flyvbjerg, 2004) when some participants suggested or introduced other relevant people with the same characteristics to form part of our research. Access to participants was through personal contacts. This research was designed to allow information gathering for exploring the recruitment and evaluation mechanisms for board of directors. The principal fieldwork was conducted with SOEs in the retailing and trade sectors in China, competitive sectors (in contrast to strategic sectors such as oil and the defence industry), where the corporate governance system is partly controlled by the state and the applicability of alternative governance forms is possible. Additionally, these sectors provide a unique lens to study economic restructuring and corporate governance system development in the context of institutional change and globalisation.

Although a relatively small sample size, the interviews can be considered to be significant as they include senior level participants who were able to comment in detail on the recruitment and evaluation issues in their boards. Each participant was contacted initially in order to make introductions and to consider arrangements of the time and location of the interview. The interview protocol developed in the light of the review of literature on recruitment and evaluation of board of directors and was used to collect detailed information about interviewees' perceptions on selection and evaluation processes, the independence issues of board of directors and so on. The profile of participants in the case studies is presented in Table 10.2. Permission from the head of these organisations (e.g., the board's chairman, or CEOs) had to be sought to conduct these meetings at the place of work. Each one-to-one interview lasted for about one hour. All interviews were conducted in China in Mandarin and simultaneously translated and transcribed into English.

This research used thematic analysis of the qualitative data. The data were coded and analysed manually. Coding involves reviewing a set of notes, either transcribed or synthesised, and dissecting them while keeping relations between the parts intact (Miles and Huberman, 1994). Transcribing, reading and re-reading the interview data provided the bulk of the information analysed with the support of the relevant literature review.

Study findings

Four major themes emerged from data analysis, namely the selection of boards of directors, the composition of boards of directors, boards of directors' training and the qualifications and evaluation of boards of directors. Each theme is presented below.

The selection of boards of directors

The following sections present how participants perceived their companies' functioning in terms of selecting and approving boards of directors and top management.

Recruitment of top management/executive directors

The following statements illustrate the formal procedures that companies followed in selecting top management:

> The process of nominating has become quite formal because the company has many outside shareholders. Under the pressure of market forces, top management and boards of directors must be competent. In the reform process, the boards have been taking an active role in executive selection. For example, a nomination committee has been established and the directors have obtained power to interview candidates before voting on them. It is a critical step taken by the SOEs because only with such a formal process, will the minority shareholders have the motivation to make investments in the enterprise. (Participant 15, Independent Director, Company B)

> In particular, top management must go through legal procedures and then hold relevant posts.(Participant 10, External Supervisor, Company B)

> The boards of directors have become more engaged in the selection of top management. Top management positions have been filled in a transparent process where the board made the final decision so that the most qualified candidates were chosen.(Participant 12, Executive Director, Company B)

> A formal nomination process includes appraisals of board members and allows greater transparency. In my company, the nomination process generally complies with the rules for listed companies. Non state shareholders can express their opinions in terms of nominating board members. (Participant 12, Executive Director, Company B)

Table 10.2 Profile of interview participants

Code Number	Industry	Tenure	Gender	Tile	Degree/Qualification
Respondent 1	Company A – International Trade	12	Male	Chairman	Bachelor
Respondent 2	Company A – International Trade	1	Male	CEO	Bachelor
Respondent 3	Company A – International Trade	12	Female	Vice Chairman	Bachelor
Respondent 4	Company A – International Trade	12	Male	Executive Director	Bachelor
Respondent 5	Company A – International Trade	12	Male	Executive Director	Bachelor
Respondent 6	Company A – International Trade	7	Male	Independent Director	Professor
Respondent 7	Company A – International Trade	7	Female	Independent Director	Master
Respondent 8	Company A – International Trade	4	Male	Chairman of Supervisory Board	Bachelor
Respondent 9	Company A – International Trade	6	Male	Internal Supervisor	Bachelor

Respondent	Company		Gender	External Supervisor	
Respondent 10	Company A – International Trade	4	Male		Bachelor
Respondent 11	Company B – Retail	4	Male	Independent Director	Professor
Respondent 12	Company B – Retail	4	Male	Executive Director	Bachelor
Respondent 13	Company B – Retail	4	Male	Director	Bachelor
Respondent 14	Company B – Retail	4	Male	Executive Director	Bachelor
Respondent 15	Company B – Retail	4	Female	Independent Director	Doctor
Respondent 16	Company B – Retail	4	Male	Supervisor	Bachelor
Respondent 17	Company B – Retail	4	Male	Supervisor	Bachelor
Respondent 18	Company C –Retail	4	Female	Director	Master
Respondent 19	Company C – Retail	4	Male	Independent Director	Professor
Respondent 20	Company C – Retail	4	Male	CEO	Master
Respondent 21	Company C – Retail	4	Male	Executive Director	Bachelor

Source: Compiled by the authors.

The directors are selected via the shareholders general meeting. Shareholders have rights to decide who will be selected as directors. (Participant 6, Independent Director, Company A)

It is not possible to recruit someone through personal relationships. We try to attract real talent to join our enterprise.(Participant 21, Executive Director, Company C)

Seen from above statements, some participants believe the nomination procedure for boards of directors and top management is transparent and formal, in accordance with the law.

Recruitment of CEO/Chairman

In terms of the nomination procedure for the Chairman and sometimes for the CEO, participants noted the process was informal and influenced by the large shareholders. For example, two participants stated:

The chairman of our company is appointed by the state agency and acts as both a government officer and the chairman of the board. He is selected without a process of consultation with the board of directors. (Participant 14, Executive Director, Company B)

It is true that the state agency selects certain people to serve on the board as Chairman or CEO. Of course, the people selected must be accepted by the public. The state has already had certain ideal candidates with good political background and competence. Although the selection is through the general assembly meeting and in the form of voting, you will find that the candidates chosen by the state always win. This is because before the general meeting, a consensus has already been reached with the large shareholders. The meeting is just a formality.(Participant 13, Director, Company B)

The findings illustrate that the large shareholders control and dominate within the SOEs. In terms of the selection of boards of directors, the state agency plays an important role in selecting the people who have a government role to serve the board as chairman or executive. The chairman of the board and executive directors are often appointed by the regional government as part of a system for promoting government officials (Takeshi, 2007). Participants also show that the state/large shareholder was keen to protect its investment by nominating competent people on the board. However, most of the candidates used to work as government officers before being selected as directors. The capability of government officials to act as entrepreneurs is doubtful. Zhang (2007) states that in contrast with capitalist firms where the manager tries to become a "capitalist," SOE managers try to be promoted as bureaucrats. Without involvement in the formal selection process, it is difficult to protect minority shareholders' interests. It is recommended that directors need to ensure that the interests of all shareholders, particularly minority shareholders, are reflected in the board's decisions (OECD, 2007).

Recruitment of independent directors

It is argued that companies should maintain the proper functioning of independent directors on the board to ensure better monitoring and control, increasing the confidence of investors in the credibility of companies. Most participants report that once the majority of independent directors were recommended by major shareholders or executive directors, they were less likely to provide any opposition to major shareholders. Problems in the recruitment process of independent directors are illustrated below

> Candidates to become independent director are selected by the large shareholders or executive board of directors. Under such a nominating system, it is difficult to guarantee that the independent directors are actually independent from the large shareholders or management. In fact, most of them maintain a good relationship with managers and executive boards of directors.(Participant 12, Director, Company B)

Personal relationships represent an important part in Chinese business society, which is illustrated in the selection process. For example, one participant comments

> Personal relationships play a big role in the nominees. Like most company directors in China, independent directors are chosen more by personal connections than business know-how. (Participant 5, Executive Director, Company A)

These findings demonstrate that the recruitment of independent directors is consistent with the selection of directors in general. It is interesting to see that the independence of directors is compromised by the friendships in the board members' appointment process, although it is claimed that the selection is not done at the expense of quality. The study reveals that majority of independent directors are selected and recommended by major shareholders and executive directors through personal contacts or friendships. Lu (2006) contends that the overwhelming majority of independent directors are nominated by major shareholders or executive directors, and as such they are unlikely to raise issues that may be uncomfortable for major shareholders. It is difficult for them to hold an opposing view to that of major shareholders or challenge the board since personal relationships are treasured in Chinese business culture. Maintaining relationships has become a prerequisite for most independent directors in honouring their obligations (Lu, 2006).

Clarke (2006) argues that truly independent directors often lack support from controlling shareholders because the latter are likely to feel threatened if the board is too independent for them to control in the way they wish to. Yuan's (2007) survey states that 2 per cent of independent directors admit that they are "vase directors"; 39 per cent of independent directors implicitly identify their role as counselor and only 37 per cent regard themselves as monitors. According to China Securities Daily's survey, 65 per cent of independent directors indicated that they never said "no" in board meetings and all of them noted that they voted yes even though they should have voted "no" on the basis of their knowledge and the merits of the proposal (China Securities Daily, 2005, cited in Wang, 2007). Independent directors cannot really operate independently owing to their relationships with the companies and are likely to have difficulty in having conflicts with the executive directors who appoint them. It is common that independent directors are very reluctant to offend their friends, such as the chairman or CEO, even though the latter may have committed something detrimental to the interests of the company and its shareholders (Xie, 2004, cited in Wang, 2007). The emphasis on informality is perceived to be inadequately transparent.

The Involvement of large shareholders

The pervasiveness of the concentrated large shareholders tends to lead to an insider-dominated system of corporate governance. The independence of boards of directors is largely compromised. For example, some participants state

> The representatives of the State-Owned Assets Supervision and Administration Commission are the people who have the right to select directors to delegate them. ((Participant 13, Director, Company B)

> Practically, the nomination process often involves the controlling shareholder, typically the state agency in the case of our company, appointing the board chairman and CEO and notifying other shareholders accordingly. Other board members are appointed by other major shareholders such as institutional investors in proportion to their shareholding, but discussed beforehand with the controlling shareholder and sometimes with the worker representatives. One or two board vacancies are sometimes left to minority and outside shareholders to elect at the shareholders' meeting. (Participant 18, Director, Company C

> There are no dominant shareholders in my company. The shareholding is dispersed in the hands of state and institutional investors. The state agency owns the largest shareholding. It has the right to compose the board and select its members. Institutional investors are other major shareholders who also have the voting right. Albeit they have a right to appoint or nominate board members, the majority of the vote is in the

hand of the state agency. Thus, board directors are selected by the major shareholders. (Participant 2, CEO, Company A)

The Communist Party is the largest shareholder, the party designates have a main role in deciding who will sit on the board. It is true that ownership is concentrated in the hands of a few shareholders. It is a Chinese characteristic. (Participant 21, Director, Company C)

These findings indicate that state interests prevail in the current governance structure. In addition to being a large shareholder, the state has control over the recruitment policy. Most of the participants point out that they were representatives of the state. Since the state is the largest shareholder, they perceive there is nothing wrong in having the power to dominate the selection of the board of directors and top management. The role of the state and its influence and engagement in controlling and managing the company are very significant because it has the responsibility for deciding the selection of the board of directors. The independence of the board of directors is threatened, although these participants express the view that they are indeed independent in the decision making.

Many participants talk about the linkage between the large shareholder and the board composition. Rather than being negative about this, their views are fairly positive because they believe the state would choose appropriate and competent candidates who would serve in the best interests of the board. The quality may not be compromised. In their views, boards ultimately function on behalf of majority shareholders. This is explained in the following statements:

It is no problem for the state to nominate the chairman and top management. There is no conflict of interests because the interests of majority shareholders and the board of directors have been very similar. (Participant 12, Executive director, Company B)

Although the representatives of the government institutions are able to veto candidates in committee, the other external directors still have chances to be elected. There was no contradiction between Party influence and the protection of minority interests. After all, we want to recruit competent people onto the board. The board of directors has the right to select the chairman and CEO and appoints top executives rather than politically as before. (Respondent 1, Chairman, Company A)

There is a link between the major shareholders and the board composition, and this is neither wrong nor disadvantageous. The large shareholders are the persons most devoted to protecting their investments and increasing them. Thus, the board composition relies on the major shareholder. Normally, the State-Owned Assets Supervision and Administration Commission has a greater role than others, this is a fact, and it nominates the chairman and CEO to represent it on the board. This does not really create a conflict of interests because the ultimate purpose of the SOEs are to create wealth for the state and thereby the public. (Respondent 20, CEO, Company C)

Typically, you find on the board that the state is keen to select some directors that represent it and add experience to the board. Although I was delegated by the State-Owned Assets Supervision and Administration Commission, I was selected mainly because the state wanted to add my experience to the board The company needs my experience, participation and open mind to express my opinion. (Participant 12, Executive Director, Company B)

These statements revealed the positive views on the recruitment of board of directors by large shareholders. It shows that the state's involvement in the selection process apparently encourages corporations to choose the most competent people to add value to shareholders. The Company Law (2005) stipulates that the shareholders' general meeting is responsible for selecting and removing directors and that the nominees must consent to be nominated by votes at the shareholders' general meeting (The Company Law, 2004). But the shareholders' general meeting with boards of directors controlled by the major shareholders lowers the effectiveness of the board in terms of the directors' supervision of management (Takeshi, 2007). Lu's (2005) research states large shareholders nominate new directors in 57 per cent of listed companies; the board of directors does so in 34 per cent of companies; the chair of the board in 6 per cent and the existing directors in 3 per cent. The empirical data shows the lack of a formal process for nomination, even though the decisions should be made by the shareholders at general meeting. Although the nomination must be done by shareholders via the general meeting, most of the participants state that nomination is actually carried out by the large shareholders because the nomination board is largely composed of the representatives of the large shareholder and the voting is just a formality. The "control by insiders" is a widespread problem among China's listed companies (Lu, 2005). The directors and managers of listed SOEs are mainly former senior managers of pre-transformed SOEs who are usually closely linked with the controlling shareholders of listed companies (Shi, 2005). The findings also show that participants could not spell out who is responsible for nominating directors. This is because China's boards of directors are often placed at institutions without a process of consultation with the board of directors (Hamid, 2005).

The involvement of minority shareholders

With regard to the relatively concentrated ownership structure, some participants explain minority shareholders have little power in selecting board of directors. For example,

> Although there is no one dominant shareholder, the ownership structure is rather fragmented because most of the shares are concentrated in the hands of a few shareholders. Minority shareholders do not have any influence in terms of the board of directors' selection. (Participant 1, Chairman, Company A)

> Minority shareholders have representatives to participate in the selection process. But since their shares are too minor, their votes cannot actually affect the final decision. (Participant 3, Vice Chairman, Company A)

> The competition is far from intensive because the ownership is concentrated in the hands of a few shareholders. The candidates are represented largely by the large shareholders. In the general meeting, these candidates will always win without any dispute. In the meanwhile, you cannot expect to find any candidates representing the minority shareholders. (Participant 19, Independent Director, Company A)

Furthermore, some participants believe the minority's interests were no different from those of the large shareholders. For instance, one participant states

> The large shareholder has the same target as that of minorities. Both of them want to select competent candidates to benefit the company's development. (Participant 11, Independent Director, Company B)

The above statements suggest the selection of the board of directors is in the hands of large shareholders, while the role of minority shareholders is unimportant. Yet the minority shareholders need clarity in their responsibilities, accountability and rights in the voting process, as the lack of clarity affects the successful implementation of an efficient corporate governance framework. Protecting minority shareholders' value should become one of the top priorities of the CSRC and all shareholders need to have the ability to nominate themselves or someone else, not an executive of the corporation, but with a chance of becoming elected (Ding et al., 2007).

Composition of board of directors

In Chinese SOEs, boards of directors are predominately composed of a pool of public servants and senior managers of companies. For example, some participants comment

> Boards of directors are appointed largely from among public servants and past employees. (Participant 13, Director, Company B)

> The board of the corporation consists of local governmental officials, the members of the Communist Party and senior managers of the company. (Participant 1, Chairman, Company A)

> Internal directors are those who take a position as senior managers and always work for the company. (Participant 18, Director, Company C)

> I was selected by the state agency. I used to work as a government officer. I am now an entrepreneur. There have been major differences between these two roles. But I think I am competent to cope with the change. (Participant 18, Director, Company C)

The findings reveal that board members are mainly composed of representatives selected by large shareholders through shareholders' meetings. Because of the high coincidence of board membership and management in China's listed companies, insider control problems are likely to prevail. Yet, boards of directors and top management positions need to be filled by a transparent process where the board makes the decision to choose the most qualified candidates. Just by doing so, the problems of manipulation through related party transactions, which sacrifice the interests of the companies and the minority shareholders, can be eliminated.

Independent directors are mostly from universities and research institutions, usually in finance, accounting or auditing. For example,

> Most of them come from the academy, often with a specialisation in finance, and their compensation is not tied to the financial performance of the company. (Participant 1, Chairman, Company A)

> The primary role of China's independent director system concentrates on monitoring and auditing financial statements of the company, and ensuring the company's information disclosure. It is necessary to recruit these directors from all areas including universities, research institutes, etc…" (Participant 14, Executive Director, Company B)

Tong (2002) states that the regulator encourages not only academics but also executives, lawyers and accountants to serve as independent directors and requires at least one of the independent directors to be in the accounting profession to serve as the chairman for the auditing committees. Some participants state independent directors are not independent at all. For example, one participant noted

> Some of the independent directors have been drawn mainly from retired/ incumbent government officers and SOE managers, and they are not really independent according to international standards. (Participant 18, Director, Company C)

Rajagopalan and Zhang (2008) argue since these independent directors have less incentive in monitoring the board activities, the only way to motivate them is to make their liabilities credible so that those who fail to exercise due diligence have to make serious financial restitution.

Board of directors' training and qualification

The training and education of boards of directors has become a crucial issue with regard to the efficiency of the board. For instance, participants point out that some board members might lack sufficient knowledge and experience to pursue their role efficiently.

> Some of the directors do not have adequate expertise and knowledge in terms of playing a control role of the board in corporate governance. (Participant 18, Director, Company C)

> Some boards of directors do not assess the Annual Report partly because they cannot understand the report.(Participant 13, Director, Company B)

> There is no training course provided by relevant regulatory authorities for members of board of directors. As a result, many members do not sufficiently know their own responsibilities as a director. (Participant 5, Executive Director, Company A)

> There is no training system in place to ensure the board of directors is qualified. (Participant 4, Executive Director, Company A)

> The training course is neither provided by the China Securities Regulatory Commission nor by the Stock exchanges. I don't think we have an opportunity to take part in the training course. (Participant 12, Executive Director, Company B)

The above statements regarding the training and education of boards of directors indicate participants believe their companies do not have structured training courses for the board of directors. On the other hand, other participants argue that the boards of directors have been well trained. This is captured in the following responses:

> Members of the board generally have obtained the expertise in doing their job. We have different expertise and experience from business

management to accounting and finance. (Participant 16, Supervisor, Company B)

Our board engaged in hiring expert and experienced top managers/board of directors who were able to provide high quality management's reporting. So the board could gain more confidence with these reports. They provided a double check within the management structure to reduce the fraud and misconduct at the company. (Participant 11, Independent Director, Company B)

Some independent directors in our company have obtained their Master or PhD degrees, have had long lasting professional careers in foreign companies. (Participant 5, Executive Director, Company A)

The finding shows the education level of the board of directors varies between companies. Qualifications and experience are important factors in determining the quality of boards of directors. Tam (2002) points out that the concept of corporate governance is misunderstood by many Chinese managers and officials as being just a modern way of organisational management. Unlike the Western board, the participants agree that China's board meetings act like an internal operating meeting. According to the IFC (2005), most board members have a lack of clear understanding of their functions and responsibilities and in turn, lack knowledge of the decision-making mechanisms used by corporate boards. The findings also illustrate that boards of directors do not fully understand the responsibilities of the job and lack knowledge to make effective decisions on the board. The overlapping of the functions of monitoring and management weakens the efficiency of the board. Most participants recognise the board of directors as the legitimate authority for conducting the supervising and control roles. But they fail to spell out how they conduct their control role in certain procedures and how exactly the control role they could exercise is constituted. The oversight is passive rather than proactive and comprehensive. It is no surprise to see although Chinese directors understand the importance of corporate governance, they are not informed of detailed guidelines and procedures of governance codes that they could follow to implement their roles (Hamid, 2005). As a result, many Chinese company boards fail to function effectively. It is clearly important that board of directors should know their rights and responsibilities.

Although China's boards of directors know they will be required to meet certain standards when they list their major companies on public markets in Hong Kong, London or New York and they are also increasingly convinced that better corporate governance lead to better business results with greater efficiency, nearly all senior Chinese officials and corporate leaders, up until now, have had no personal experience with this and no frames of reference (Barton and Huang, 2007). They know they need to do it, but most just do not know exactly how to go about it (Barton and Huang, 2007). Since there is a lack of a market for professional managers, the government needs to put a greater emphasis on corporate governance awareness and adoption by introducing training programmes for managers, senior executives and directors (Cheung et al., In press). Continued training and education of both companies and investors constitute a focal part supporting the creation of an efficient corporate governance system in conjunction with new rules and regulations in the reform period (Cha, 2001). China's CSRC regularly conducts training programmes to educate directors for listed companies, although these short training programs can provide only very general guidance (Rajagopalan and Zhang, 2008). According to Barton and Huang (2007), the Chinese officials at the highest levels recognise the need to put in place what might be called a modern system of corporate governance. For instance, many companies listed on the domestic stock markets have invited well-known social personages and professionals to become independent directors, who account for as much as 50 per cent of the board membership in quite a few companies such as the Little Swan and Inner Mongolian Baotou Iron and Steel Company (Lu, 2005).

Evaluation of board of directors

Another interesting issue is related to the evaluation of boards' members. All the participants believe their boards do not have a formal explicit mechanism for assessing directors. For example,

> We do not have an official mechanism for directors' appraisal. (Participant 8, Chairman of Supervisory Board, Company A)

> I do not think that we have a mechanism to evaluate directors except in terms of meeting attendance. If some directors do not attend the meeting without excuse, we assume they do not have good performance. (Participant 1, Chairman, Company A)

One participant illustrates there was no significant changes in his board:

> You can look at our board it does not change dramatically, we do not change the whole board, but you get one or two changes. (Participant 2, CEO, Company A)

When being asked about the mechanism for directors' evaluation, participants stress that some sort of directors' evaluation is conducted implicitly between major shareholders and the board's chairman. For example, the following examples spell out the evaluation procedure of board of directors.

> The director, who attends the board meetings to engage in the discussion, is different from the member who attends meetings just for being

there. The board members' appraisal is conducted by the board chairman. (Participant 18, Director, Company C)

Directors are appraised in an informal way. (Participant 12, Executive Director, Company B)

We do not have a mechanism for directors' appraisal, however, directors are judged implicitly in some way.(Participant 4, Executive Director, Company A)

We appraise directors informally. It is done quite often between the board directors and large shareholders' representatives serving as members on the board. (Participant 8, Chairman of Supervisory Board, Company A)

Participants point out how Chinese culture affects the evaluation process. For example,

Often the Chairman of the board consults with other directors about the evaluation. However, in China such discussion is done in friendly way so that it does not harm anybody.(Participant 13, Director, Company B).

The evaluation of the board of directors is an important aspect in assuring the best practices of the board. The results show that the participant companies do not have a systematic mechanism for evaluating the board of directors in terms of their skills, knowledge and capabilities before electing them to serve on the board. The Code of Corporate Governance for Listed Companies in China states the duties and responsibilities of directors are to "faithfully, honestly and diligently perform their duties for the best interests of the company and all the shareholders. Directors shall attend the board of directors meeting in a diligent and responsible manner, and shall express their clear opinion on the topics discussed" (Lu, 2005). The study reveals that attending all board meetings are one of the most important criteria for evaluation of board of directors.

The findings also show the influence of large shareholders in evaluating the directors. The respondents stress the unclear methods in assessing directors and point out the obvious role of the state agency in approving the appropriate candidates. The assessment of board of directors is informal and carried out by the chairman. Most frequently, directors are reelected for several consecutive terms and in turn, the composition of the board has little changes from year to year. The lack of formal procedures in the evaluation of the board of directors underscores the function and efficiency of the remuneration committee. What is more, Chinese directors are insulated from responsibilities for their company's economic performance because their compensation is not linked to it, and they cannot be dismissed prior to the expiration of their terms without "cause," although what constitutes "cause" is not defined (Feinerman, 2007).

Discussion of study findings

China needs an independent, competent and engaged board, which is capable of exercising its strategic and monitoring functions. It requires a functioning recruitment process that achieves the right balance between the competence and independence of directors and drives their accountability and effectiveness. The findings indicate that the problems start at a very basic level, namely from the selection process. Since board nomination is the first crucial element in corporate governance, it must be combined with transparency and with clear financial goals. Competence must be the key factor in deciding who will serve on the board. According to Mallin (2004), the nomination committee must carry out a systematic procedure to evaluate the existing balance of skills, knowledge, and experience on the board and utilise this when preparing a candidate profile for new appointments.

Rather than being appointed by the state with a government function, it is argued that boards of directors' recruitment processes should be sufficiently transparent to ensure that the most qualified candidates are chosen. During the process of reform and development, companies have brought in institutional investors who require the skills and expertise of top management. The board therefore must take a more proactive role in the selection process and the control rights should be given back to the management and the board. A formal procedure should be established to ensure that the directors should be given incentives to interview candidates before being asked to vote on them (Hamid, 2005).

The findings suggest there is a need to educate both board of directors and investors in executing corporate governance to create an efficient system. CSRC have hired several corporate governance experts form Hong Kong to promote higher standards (Ewing, 2005). In addition, the Qualified Foreign Institutional Investor scheme (QFII) programme is likely to improve China's corporate governance by directly introducing foreign institutional investors who have experience of governing the companies. Another solution to the shortage of qualified independent directors is to appoint more foreign directors to fill the boardrooms (Rajagopalan and Zhang, 2008). Tenev and Zhang (2002) suggest China needs an institute of company directors independent from the regulator to provide training for directors and establish benchmarking for remuneration and functions of boards of directors and so on.

The results show companies have neither a formal and systematic process nor guidelines for board of directors' evaluation. The lack of formal procedures can reduce the effectiveness of the board, as underperforming directors may not be replaced. It is important to have a formal mechanism in evaluating directors to make them more accountable and engaged to companies.

Conclusion

The chapter has provided an overview of the selection and evaluation of boards of directors in Chinese SOEs. The main problems stem from the large shareholder's involvement in recruitment and evaluation, lack of effective monitoring mechanisms and the lack of independence of board of directors. The insiders, such as the controlling shareholder, board of directors and senior managers, dominate and control the board. Although the shareholders' general meeting forms a basic framework of corporate governance in China and the boards of directors have the right to select top management, the meeting normally can be manipulated by the major shareholders, because of their overwhelmingly large voting rights. The board of directors comprises insiders who are selected by the "key person" on behalf of the state agency or the controlling shareholder (Wang, 2007). The management selection mechanism is problematic as the state agency can exercise control through directors and managers by delegating a representative of the corporation to attend the shareholders general meeting. These representatives can nominate and replace candidates for directors of the board since the voting power of these large shareholders is significant and have the ultimate decision-making power over all corporate affairs including control, execution and supervision (Tan and Wang, 2007). Although managers of SOEs are formally appointed by boards of directors, all the decisions on appointments must be approved by large shareholders. It is argued that candidates appointed by the state, who were government officials previously, may not necessarily align their own interest with that of the state. Chinese SOEs have started to recognise the importance of selecting qualified management with business knowledge and corporate governance expertise during the reform (Hua, 2003). The greatest challenge is to find the appropriate balance between the government's responsibilities as an active owner, while refraining from undue political interference in the management of the company (OECD, 2007).

Independence of board of directors can greatly influence the monitoring function of the board of directors. Increasing this independence is extremely important to protect minority shareholders. Yet the independence of boards of directors is undermined by the pervasive personal relationship-based culture in contemporary Chinese society. This unique business culture can limit the applicability of best practice developed in the developed countries. It is important to foster a business culture in which directors know what is expected of them and are motivated to carry out due diligence (Rajagopalan and Zhang, 2008). In order to conduct effective oversight and give advice, independent directors need to speak up and be able to challenge top managers by asking tough questions (Hua, 2003).

The evaluation of board of directors tends to be informal and in the hands of CEOs and chairman. In order to achieve greater accountability and transparency in the board, it is recommended that evaluation processes must be carried out by independent directors, that the remuneration packages should be disclosed and that the compensation of board of directors must be allied to their performance in order to motivate them to meet economic goals.

China has a long way to go on corporate governance matters. Although the notion of "best practice" has been gradually accepted by the Chinese board, change cannot happen overnight. There needs to be established an efficient institutional environment, rendering boards of directors with full authority to manage the nomination and evaluation process, and reinforcing the education of both board of directors and regulators.

Note

1. This refers to the status in which the shares of China's listed companies in the two stock markets in Shanghai and Shenzhen fell, the two categories being nontradable shares (accounting for roughly two-thirds of domestically listed companies' total shares, including state-owned shares and legal person shares) and tradable shares (referring to public shares accounting for the rest).

References

Barton, D. & Huang, R. H. (2007) Governing China's boards: An interview with John Thornton. *The McKinsey Quarterly*, 98.

Beltratti, A. & Bortolotti, B. (2006) *The nontradable share reform in the Chinese stock market*, University of Torino and Fondazione EniEnrico Mattei.

Braendle, U. C., Gasser, T. & Noll, J. (2005) Corporate governance in China – Is economic growth potential hindered by Guanxi? *Business and Society Review*, 110, 389–405.

CFA Institute (2007) China Corporate Governance Survey. CFA Institute.

Cha, L. (2001) The future of China's capital markets and the role of corporate governance. *The China Business Summit*. Beijing.

Chen, J. (2005) *Corporate Governance in China*, London and New York, Routledge Curzon.

Chen, J. J. (2004) Determinants of capital structure of Chinese-listed firms. *Journal of Business Research in International Business and Finance*, 57, 1341–51.

Cheng, C. (1998) A study of the motivation and constraint mechanisms of the management of the state owned enterprises. *Journal of Finance and Economics*, 32, 27–31.

Cheng, S.-W. (2007) Standing committee of the National People's Congress. *Financial Times*. London.

Cheung, Y.-L., Jiang, P., Limpaphayom, P. & Lu, T. (2008) Does corporate governance matter in China? *China Economic Review*, 19(3), 460–79.

China Securities Daily (2005) Zhongguo Dudong Diaocha Ji Zhidu Fansi [Survey on China's independent directors and reflections on the institutions]. *Zhongguo Zhengquan Bao [China Securities Daily]*.

Clarke, D. C. (2003) Corporate governance in China: An overview. *China Economic Review*, 14, 494–507.

Clarke, D. C. (2006) The independent director in Chinese corporate governance. *Delaware Journal of Corporate Law*, 31, 125.

The Company Law of the People's Republic of China (1994), National People's Congress of the People's Republic of China.

The Company Law of the People's Republic of China (2005), National People's Congress of the People's Republic of China.

Cooper, M. C. (2002) Returning shares to the people? The politics of the stock market in China. Connecticut, Yale University.

CSRC (2005) Administrative measures on the split share structure reform of listed companies. In CSRC (Ed.) China Securities Regulatory Commission (CSRC). Beijing, CSRC.

Ding, Y., Zhang, H. & Zhang, J. (2007) Private vs. state ownership and earnings management: Evidence from Chinese listed companies. *Corporate Governance: An International Review*, 15, 223–38.

Ewing, R. D. (2005) Chinese corporate governance and prospects for reform. *Journal of Contemporary China*, 4, 317–38.

Feinerman, J. V. (2007) New hope for corporate governance in China? *The China Quarterly*, 590.

Finkelstein, S. & Mooney, A. C. (2003) Not the usual suspects: How to use board process to make boards better. *Academy of Management Executive*, 17, 101–13.

Firth, M., Fung, P. M. Y. & Rui, O. M. (2007a) How ownership and corporate governance influence chief executive pay in China's listed firms. *Journal of Business Research*, 60, 776–85.

Firth, M., Fung, P. M. Y. & Rui, O. M. (2007b) Ownership, two-tier board structure, and the informativeness of earnings – Evidence from China. *Journal of Accounting and Public Policy*, 26, 463–96.

Flyvbjerg, B. (2004) Five misunderstandings about case-study research. In Seale, C., Gobo, G., Gubrium, J. F. & Silverman, D. (Eds.) *Qualitative Research Practice*. London, Sage.

Garnaut, R., Song, L., Tenev, S. & Yao, Y. (2005) *China's ownership transformation: Process, outcomes, prospects*. Washington, DC, The International Finance Corporation (IFC) and the World Bank.

Glaser, B. G. & Strauss, A. L. (1967) *The Discovery of Grounded Theory: Strategies for Qualitative Research*, Transaction Publishers.

Green, S. (2004) The privatization two step at China's listed firms. *Stanford Center for International Development*.

Hamid, J. (2005) Step by step corporate governance models in China: The experience of the International Finance corporation. Washington, DC, International Finance Corporate, World Bank.

Hovey, M. (2005) Corporate governance in China: An empirical study of listed firms. In *Department of Accounting, Finance and Economics*. Griffith, Griffith University.

Hovey, M. & Naughton, T. (2007) A survey of enterprise reforms in China: The way forward. *Economic Systems*, 31, 138–56.

Hu, R. Y. (2005) Overview of Governance of State-owned Listed Companies in China. *OECD – Second Policy Dialogue on Corporate Governance in China*. Beijing, OECD.

Hua, C.-Y. (2003) Corporate governance, board compensation and firm performance: An investigation of corporate governance in Taiwan's high-tech industry. California, Golden Gate University.

Hua, J. Y., Miesing, P. & Li, M. F. (2006) An empirical taxonomy of SOE governance in transitional China. *Journal of Management and Governance*, 10, 401–33.

Huchet, J. F. & Richet, X. (2002) Between bureaucracy and market: Chinese industrial groups in search of new forms of corporate governance. *Post-Communist Economies*, 14, 169–701.

IFC (2005) *Corporate Governance Models in China.* Hong Kong, International Finance Corporation.

Johnson, S. & Shleifer, A. (2004) Privatization and corporate governance. In Ito, T. & Krueger, A. O. (Eds.) *Governance, Regulation and Privatization in the Asia–Pacific Region.* Chicago, The University of Chicago Press.

Koppell, J. G. S. (2007) Political Control for China's State-Owned Enterprises: Lessons from America's Experience with Hybrid Organizations. *Governance*, 20, 255–278.

Lawler, E. & Finegold, D. (2005) The changing face of corporate boards. *Sloan Management Review*, 46, 67–70.

Leung, E., Liu, L., Shen, L., Taback, K. & Wang, L. (2002) Financial reform and corporate governance in China. In Myers, S. C. (Ed.) *50th Anniversary Proceedings.* Cambridge, MA, MIT Sloan School of Management.

Li, D. D. & Wu, C. (2002) The colour of the cats. *The Economic and Social Review*, 33, 133–46.

Lin, C. (2000) Corporatisation and corporate governance in China's economic transition. *Economics of Planning*, 34, 5–35.

Lin, C. (2001) Corporatisation and corporate governance in China's economic transition. *Economics of Planning*, 34, 5.

Lin, T. W. (2004) Corporate governance in China: Recent developments, key problems, and solutions. *Journal of Accounting and Corporate Governance*, 1, 1–23.

Liu, S. (2005) Corporate governance and development: The case of China. *Managerial and Decision Economics*, 26, 445.

Lu, T. (2005) *Defects in China's Independent Director System: A Case Study of Leshan Power Company.* Beijing, Institute of World Economy & Politics, Chinese Academy of Social Science.

Lu, T. (2006) *Corporate Governance in China.* Beijing, Chinese Center for Corporate Governance, Institute of World Economics and Politics.

Mallin, C. A. (2004) *Corporate Governance.* Oxford, Oxford University Press.

McNally, C. A. (2002) China's state-owned enterprises: Thriving or crumbing? *The AsiaPacific Issues*, 59.

Miles, M. & Huberman, A. (1994) *Qualitative Data Analysis (2nd Edn.)*, Thousand Oaks, Sage.

Naughton, B. (1995) *Growing Out of the Plan: Chinese Economic Reform, 1978–93.* , Cambridge, Cambridge University Press.

Nee, V., Opper, S. & Wong, S. (2007) Developmental state and corporate governance in China. *Management and Organization Review*, 3(1), 19–53.

OECD (2005) *Comparative Report on Governance of State Owned Assets.* Paris, OECD.

OECD (2007) Conclusions and key findings – The Third OECD-China Policy Dialogue on Corporate Governance. *The Third OECD-China Policy Dialogue on Corporate Governance.* Shanghai, OECD.

People's Daily (2006) China's share reform process slows down. *People's Daily.* Beijing.

Qu, W. & Leung, P. (2006) Cultural impact on Chinese corporate disclosure – A corporate governance perspective. *Managerial Auditing Journal*, 21, 241.

Rajagopalan, N. & Zhang, Y. (2008) Corporate governance reforms in China and India: Challenges and opportunities. *Business Horizons*, 51, 55–64.

Rapley, T. (2004) Interviews. In Seale, C., Gobo, G., Gubrium, J. F. & Silverman, D. (Eds.) *Qualitative Research Practice*. London, Sage.

Shi, C. (2005) The international corporate governance developments: The path for China. *Australian Journal of Asian Law*, 71, 60–94.

Takeshi, J. (2007) Corporate governance for listed companies in China: Recent moves to improve the quality of listed companies. *Nomura Capital Market Review*, 10, 36–52.

Tam, O. K. (2002) Ethical issues in the evolution of corporate governance in China. *Journal of Business Ethics*, 37, 303.

Tan, L. H. & Wang, J. (2007) Modelling an effective corporate governance system for China's listed state-owned enterprises: Issues and challenges in a transition economy. *Journal of Corporate Law Studies*, 7, 143–83.

Tenev, S. & Zhang, C. (2002) *Corporate Governance and Enterprise Reform in China*, Beijing, China Financial and Economic Publishing House.

Tian, J. J. & Lau, C. M. (2001) Board composition, leadership structure and performance in Chinese shareholding companies. *Asia Pacific Journal of Management*, 18, 245–63.

Tong, D. (2002) Making companies as better citizens: Advancing corproate governance in China. *2002 Annual Conference Borsa Italiana*. Milano, International Corporate Governance Network.

Tucker, S. (2006) China told to refine corporate governance. *Financial Times*. Sydney.

Voß, S. & Xia, Y. W. (2006) Corporate governance of listed companies in China. *IFSAM VIIIth World Congress 2006*. Berling, IFSAM.

Wan, J. & Yuce, A. (2007) Listing regulations in China and their effect on the performace of IPOs and SOEs. *Research in International Business and Finance*, 21, 366–78.

Wang, J. Y. (2007) The strange role of independent directors in a two-tier board structure of China's listed companies. *Compliance & Regulatory Journal*, 47–55.

Wu, J. L. (1999) *China's Economic Reform: Strategies and Implementation*. Shanghai, Shanghai Far East Publishing House.

Xie, C. (2004) Duli Dongshi Falv Zhidu Yanjiu [A Study of the Independent Director System]. *Falv Chubanshe [Law Press China]*. Beijing.

Xu, L. (2004) *Types of Large Shareholders, Corporate Governance, and Firm Performance: Evidence from China's Listed Companies*. Hong Kong, Hong Kong Polytechnic University.

Yao, Y. (2004) Political process and efficient institutional change. *Journal of Institutional and Theoretical Economics*, 160, 439–53.

Young, M. N., Peng, M. W., Ahlstrom, D., Bruton, G. D. & Jiang, Y. (2008) Corporate governance in emerging economies: A review of the principal–principal perspective. *Journal of Management Studies*, 45, 196–220.

Yuan, J. (2007) Formal convergence or substantial divergence? Evidence from adoption of the independent director system in China. *Asian-Pacific Law & Policy Journal*, 9, 71–104.

Yuan, J. & Yuan, C. (2007) How to improve China's enterprise internal control system: Based on the perspective of corporate governance. *The Business Review*, 7, 91.

Zhang, L. Y. (2002) The role of the state in China's transition to a market economy. *Modern State Structures in the Chinese World*. Asia Research Centre in London School of Economics and Political Science.

Zhang, W. Y. (2006) China's SOE reform: A corporate governance perspective. *Corporate Ownership and Control*, 3, 132–150.

Zhang, Z. (2007) Legal deterrence: The foundation of corporate governance – Evidence from China. *Corporate Governance: An International Review*, 15, 741.

11
The Imperative of Rapid Adaptation to Climate Change: Are the Lights On in the Boardroom?

Malcolm McIntosh

Introduction

Corporate governance is challenged on several fronts as we come to the end of the first decade of the twenty-first century. "Are the lights on the boardroom" alludes to the work rate of board members, to their ability to be connected to extreme global change and to be educated enough and competent when faced with a world that is changing around them. After all, the evidence states unambiguously that most board members of global corporations are linked, are incestuous, and share each others' boards, interests, clubs and limitations (Kakabadse and Kakabadse, 2008). How then can they cope with the onslaught – and what is that onslaught?

The challenges are three. First is the challenge of climate change, and the question "doesn't climate change change everything?" The answer is an unequivocal "yes" if the science is to be believed, and there are a dwindling lunatic fringe who challenge the whole notion but a substantive minority who reasonably question. First, the premise that the major cause is human activity and, second, whether we should or could mitigate or adapt. The second challenge comes from the relationship between economics and ecology. If the environment has been so damaged by our love affair with the current model of economics, then our largest economic institutions, which include global corporations, are significantly challenged because they are the children of a seriously faulty system. And the third challenge may ultimately be providing the best drivers for change in the boardroom, because it is through a combination of stakeholder empowerment, social networking and systems thinking that conventional models of power, responsibility, accountability and governance are being rethought.

Doesn't climate change change everything?

If humanity has but a few years to adapt to the inevitability of climate change, or if it is upon us now, then it is our institutions that are most challenged and it is in them that we see the greatest inertia and disinclination to change. MIT organisational learning guru Peter Senge has said that "facing up to climate change requires a revolution in business thinking" (Senge et al., 2008, p. 44) and Stuart Hart has written about "capitalism at a crossroads" (Hart, 2005) and in this chapter we look at SEE Change: moves towards the low carbon sustainable enterprise economy (McIntosh, 2008).

This is true for OPEC (the Organisation of Petroleum Countries) whose raison d'etre is to maintain prices for their members, when it is known that the misuse of fossil fuels is the primary cause of climate change. It is true of Wal-Mart, the world's largest retailer, who relies on boundaryless procurement and the movement of goods around the world as if there were no crisis. We will return to the case of Wal-Mart later, as they are a fascinating case study in leadership and change. And it is true for an extractive industry giant like Anglo American whose origins lie in the colonial domination of Africa and whose future lies in the increased extraction of raw materials from the Earth's surface.

Climate change challenges global corporations on all levels but the reason climate change changes everything in corporate governance is because it calls for the internalisation of externalities, which raises costs for companies, which in turn calls for dramatic upstream redesign and rethinking so that these are no longer end-of-pipe problems – for that is what the issues of waste management and pollution represent.

But what is the evidence that supports the contention that we need a new model of capitalism? The 4th assessment of the IPCC (Intergovernmental Panel on Climate Change) states

> Warming of the climate system is unequivocal, as is now evident from observations of increases in global average air and ocean temperatures, widespread melting of snow and ice and rising global average sea level. (IPCC, 2007, p. 2)

If this is not seen as an extreme threat to all human life on Earth and does not represent a challenge to those who have the power and authority to make change happen, then there has been a failure of communication and understanding, or a socio-pathological denial, or that humanity is destined to fail itself. In *"Collapse: How Societies Choose to fail or Survive,"* Jared Diamond, a geographer, addresses exactly these threats in societies that have passed away leaving, in some cases, barren landscapes, discarded temples and signs of immense effort and apparent civilisation (Diamond, 2005). If our corporations die because they fail to face the current realities, what will be there to show they ever existed? In *"The Living Company,"* Arie de Geus, a former senior Royal Dutch Shell executive, points out that the most successful corporations are those that metamorphose (De Geus, 2002). They are embodied by the world's two oldest companies, Finland's Stora Enso and Japan's Mitsubishi, both of which have adapted to changing conditions and trade patterns moving in and out of industrial sectors while retaining and maintaining their corporate integrity. Can our leviathans adapt and adopt contrary sectors as we move towards a low carbon sustainable enterprise economy? Does BP's redesign as "Beyond Petroleum" and their subsequent rowing back to fossil fuels signal the inability of a corporate giant to adapt, a failure of corporate strategy and governance, or was it that the time is not yet for their death? Or are we moving towards a post-fossil fuel economy where we make better and more sustainable use of our vast fossil fuel reserves through carbon capture and sequestration and significantly increased efficiency. The latter scenario makes absolute social sense but the business case for using less is more difficult to argue unless there are incentives for rewarding investment through quality rather than quantity. This challenges the current model of industrial capitalism, and the growth model, and all those in the boardroom that have been weaned and wedded to these principles. But, as the climate change imperative comes home to roost, we may be seeing the beginnings of change in the boardroom.

According to a survey of global executives by McKinsey in 2008, environmental issues are increasingly seen as opportunities rather than risks (McKinsey Quarterly, 2008). However, the actual change process may be slow amongst these same executives was also reported by McKinsey the same week:

> Efforts to reduce climate change can profoundly affect the valuations of many companies, but executives so far seem largely unaware. As global warming spawns new regulations, technological remedies, and shifts in consumer behavior, its effect on the valuations of many sectors and companies is likely to be profound. The shocks to some industries could be severe – potentially as severe as, for example, the effect of the introduction of wireless telephony on the telecommunications sector during the 1990s and of shifting oil prices on the oil and gas sector during the 1970s and 1980s. Yet executives have so far paid scant attention, either because they don't understand the effects of climate change on their businesses or they believe them to be too uncertain or distant to model.

One company that has smelt the coffee and woken up is Wal-Mart. That company's CEO and Chairman, Lee Scott, has become messianic in his mission to change his company's priorities *and* boost competitiveness. In April 2008, he said: "They (pension funds) are looking 40 years out. In that world, carbon really is a risk" and "If you really want your share price supported by these large funds of money, you'd be prudent to reduce your environmental footprint" (Langford and Wagler, 2008). Lee Scott's epiphany came about because of Hurricane Katrina, which caused him to take stock both of the state of the planet and his company: "As we watched and experienced how the world reacted to our efforts following Katrina, it was time for me to send a message to our associates about who we can become as a company. Our associates need to know how we can make a difference. It's a personal thing on our part. I felt it was the right time to share a bigger picture that tells a bigger story" (CNN Money, 2005).

Another company that has also completely changed its raison d'etre and operating policies is floor-covering company Interface. Their CEO, Ray Anderson, says: "Mission Zero is the company's promise to eliminate any negative impact it may have on the environment, by the year 2020, through the redesign of processes and products, the pioneering of new technologies, and efforts to reduce or eliminate waste and harmful emissions while increasing the use of renewable materials and sources of energy."

There are many paradoxes in the journey towards a low carbon sustainable enterprise economy and these two US companies are two such examples. Both are examples of leadership from the top, and both came about because one of the CEOs had an epiphany through reading a book (Ray Anderson read Paul Hawken's *The Ecology of Commerce*) and the other CEO, Lee Scott, watched as his company dealt with the aftermath of Hurricane Katrina in 2005 rather better than the US government's FEMA (Federal Emergency Management Agency) and recognised not only the power and responsibility of the corporation but also the power and authority of changing weather patterns.

Economics and ecology

Nicolas Stern, former World Bank Chief Economist, reported to UK Chancellor Gordon Brown in 2007 on the links between economics and ecology (it is worth quoting at some length):

> There is still time to avoid the worst impacts of climate change, if we take strong action now.... The scientific evidence is now overwhelming: climate change is a serious global threat, and it demands an urgent global response.... This Review has assessed a wide range of evidence on the impacts of climate change and on the economic costs, and has used a number of different techniques to assess costs and risks. From all of these perspectives, the evidence gathered by the Review leads to a simple conclusion: the benefits of strong and early action far outweigh the economic costs of not acting.... Using the results from formal economic models, the Review estimates that if we don't act, the overall costs and risks of climate change will be equivalent to losing at least 5% of global

GDP each year, now and forever. If a wider range of risks and impacts is taken into account, the estimates of damage could rise to 20% of GDP or more. In contrast, the costs of action – reducing greenhouse gas emissions to avoid the worst impacts of climate change – can be limited to around 1% of global GDP each year.... If no action is taken to reduce emissions, the concentration of greenhouse gases in the atmosphere could reach double its pre-industrial level as early as 2035, virtually committing us to a global average temperature rise of over 2°C. In the longer term, there would be more than a 50% chance that the temperature rise would exceed 5°C. This rise would be very dangerous indeed; it is equivalent to the change in average temperatures from the last ice age to today. Such a radical change in the physical geography of the world must lead to major changes in the human geography – where people live and how they live their lives. (Office of Climate Change, 2007)

The Stern Review has been effective in changing the minds of even the most calcified boardroom brain because it was written in sober language by an economist and because it crosses the boundaries of economics and ecology, even though it was essentially a summation of the knowledge gained about the world's ecosystems since the 1970s. Reports from the City of London when the Stern Review was published in 2007 triggered a response that hitherto fore had been less than understanding of the enormity of the climate change challenge. The Review could be read in summary and also at length, it was written by an economist and, more than anything, it spelt out the disadvantages of medium- and long-term delay over short-term action. And, that action was required now – which for financial analysts who have an attention and investment time span of months or at most a few years, unlike many institutional investors who think in terms of decades, has been the catalyst for reaction and some action.

The challenge of stakeholder empowerment, social networking and systems thinking

In 1984, Ed Freeman published *Strategic Management: A stakeholder approach (Freeman, 1984)* and stakeholder theory has dominated much of the discourse on corporate responsibility and corporate citizenship since. In 1992, Malcolm McIntosh made reference to "stakeholder empowerment" (McIntosh, 1993) and particularly since the introduction of inexpensive global communications technology pressure has increased on companies to be more open, more transparent, more accountable, and to respond to a multiplicity of demands from various stakeholders, internal and external, primary and secondary (Andriof and McIntosh, 2001).

The evolution of stakeholder thinking and company engagement has led to the understanding that a company's intelligence may lie with its external stakeholders rather than in the minds of internal strategists, policy makers, designers, and marketers. This has led to companies seeking to engage with their customers for advice on future products. One classic example of this outward facing model of strategic management is captured by the decline of the UK car industry over the last few decades and the near decline of the US auto industry in the last few years such that, as I write, GM is negotiating to merge with Chrysler and is seeking a bailout from the US government. In both cases, the UK and the US, the industry continued lemming-like to make products with outdated designs and technology that customers no longer wanted or needed. Overtaking on the outside the Japanese auto industry has succeeded in transforming the sector coming from nothing to second in four decades by, first, asking customers what they want, and second, by developing sophisticated technology that saves the customer money and the planet at the same time. Both the UK and US auto industries are case studies in boardroom inertia – the light only came on when it was too late by which time others had taken the lead. Both are also case studies in imperial decline – for the auto companies themselves and the countries they represent.

Stakeholder empowerment, the death of deference to corporate giants (and to anything with apparent authority), and an increasingly open know-ledge-based economy challenged companies to be more transparent in all their dealings not just on financial performance but also in their social and environmental impact. This has led to a boom in corporate social, environ-mental and sustainability reporting particularly in Fortune 500 companies. Concomitant with this has been the birth over the last ten years of the social auditing industry and the growing professionalization of social audi-tors and verification and compliance officers. The issue here concerns trust, its construction and its management. Can it be nurtured, grown, bought, sequestered or ignored?

Building on the necessity for companies to be focused on their finan-cial performance and mindful of their social and environmental impact in 1989, John Elkington usefully coined the term "triple bottom line" and popularised it in a best-selling book *Cannibals with Forks: The Triple Bottom Line of 21st Century Business* (Elkington, 1994). The management of three bottom lines has proved a strategic and management headache for those companies that have engaged with this SEE change (McIntosh, 2008), not least because it has involved new management competences and skills. At the boardroom level it has often led to the strategic decision to apportion responsibility for this highly complex three-way split to corporate or public affairs, public relations or a separate back office disconnected to the main stream activities of the company. Only in a few companies has it become a boardroom issue such that it has led to a real rethinking of the purpose of the company and its role in wider society – or indeed how that company can help save the planet or humanity. It was argued that this was not the role of the company, that it flew in the face of the rules that govern company incorporation and that it diverted attention from rewarding investors.

Apart, that is, from more enlightened leading companies like Wal-Mart, Interface, Royal Dutch Shell, Pfizer, Unilever, BP and Anglo American who have begun the tasks of dealing with the three conditions set by McIntosh et al. in their definitions of corporate citizenship in 1998 and 2003: (i) That companies should understand and be able to articulate their role scope and purpose, (ii) That they should be in compliance with any laws that exist in their areas of operation and (iii) That they should understand their financial performance and social and environmental impact (McIntosh et al., 1998, 2003). These conditions do not sound radical then and they do not sound radical now, but if all companies acted on these three principles, and if there was supporting regulation that was enforced through due legal processes, the business environment and the world would be a significantly different place. The first condition has, in the last ten years, produced the social and environmental reporting industry as companies grapple with the task of explaining what, how and where they do what they do to a sceptical world. The second condition has led to a dramatic increase in due diligence audits and a boom in compliance officers as companies anxiously wait to find out if they are transgressors of what are sometimes very basic laws and international agreements – for instance on child labor. The third condition has led to creative learning and multiple partnerships with civil society around how we might understand, measure and report on a company's social and environmental footprint.

Some of the leading companies have become signatories to the UN Global Compact's ten principles of human rights, labour standards, environmental protection and anti-corruption. At the end of 2008, they numbered about 5000 companies from most countries, including many from emerging economies. The issues that have arisen on a practical and intellectual level – and have taken the greatest effort of understanding and engagement by companies, civil society groups and the UN itself – have been around two terms used in Principles One and Two of the Compact, namely what is a company's "sphere of influence" and what does "complicity" mean in the context of business? These, of course, go to the heart of the three conditions given by McIntosh et al. in their definition of good corporate citizenship. Partly to address these questions, John Ruggie from Harvard's Kennedy School was appointed by UN Secretary-General to be a Special Representative on business and human rights through to 2011 (Business & Human Rights Resource Centre, 2008). His current mandate is to define the relationship between business, government and civil society on human rights.

As we near the end of the first decade of the twenty-first century it is important to note that the lights *are* on in some boardrooms in some of our largest corporations, private, public and social and in some sectors. The sectors that lead are those that have long investment trajectories and have to go to where their raw material lies, as in the extractive industries; the retail sector, because they are exposed on the high street to scrutiny; and pharmaceuticals, because of the issues they deal with – life and death, health and vitality, equality and diversity, rich and poor.

Coming to terms with "the role scope and purpose" of the company and understanding its "sphere of influence" have led to increased attention being paid to systems. What is the relationship, for instance, between Unilever's sales of Dove products and the health of nations, the resilience of local communities and the state of the planet? Dove soap and related products is the most ubiquitous personal hygiene brand on the planet and is sold in 156 countries (McIntosh, 2003, pp. 61–71). In a groundbreaking piece of research, 2008, Unilever and Oxfam worked together to look at the company's impact on Indonesia (Unilever, 2008). The learning that took place within each organization and together as a partnership included the following points:

- UI's core workforce includes approximately 5000 people, of whom 60 per cent are direct employees, and 40 per cent are contract workers. Indirectly, the full-time equivalent (FTE) of about 300,000 people make their livelihoods in UI's value chain.
- More than half of this employment is found in the distribution and retail chain. This includes an estimated 1.8 million small stores and street vendors.
- The closer and more formally workers in the value chain are linked with UI's operations, the more they benefit from the company. Contracting out employment may reduce a company's ability to monitor the situation of contract workers or suppliers' employees, and thus results in gaps between corporate policy and practice.
- Two-thirds of the value generated along the chain is distributed to participants other than UI (producers, suppliers, distributors and retailers). Taxes paid by UI to the Indonesian government account for 26 per cent of the value generated in the chain.
- The value created by poorer people working at either end of the value chain is much lower than the value captured by those who are in direct interaction with UI.
- Participation in value chains such as UI's does not automatically guarantee improvements in the lives of people living in poverty.

This report represents a detailed analysis of the situation, and, while some would argue that Unilever probably knew much of what was subsequently revealed and that they should have known this anyway, the fact is that this was a successful example of a partnership between a global company and a global NGO and the information has been presented as a coherent story of the company's role scope and purpose (Smith and Crawford, 2008).

The lights may not be on in all boardrooms but there are some who must be applauded for at least beginning to engage. That most companies are laggards is shown by the relatively low number of signatories to the UN Global Compact at 5000, when UNCTAD reported in 2006 that there were 70,000 transnational corporations with 690,000 affiliates employing 57 million people worldwide (UNCTAD, 2006).

The Unilever Oxfam case study is an example of stakeholder engagement and systems thinking. The fact that the results can be read anywhere in the world that has electricity and internet connectivity (which I concede is not true for 40 per cent of the world's people) is a sign of social networking and electronic interconnectivity. Many forget that we have seen a revolution in the last two decades in terms of the knowledge empowerment of stakeholder groups, however small, throughout the world. What Manuel Castells has referred to as the "techno-meritocratic culture rooted in academia and science," but now including all who wish to look, has challenged the bastions of boardrooms (Castells, 2001, p. 39). No longer can they be the sole holders of evidence about the impact of their operations.

So, now "everyone is a media outlet" according to Clay Shirky in *Here Comes Everyone* (Shirky, 2008, pp. 55–80) or as Andy Warhol predicted: "in the future everyone will have 15 minutes of fame." For companies, this apparent democratisation of information comes with benefits and downsides. It allows them to publicise themselves, honestly and not so honestly, and for critics to do the same, honestly and not so honestly. Managing the ether-space is crucial to managing any organisation and there is evidence that many board members, because of age and wealth, are not as internet savvy as many of their stakeholders. British Prime Minister Tony Blair on leaving office in 2007 commented that he had to learn how to send his own emails.

More importantly for boardrooms, and whether the lights are on, is the contemporary discourse concerning what is meant by a company in a world awash with connectivity and stakeholder empowerment and with a better understanding of systems, interorganisational learning networks and nested networks (Ruggie, 2002). This analysis relates to the earlier point in this chapter concerning "spheres of influence" as referenced in the UN Global Compact. For some commentators, system thinking provides a redefinition of the company as a complex adaptive system that certainly does not operate on the rational deterministic lines that much management theory has tended to teach over the last one hundred years. In this world, management, and of course the boardroom, does not necessarily have the control over the company that it thinks it has (McIntosh, 2003; Monks, 1998). In this world, companies must expect the unexpected and learn to love surprise and ambiguity as they recognise that their company is a network nested amongst others, the most important network being Earth's planetary ecosystem on which all life on Earth depends.

So, the lights need to go on in the boardrooms, particularly those boardrooms that could have some control over the state of the planet. They need to listen to board members from Wal-Mart, Interface and Unilever (a surprising collection for many people working in this field) and recognise what the UK Astronomer Royal and President of the Royal Society said in 2004 that this may be *Our Final Century* and the end of civilization and the human race (Rees, 2004). As former NASA scientist James Lovelock, the inventor of the Gaia hypothesis, says: "The evidence coming in from watchers around the world brings news of an imminent shift in our climate towards one that could easily be described as Hell.... We have made this appalling mess of the planet and mostly with rampant liberal good intentions" (Lovelock, 2006, p. 147).

Ongoing research at Coventry University's Applied Research Century in Human Security in twelve countries involving hundreds of commentators due to be published in July 2010 on the 19th anniversary of the UN Global Compact points to three main issues that need confronting: market failure, which was highlighted by the Stern Review in the *Economics of Climate Change* (Stern, 2007); scientific illiteracy, which means two things – that most people do not fully understand global warming, and do not have a systems view of the world because of the enlightenment tendency to atomise rather than integrate knowledge; and, institutional inertia, which refers to all organs of society, public, private and civil – how many governments have adapted to climate change, how many companies have adopted Interface's strategy, and how many golf clubs' missions are to save the world *and* play golf? The answer may be that companies are better at change than government or civil society – but the evidence is limited so far on all three fronts.

To finish, a good example of the difficulties of change can be found in Europe's largest, and the world's fifth largest, employer – the UK's National Health Service – which at a corporate level employs more than a quarter of a million people and whose supply chains stretch around the world. Radical organisational change requires five components to be successful: leadership, new systems, new strategies, knowledge, and feedback and rewards for change agents – a virtuous and self-empowering circle. This is an organisation where the lights are most definitely on in the boardroom when it comes to climate change. They have made the links between climate change, eco-efficiency, community engagement, staff morale, procurement and health care at a strategic level. So, they have leadership from the top but what they do not have yet is strategy that is driven from a systems perspective, which means that across the NHS there is not enough linkage between energy efficiency and building programmes, recycling and waste management, health care and employability. Two examples suffice to illustrate this and should turn the lights on in boardrooms around the world. At a daylong meeting of NHS internal change agents run by the UK government's Sustainable Development Commission in 2008, two comments rang out. The first was from the human resources manager at one of the UK's largest hospitals who said that recycling was a human resources issue. He argued that if he could ensure that he employed the right sort of people, with an understanding of the issues, his hospital would not have a waste management problem because the issues would be dealt with upstream before the problem is created. The second comment came from the energy manager of a vast hospital complex who was grappling with the need for a new energy system and had been looking at all manner of alternatives to the traditional generation of heat and light from the last two hundreds years. While he wanted to radically reduce the hospital's carbon footprint by bringing CO_2 emissions down by 80 per cent, which he knew he could do, he was not connected to the building and refurbishment programme, and, even more important, his financial trajectory for investment was 2–3 years, and at a maximum of 5 years, when he knew that the pay back on a really eco-efficient energy system would be 10–20 years.

When the lights go on in the boardroom on climate change, there must also be a radical systems based rethink of the whole operation, which must in turn lead to a new strategic approach. Another NHS manager pointed out when the personal light bulb goes *on* for an individual who has an epiphany, and starts to do the right thing, there must be instant gratification for saving the planet when they turn *out* the lights on leaving the room. Knowledge empowerment requires reward especially when swimming against the tide. For Ray Anderson, Lee Scott and the NHS, and you and me, the lights are on, and we may be the wisdom of crowds, but have the lights come on in boardrooms around the world?

References

McKinsey: Available at http://uk.f865.mail.yahoo.com/dc/launch?.partner=bt-1&. rand=0mngajd5oqnea, accessed 9 November 2008.

Interface: Available at http://www.interfaceinc.com/who/founder.html, accessed 8 November 2008.

Andriof, J. and McIntosh, M. (2001), *Perspectives on Corporate Citizenship*, Greenleaf Publishing, Sheffield.

Business & Human Rights Resource Centre (2008), "UN Special Representative on business & human rights," available at http://www.business-humanrights.org/ Gettingstarted/UNSpecialRepresentative, accessed 8 November 2008.

Castells, M. (2001), *The Internet Galaxy: Reflections on the Internet, Business, and Society*, Oxford University Press, Oxford.

CNN Money (2005), "Wal-Mart calls for minimum wage hike: CEO Lee Scott tells executives he's urging congressional action in a bid to help 'working families," available at http://money.cnn.com/2005/10/25/news/fortune500/walmart_wage/, accessed 8 November 2008.

De Geus, A. (2002), *The Living Company: Growth, Learning and Longevity in Business*, Nicholas Brealey, London and Boston.

Diamond, J. (2005), *Collapse: How Societies Choose to Fail or Succeed*, Penguin, London.

Elkington, J. (1994), *Cannibals With Forks: The Triple Bottom Line of 21st Century Business*, New Society Publishers, Gabriola Island, BC.

Freeman, R. E. (1984), *Strategic Management: A Stakeholder Approach*, Pitman, Boston.

Hart, S. L. (2005), *Capitalism at the Crossroads : The Unlimited Business Opportunities in Solving the World's Most Difficult Problems*, Wharton School Publishing, Upper Saddle River, NJ.

IPCC (2007), Fourth Assessment Report, available at www.ipcc.ch.pdf/assessmentreport, accessed 7 November 2008.

Kakabadse, A. and Kakabadse, N. (2008), *Leading the Board the Six Disciplines of World Class Chairmen*, Palgrave McMillian, Basingstoke and New York.

Langford, C. and Wagler, J. (2008), "Green on green," CEO Scorecard, Financial Post, available at http://www.silobreaker.com/DocumentReader. aspx?Item=5_921475087, accessed 8 November 2008.

Lovelock, J. (2006), *The Revenge of Gaia*, Penguin, London.

McIntosh, M. (1993), *Good Business? Case Studies in Corporate Social Responsibility*, SAUS, Bristol.

McIntosh, M. (2003), *Raising a Ladder to the Moon: The Complexities of Corporate Social and Environmental Responsibility*, Palgrave Macmillan, London.

McIntosh, M. (2008), "Editorial," *Journal of Corporate Citizenship*, 30, 3–9.

McIntosh, M., Leipziger, D., Jones, K., and Coleman, G. (1998), *Corporate Citizenship: Successful Strategies for Responsible Companies*, Financial Times Prentice Hall, London.

McIntosh, M., Thomas, R., Leipziger, D., and Coleman, G. (2003), *Living Corporate Citizenship*, Financial Times Prentice Hall, London.

McKinsey Quarterly (2008), "From risk to opportunity – How global executives view sociopolitical issues: McKinsey Global Survey Results," available at http://www. mckinseyquarterly.com/Strategy/Strategic_Thinking/McKinsey_Global_Survey_ Results_From_risk_to_opportunity_How_global_executives_view_sociopolitical_ issues_2235, accessed 8 November 2008.

Monks, R. A. G. (1998), *The Emperor's Nightingale: Restoring the Integrity of the Corporation*, Perseus Books, Reading, MA.

Office of Climate Change (2007), "Stern team," availabe at http://www.occ.gov.uk/ activities/stern.htm, accessed 8 November 2008.

Rees, M. (2004), *Our Final Century: Will the Human Race Survive the Twenty-first Century?*, Heinemann, London.

Ruggie, J. G. (2002), "The theory and practice of learning networks: Corporate social responsibility and the global compact," *Journal of Corporate Citizenship*, 5, 27–36.

Senge, P., Smith, B., and Kruschwitz, N. (2008), "The next industrial imperative," *strategy + business*, 51, 44–55.

Shirky, C. (2008), *Here Comes Everybody: The Power of Organizing Without Organizations*, Penguin, London.

Smith, C. N. and Crawford, R. J. (2008), "Unilever and oxfam: Understanding the impacts of business on poverty," *Mainstreaming Corporate Responsibility, Journal of Business Ethics Education*, 5.

Stern, N. H. (2007), *The Economics of Climate Change: The Stern Review*, Cambridge University Press, Cambridge.

UNCTAD (2006), "Statements by Supachai Panitchpakdi, Secretary-General of UNCTAD", 10th World Summit of Young Entrepreneurs, São Paulo, Brazil, 17 March 2006, available at http://www.unctad.org/Templates/webflyer.asp?docid=6900&intItemID=3549&lang=1, accessed 8 November 2008.

Unilever (2008), "A case study of Unilever in Indonesia," available at http://www.unilever.com/ourcompany/newsandmedia/unileverindonesia.asp, accessed 8 November 2008.

Index